משנה

ArtScroll® Series

Rabbi Nosson Scherman / Rabbi Gedaliah Zlotowitz
General Editors
Rabbi Meir Zlotowitz ז״ל, *Founder*

Published by

ARTSCROLL®

Mesorah Publications, ltd

YOU Revealed

A TORAH PATH TO A LIFE OF SUCCESS

NAFTALI HOROWITZ

FIRST EDITION
First Impression ... November 2020

SECOND EDITION
Five Impressions ... August 2021
Sixth Impression ... February 2022

Published and Distributed by
MESORAH PUBLICATIONS, LTD.
313 Regina Avenue / Rahway, N.J 07065

Distributed in Europe by
LEHMANNS
Unit E, Viking Business Park
Rolling Mill Road
Jarow, Tyne & Wear, NE32 3DP
England

Distributed in Australia and New Zealand by **GOLDS WORLDS OF JUDAICA**
3-13 William Street
Balaclava, Melbourne 3183
Victoria, Australia

Distributed in Israel by
SIFRIATI / A. GITLER — BOOKS
POB 2351
Bnei Brak 51122

Distributed in South Africa by
KOLLEL BOOKSHOP
Northfield Centre, 17 Northfield Avenue
Glenhazel 2192, Johannesburg, South Africa

ARTSCROLL® SERIES
YOU

To contact the author
he can be reached via e-mail at youreveaIedbook@gmail.com

ITEM CODE: YOUH

ISBN 10: 1-4226-2746-2 / ISBN 13: 978-1-4226-2746-4

Typography by CompuScribe at ArtScroll Studios, Ltd.

Printed in the United States of America
Bound by Sefercraft, Quality Bookbinders, Ltd., Rahway N.J. 07065

Rabbi Yitzchak David Grossman
Chief Rabbi of Migdal Ha'emek
Member, Chief Rabbinate Council
Dean, Migdal Ohr Institutions

הרב יצחק דוד גרוסמן
רב העיר מגדל העמק
חבר מועצת הרבנות הראשית
נשיא מוסדות מגדל אור

בס"ד

יום ד' לסדר "והתחזקתם ולקחתם מפרי הארץ" ח"י סיון תש"פ

שלום רב לאוהבי תורתך,

הנני להכיר ולהוקיר את ידידנו ומכובדינו הדגול מגזע אראלים ותרשישים, בר אוריין ובר אבוהון. פה מפיק מרגליות, חיכו ממתקים וכולו מחמדים. שמו נישא לשבח ולתהילה חוכה לקדש שם שמים ברבים.

הרב **ר' נפתלי הורוויץ** שליט"א

שש אנוכי על אמרותיך כמוצא שלל רב, לראות עלים לתרופה, פרי ביכורים מעשי ידיך להתפאר בחיבור ספר נפלא ביותר, להוכיח ולהראות את גדל הכוחות ועוצמת הכשרונות, אשר הקדוש ברוך הוא העניק ונתן לכל הברואים. כוחות ספונים וטמונים בעומק, ונסתרים מעין כל, ומגלגלין זכות על ידי זכאי, בזכות אבותיך הקדושים זי"ע. זכית להוציא לאור את הספר הנכבד **"אתה"**. אשר יסודתו בהררי קודש מדברי חז"ל וסיפורים ועובדות בהתחזקות באמונה ובטחון, במתן מוטיבציה ועידוד וחיזוק לעוסקים בענייני מסחר ומשא ומתן כראוי וכהלכה.

כיהודה ועוד לקרא, ראיתי לנכון להעתיק מאמר חז"ל ללמוד וללמד מה גודל כוחו וסגולתו של כל אחד ואחד. ובלשון הזוהר של הרמב"ם זי"ע בהלכות תשובה פ"ג, ה"ד "לפיכך צריך כל אדם שיראה עצמו וכו'... וכן כל העולם חציו זכאי וחציו חייב. חטא, חטא אחד, הרי הכריע את עצמו ואת כל העולם כולו לכף חובה וכו'... עשה מצווה אחת, הרי הכריע את עצמו ואת כל העולם כולו לכף זכות, וגרם לו ולהם תשועה והצלה".

יהי רצון שיזכה מע"כ להפיץ מעיינותיו חוצה מתוך בריות גופא ונהורא מעליא וכל מילי דמיטב. הצלחה וברכה בכל העניינים, אך טוב וחסד ימצאוכם כל הימים.

בברכת התורה ולומדיה,

הרב יצחק דוד גרוסמן

P.O.B. 345
Migdal Ha'emek ISRAEL 23028

Tel: 073-2227070 :טל
Fax: 04-6546847 :פקס

ת.ד. 345
מגדל העמק 23028

Rabbi Uri Zohar

בס"ד

חודש סיון
תש"פ
עיה"ק ירושלים
תובב"א

לכל מאן דבעי

לדעתי אין ספק כדאי לקרוא
את ספרו של הרב נפתלי הורוביץ שליט"א
מאמין ש"....הזמן קצר והמלאכה מרובה..."
אולם אני מצרף חתימתי להסכמות
של הרבנים החשובים שליט"א
בברכת "שרגא כי יהדרא מאי מינה"
ובתקוה ותפילה שהספר הזה
יקרב לבבות לאבינו שבשמים
א.כ.י.ר.

באהבה רבה אורי זהר

רב אברהם חיים פייער
ירושלים, עיר כלילת יופי משוש כל הארץ

BS"D 12th day of Adar, 5779

The tremendous development of Torah true Judaism we witness today surpasses our wildest dreams. Yet, something fundamental is missing. Many individuals struggle to find a sense of clear meaning and mission in their Torah study and divine service. A lack of clear purpose and concrete goals undermines our accomplishments.

This work, **"YOU"** addresses this issue head on. **For those who feel lost**, this book is a real "find". For those who have found their life's path this sefer will make their vision sharper and more focused, helping them to realize their maximum potential.

Rabbi Avrohom Chaim Feuer

Rabbi Avraham Schorr
רב דביהמ״ד נזר גדליהו
1860 52nd Street
Brooklyn, NY 11230

בס״ד

לאדם יש ברירה לפרש האני של האדם בטעות, לחשוב כי האני הוא הגוף החלק הגשמי של האדם, וממילא עד כמה הוא יכול ליהנות מהנאת העולם הזה הוא ממלא תפקיד של האני, אבל דברי הלל מכחיש את זה, שאמר אם אני כאן הכל כאן, ובודאי הלל שהתייחס אל הגוף כאילו מדבר מגוף שלישי, כדברי המדרש בפרשת אמור, לא החשיב הגוף כאילו הוא הכל, רק הלל מכוון לאני האמיתית של האדם שהוא הנשמה הקדושה שהוא האני האמיתי, החלק אלקי ממעל, ואם זה האני הוא כאן אז הכל כאן.

ספר זה שחיבר ידי״נ היקר הרב הח׳ ר׳ נפתלי הורוויץ שיחי׳ לאוי״ט בא ללמד האדם בשפה המדוברת מה האני שמונח בתוך האדם ולליידע ולמצוא האני, ובזה הוא מאיר להאדם מה תפקידו בעולמו, ומה הוא האני האמתית שלו. ויהי׳ לתועלת גדול לכל אחד להתעלות בעבודת השם כראוי.

בברכה שמטרתו ושאיפתו בהדפסת הדברים יהי׳ לתועלת גדול, ועל ידי הלימוד והקריאה בהספר ישתנו אנשים לראות העולם במבט אחר ויתעלו למעלה מהבלי העולם המחשיכים ראות האדם.

בברכה ובידידות,
אברהם הלוי שאהר

Rabbi Simcha Bunim Cohen
K'hal Ateres Yeshaya
Lakewood, New Jersey

שמחה בונם קאהן
קהל עטרת ישעי'
לעקוואד ,ניו דזערסי

כ' אלול תשע"ב מכתב ברכה

ראיתי מה שכתב ידידי כהרה"ג ר' אברהם הלוי שוהר שליט"א אודות
הספר החשוב מה שכתב ידידי הרה"ג הגדול בתורה ויראת שמים
ר' נפתלי הורוויץ שליט"א. והגם שלא היה לי פנאי לקרות כל הספר
שמלא תוכן ויסודות איך האדם צריך לחשוב. ואמ"ו רשכבה"ג מרן
הגר"מ פיינשטיין זצ"ל אמר שליתן הסכמה על ספר צריכין
לקרות כל מילה ומילה. אבל הגאון ר' אברהם שליט"א כתב בהסכמתו
שהספר יהיה לתועלת גדול לכל אחד להתעלות בעבודת השם,
וכשהכרתי את הרה"ג ר' נפתלי שליט"א ראיתי גברא רבא מלא השקפות
התורה ולב טהור לעזור ולחזק אחינו בני ישראל

ברכתי שתהא הספר נתקבל אצל אחינו בני ישראל

בברכת כתיבה וחתימה טובה
ידידך האוהבך בלב ונפש
שמחה בונם הכהן קאהן

908 EAST COUNTY LINE ROAD | LAKEWOOD NJ 08701 | 732-367-2267

Contents

Acknowledgments

The lessons, ideas, and techniques found in this volume are the direct result of Hashem's infinite kindness. *For everything is from You, and what we give is from Your hand (Divrei HaYamim I* 29:14*).* I thank Him with all of my heart for allowing me to help others. The *siyata d'Shmaya* that enabled this book to be written was apparent and obvious throughout the process.

This book is dedicated to the memory of my late parents, Shmuel Ahron ben Harav Yitzchok *z"l* and Chana bas Harav Yisroel *a"h,* who never allowed us children to forget who we were and what we were on this world to accomplish. In addition, it is dedicated to my Rebbe *zt"l,* Harav Hagaon Yosef ben Ahron Moshe Leifer, the holy Verdaner Rebbe, who left this world while this book was being edited, leaving me and my family as broken and lost orphans. I had the merit of a deep relationship with the Rebbe *zt"l* for close to 30 years; his deep *yiras Shamayim* and love for every Jew has forever changed anyone that ever merited to meet him. Lastly, I wish to acknowledge my debt to my Rebbe and cousin whom I never merited to meet, the holy Piaseczna Rebbe, Rav Klonimus Kalman ben Elimelech *hy"d.* The Rebbe's Torah and life directives continue to have a profound influence on me. May his legacy of fervent service to Hashem and the influential *sefarim* that he wrote be a merit to his holy *neshamah.*

This book would not have come to be were it not for my *yedid ne'eman* and accomplished author, **Naftali Weinberger**. Naftali first presented the idea to write a book, made the introduction to ArtScroll, and took a personal interest in this project from the start.

I want to express my *hakaras hatov* to my son-in-law, **Rav Yisroel Aryeh Wachsman**, for serving as my information sieve. With his sharp eye, brilliant mind, and Torah knowledge, he sifted through each chapter to ensure the accuracy of all Torah sources.

I extend my deepest appreciation to my *yedid nefesh*, **Moshe Hazan**, who opened my eyes and mind to the beauty of *Toras HaNistar* and served as my sounding board on several key chapters.

My appreciation to **Rabbi Yaacov David Schulman** for allowing me to use excerpts from his translation of the Piaseczna Rebbe's *sefer Hachshoras Avreichim*. My appreciation to Kehot Publishing for allowing me to use excerpts from their copyrighted work *Lessons in Tanya*.

To my remarkable editor **Mrs. Chana Nestlebaum**, who added great enhancement, refinement and elegance to my words. To my dear friend **Lawrence Burian** for the hours he spent providing valuable input for this book. To **Gedaliah Zlotowitz** and **Avrohom Biderman**, who shared my vision for this book early on, encouraged me to begin writing, and then embraced the final product. To my esteemed neighbor **Rabbi Nosson Scherman** for endorsing and encouraging my work. To the remarkable staff at ArtScroll: **Mrs. Judi Dick** who perfected each chapter and encouraged me to clarify many important points; **Chanie Ziegler** who designed the inviting page layout, and to **Mendy Herzberg** for timely and efficient coordination during the entire publishing process.

My *Eishes Chayil* supported and encouraged this project with the fervent wish that it would promote our joint efforts to make a *kiddush Hashem* and help *Klal Yisrael*. My children were there for me every step of the way by offering words of encouragement and by putting up with a father who was sometimes preoccupied when they needed him. May the *zechus* of *zikui harabim* stand in their merit always.

Introduction

◆ Why I Wrote This Book and What You Can Expect From It

As a rule, authors write the introduction to their book when they have completed the manuscript. However, I am writing it at the very beginning, perhaps because I need to explain to *myself* why I am investing the time and effort that this project will require. Consider this introduction as my "pre-commitment letter" to myself, a concept that I intend to address in a later chapter. So here I am, sharing my letter with you.

Through it, I hope you will get to know me well enough to trust the insights I will be offering in the chapters to come. In any book that touches upon life's perspectives and values, the words are only as valid as the person who's speaking them. Therefore, I will tell you about my background and how I gained the knowledge I'll be sharing with you.

◆ Why This Path?

I grew up constantly being reminded of what is expected of me. My family tree links me directly to holy *tzaddikim* such as Rav Elimelech of Lizhensk, the Maggid of Kozhnitz, and Rav Naftali of Ropshitz. My holy Zaides before me dedicated their lives to rising up to greatness and inspiring others to do the same, and I believe that it's my obligation to live up to this heritage.

My rebbeim encouraged me to take the path of teaching Torah or becoming a Rabbi, but my heart told me that I needed to reach people in a different way. It was my cousin and Rebbe, the great Rav Hershele of Spinka *zt"l,* who confirmed what my soul had been telling me. He encouraged me to become successful in the business world with the words *"Klal Yisrael darf givirim,"* the Jewish nation needs successful people. Upon leaving his holy presence at that meeting, quite stunned I will add, I realized that my mission was clear: Work at being successful and then teach others how to do the same. And so, my course was set, and with extraordinary assistance from Hashem, and against many odds, I climbed rung by rung from my beginnings as a print salesman to where I am today — a managing director at the nation's largest investment bank, a lecturer, and counselor to those seeking guidance. This directive, I will underscore, was not intended as a guide for Jewish men in general, since the Rebbe *zt"l* often encouraged others to embrace the path of full-time Torah study. The directive was meant for me personally because my Rebbe's *Ruach Hakodesh* enabled him to see where my life's mission was to be found.

Climbing is always a struggle, but Hashem blessed me along the way. I began my climb weighed down by many of the personal challenges that people often cite as causes for failure: fear of rejection, low resiliency, and inconsistent self-confidence, just to name a few issues. My ongoing journey is to overcome each of these obstacles as they continue to confront me in various forms, and to show others that they can do the same. My disadvantages are now my advantages, because dealing with them unflinchingly placed me in a more powerful position to teach others. Someone blessed with a natural skill is not always able to teach that skill to anyone else. He just does it, with little need for thought, and it works. Asking such a person for advice is like asking a lottery winner to tell you how he won so that you can win as well. "Well, I went into the bodega, put down a dollar, the machine picked my numbers and I won!" There's not much you can do with that information. On the other hand, someone who was compelled to learn a skill through trial and error, who made loads of mistakes and paid close attention to what worked, what didn't work and why, can guide others down the same path. Perhaps my advice resonates with people because they see me as no different or more special than they are.

◆§ We're in It Together

Over the past twelve years, I have had the *zechus* to lecture to thousands across the globe and to counsel many more individually either by phone or in person. The topics include all areas of self-development: career, personal growth, and faith. Some people simply want help in making sense of their complicated lives. Wherever I go, I find that people are searching — searching for answers, meaning, direction, and mostly, a path to successful living.

My role in helping people began in 2007 when, during that difficult period of economic meltdown, I watched far too many lose their jobs in the mortgage industry and other fields. I knew that I could help, that I had to help. The question was: Where would I find the time to do so? At that time, I was active in the world of *kiruv* (Jewish outreach), running a learning program in Manhattan while managing a busy Wall Street practice and being a father to a growing family. I discussed the matter with an advisor whose wisdom I seek whenever I need to hear the Torah's true perspective on an issue. His exact words were, "Helping Jews with their livelihood is life-saving work, and takes precedence over everything else." And so, I scaled back my *kiruv* work and began to try to bolster those who faced challenges when unemployed.

I became involved in EPI (Emergency Parnassah Initiative), Agudath Israel of America's PCS (Professional Career Services), Mesila (an organization that helps families develop strategies to achieve financial stability), and many other wonderful organizations that are geared to enabling our fellow Jews find jobs and earn a respectable living. Eventually, I developed a fairly extensive curriculum and was called upon by numerous communities around the world to come educate and motivate their constituents. As a heartwarming side note, I have had the pleasure of meeting Jews from across the globe and have seen the support that our communities provide for those who are going through rough times. *Mi k'amcha Yisrael* — Who is like Your (G-d's) nation, Israel!

The more I lectured, the more I was approached by individuals requesting that I counsel them one-on-one in multiple areas of their lives. Through that personal interaction, I learned about behaviors that impact *parnassah,* marriage, faith and relationships and what people can do to improve their situation. I learned about proper *hishtadlus,* which along with our fervent *Tefillos,* will *b'ezras Hashem* lead to *siyata d'Shmaya;* the catalyst of all success and accomplishment.

As this book is being prepared for publication, a new crisis period is emerging with the universal upheaval caused by the Covid19-pandemic. I hope that by the time this volume reaches the bookstores, the epoch will have become a chapter in history — hopefully the last before the arrival of Mashiach. However, the emotional and financial challenges people are facing now may seem to many to be unprecedented and perhaps beyond the scope of any advice we might be able to offer. In reality, however, the Torah's truth remains true in every situation. The lessons that have always carried our nation through the myriad of challenges that we and prior generations have faced are equally applicable, and more vital than ever in facing the astronomical challenges before us now.

I am humbled that Hashem has allowed me to play a role in instructing and counseling thousands, with help from Above, to re-engineer their approach to living successfully. I often meet people who tell me, "You taught me something that changed my entire perspective and I went and made something of myself." All I taught them was an approach that is rooted in the very Torah that is found in every Jewish home (and heart). They took the initiative to act upon that approach and from that point forward, they saw improvement in their situation. Such success stories no longer surprise me. Torah works.

The pleasure I derive from helping my fellow Jews in this way cannot be adequately expressed in words. I grew up knowing what it means to live with stress and financial strain. As a child I saw the worry on my parents' faces when challenged with the question of how to make ends meet, and their anxiety when they experienced the instability of the world around them. As a result, the struggles of others deeply affect me and I sometimes find myself crying along with them as they unburden their hurt and worries. I empathize with the pain of someone who watches those around him moving forward in life as he experiences the shame and frustration of his own life being stuck in neutral, or even worse, in reverse. Many fear that they will never live up to their own potential, and when they ultimately leave this world they will be regarded as failures.

◆§ Don't Bury Your Potential!

In my lectures, I often tell my "toothpaste story." Several years ago, when my wife and children had already moved upstate for the summer, I arrived home late one night from learning, as I tend to do when I'm coming to an empty house. I headed upstairs and, as my dentist always advised, I went to brush my teeth before going to sleep. There on the bathroom vanity sat a tube of toothpaste that looked like it had seen better days. The thought of shlepping down two flights at that late hour to get a fresh tube from our storage room didn't appeal to me; I squeezed the tube and enough came out to do the trick. The next morning, I needed to get to Shacharis on time, so again I squeezed, and out came toothpaste. I made a mental note to go to the storage room that night before heading upstairs, and of course I forgot. Again I squeezed, this time even harder, and again enough came out. Next morning... you guessed, Shacharis. Now I began to challenge myself. How long could I keep getting toothpaste out of a tube that, in my estimation, was already depleted two nights earlier? The answer turned out to be more than a week!

When that tube finally gave out (I won't even tell you what it looked like when I was done with it) I stopped and thought, imagine how much toothpaste lies in the landfills of this country, inside tubes that people regarded as empty when in truth there was plenty left inside. Perhaps enough to meet our country's tooth-brushing needs for several years. All it took on my part was a bit more work. Squeezing.

Why am I telling you this story? Because I quickly realized that this wasn't a lesson about toothpaste at all. Toothpaste costs $3.00 a tube, so wasting some is not a big deal. This is a lesson about you and me. I thought about how much untapped potential lies in the cemeteries of our nation; about how much more people are capable of accomplishing. Yet that greatness remains buried inside them, because they never squeezed it out of themselves. Perhaps at one point they decided, "This is all that I am and all that I can be" or that, "There are great people in this world but clearly I wasn't meant to be one of them."

Sometimes Hakadosh Baruch Hu squeezes us because He knows what is inside of us and wants us to bring it forth into the world. However, our lives are far better when we learn to squeeze ourselves. Growing is difficult, yet the rewards are eternal. Changing ourselves takes perseverance and hard work, but there is no greater feeling than that of self-actualization, the achievement of one's full potential, in any given area of life.

I wrote this book because you have the potential to leave this world at the end of a good, long life, with the knowledge that you left none of your capabilities untapped. The gift of life is so very precious, priceless indeed, and it should therefore never be wasted.

Searching in the Right Place

Like most people, I never saw myself as an author, and quite frankly I still don't. Why then am I writing a book? Over the years many people have asked me to put my ideas on paper, but my already hectic schedule made this seem impossible. Then something began to happen that made me realize that I *had to find the time no matter how difficult this might be.*

During the past few years, I have witnessed an alarming trend. More and more *bnei Torah* are turning to secular authors, "gurus," and seminars to help them develop the building blocks of successful living. This is a terrible mistake on the part of these *bnei Torah.*

These resources often have no long-term benefit. I have met with countless individuals, Jewish or otherwise, who have paid good money to attend a secular, two-day motivational seminar only to admit to me a year later that despite implementing the ideas they were taught, "It just didn't work." The reason for this is simple. Real and lasting change requires that we "own" the information and then apply it by working on our inner self — the essence of who we are. Spoon-fed inspiration wears off quickly, leaving the person with an even deeper sense of having failed because he/she was unable to follow through. Sure, these gurus fill seats and sell books/CDs, but that only serves as a testament to how desperate people are to improve their lives.

We say that *"chochmah b'goyim taamin,"* wisdom exists among the nations of the world. However, topics such as self-esteem, motivation, resilience, the meaning of life, and achieving our aspirations are not mere *chochmah*, they are Torah! These concepts are among the essential elements of human existence and we can learn about them only from the Torah. *"Torah b'goyim al taamin,"* do not believe that the nations of the world possess Torah wisdom. For a Torah Jew to learn such fundamental ideas from secular sources is like trying to fuel a jet engine with car gasoline.

Real change only comes with work, and by opening our minds to information and ideas that are transformative and build the essential self. Those ideas are found in the Torah, the blueprint of creation, which enables us to understand how Hashem meant for us and the world around us to operate. On that basis, we can make the necessary adjustments to our character traits and daily routine. In contrast, people often seek shortcuts. They seek to alleviate the symptoms, which are in fact the challenges Hashem has given us to improve our underlying self.

The materials that form our building blocks are found in *Chovos HaLevavos, Ramchal, Sefer HaTanya, Nefesh HaChaim,* the writings of the Chofetz Chaim, Rav Klonimus of Piaseczna, *the Nesivos Shalom* of Slonim, the Alter of Kelm, Rav Elchonon Wasserman, Rav Nachman of Breslov, and so many others. Our *mesorah* is so rich and our Torah addresses every aspect of our lives. It is for us to be a light unto the nations, not for secular sources to provide the essential values of how to live our lives.

Think about it. How ludicrous is it that we, a nation of immortality, purity, and loftiness, seek guidance from a world that is struggling? Are our definitions of successful living the same as theirs? Even the nations around us are waking up to the fact that their lives would be greatly enhanced through a deeper connection to spirituality as illustrated by the following story:

> *A kiruv organization once asked me to lecture to a highly respected finance fraternity at a prominent East Coast university. Assuming that only Jewish students were invited, I was shocked when upon entering the room, I saw that half the crowd was not Jewish! How could I deliver my usual, Torah-based talk? I decided that the diversity of the crowd should not deter me from delivering my intended message. I therefore spoke what I know works best — pure Torah. The talk was based on a writing of Rav Elchonon Wasserman, hy"d. When I was done, the entire room charged up to the podium; Jews AND non-Jews wanted more — much more! Like starving children, they begged. The non-Jews wanted to know where they could read more about these concepts. In their words: "This is more brilliant and truthful than anything we have ever learned."*

This should not come as a surprise. Torah is the blueprint of the universe; *everything*, every bit of authentic wisdom, is to be found in the Torah. We only need to know how to search.

It is my fervent hope that this book will convince you, the reader, to realize that you have no need to look beyond your library of *sefarim* when seeking answers to life's greatest challenges. I will be sharing the small selection of sources that I have merited to study, but please know that the Torah is infinite and I have barely scratched the surface. This book is also meant to demonstrate that the Torah is timeless and therefore relevant and applicable to the challenges of today; that yes, Torah knowledge will build YOU and make you better at everything. The Torah is the only path to success.

I ask that this book be the beginning of you believing that you are capable of more than you may have thought until now and that there is still so much more toothpaste in you. This book is a compilation of thought-provoking Torah-based lessons and ideas that I have shared with audiences and individuals over the past decade and which have motivated people to change, and to make more of themselves than they ever imagined possible. These are concepts that I have taught myself and that I have seen in others around me and are worth emulating.

In case the book's title hasn't made it clear, this book is about you becoming YOU — the YOU that is buried inside of you, the YOU that shines bright in some areas of your life and is nowhere to be found in others. We all came to this world with a purpose, and realizing that purpose is highly dependent on you becoming YOU. This book is about reaching your potential. The more you live up to your own potential the more successful, fulfilled, and happy you will be in every area of your life.

This book will draw many examples from the topic of *parnassah* and business because that is the primary motivating factor that brings people to my door or fully engaged at a lecture. It can be proven, however, that a person who builds himself will see results and improvement in all areas of his life, even if his primary and initial motivation is to earn more money.

Those who struggle in the area of *parnassah* often struggle in other areas as well, and therefore, quite often, when people come to seek counsel regarding their career or business, the topic quickly turns to deeper aspects of their lives such as marriage, self-esteem, confidence, Yiddishkeit, and their upbringing. The many aspects of our lives are intertwined and each area has a major impact on the others.

The most effective way to restore something to its optimal state is to understand how the object was designed to function in the first place, and then understand what has gone wrong. Based on this, we can make adjustments. Some of what you will read in this book may prove quite familiar, but when you view it through a new lens, I hope you will gain a clearer understanding of how the various components of YOU fit together and interact. I also hope to help you gain a deeper awareness of the thought patterns and *middos* that may be impeding your growth in the various areas of your life.

In the words of the Ramchal in his introduction to *Derech Hashem*:

> *When one knows a number of things, and understands how they are categorized and systematically interrelated, then*

the person has a great advantage over one who has the same knowledge without such distinction. It is very much like the difference between looking at a well-arranged garden, planted in rows and patterns, versus seeing a wild thicket or forest growing in confusion.

This book and my lecturing and counseling are but a small token of expression of my *hakaras hatov* to Hakadosh Baruch Hu for all that I have in my life and the growth opportunities provided by the challenges that I faced along the way. It is quite clear to me that anyone who is able to entertain any thought of *"kochi v'otzem yadi"* — the power and the strength of my hand [has brought my success] — is blind and out of touch with reality.

And now let's talk about YOU.

Just before YOU were born,
A candle burned above your head, allowing you to see from one end of the world to the other.
You took an oath to be righteous and not wicked, but at the same time to see yourself as imperfect even if the entire world saw you as righteous.
The candle allowed you to see your full potential; all that you could be.
The first aspect is what drives you toward perfection.
The second is why you will never see yourself as good enough.

(Based on the Talmud in *Niddah* 30b)

1

The Journey Begins

Congratulations for taking this important step forward in your quest for self-actualization, a major breakthrough toward achieving your full potential.

You are among those people who deeply cherish life, the greatest gift that you will ever receive. You have internalized the fact that the Grantor of this gift, Hakadosh Baruch Hu, knows in His infinite wisdom that the potential for greatness lies within you. You appreciate the extraordinary opportunity that life offers and want to make the very most of it.

There is nothing more rewarding and uplifting than months and years filled with the toil entailed in overcoming challenges and achieving growth. It is deeply satisfying to look back after a period of time and realize, as if all at once, that you are not the same person that you once were; you have scaled mountains that once seemed beyond your reach. Situations that would have made you angry, depressed, or anxious now seem to roll off your back. Obstacles that would have made you stumble no longer pose a challenge. Time that was once wasted on trivialities and distractions is now being used to further your important mission. Days that were once spent in despair, depression, and frustration are now driven by a sense of purpose. The deep fulfillment that you will feel the day you look back and marvel at how much you have grown is indescribable.

On the other hand, no one wants to look back at the life they lived and the choices they made, and think, "I could have accomplished so much more." Regret is a bitter pill indeed, especially if it comes when it is too late to do much about the status quo. Avoiding this fate lies within our hands, and we can choose to change with the very next decision we make.

☙ Be Prepared

In the coming chapters we will be asking you to do some work, because reading alone will not have the intended effect. Sometimes that work may not be easy, and as we will learn, that's a good thing. Growth, and therefore fulfillment, will primarily be found outside of the comfort zone. Nevertheless, the toil will be worthwhile; it will bring fulfillment to your life to a degree you may never have thought possible.

Be prepared, however, because as with any worthwhile endeavor, the Satan will not be pleased with your journey and he will not lie dormant. His goal is to ruin your life in every way imaginable, and he will rear his ugly head as soon as you begin taking positive steps. We will therefore spend time disarming some of his insidious tactics by addressing several issues that he may raise. Even if there are those that don't pertain to you, I encourage you to learn about them so that you can help others on their journey. These are some of the issues/excuses that many people have proffered, and it is important that we address them at the outset, because the Satan must not be allowed to have his way.

Satan says: ***"You're average, nothing special. Achievement and fulfillment were meant for those better than you."***

We respond: ***Hakadosh Baruch Hu didn't create anything that doesn't have the potential for spectacular greatness.***

Some may see themselves as destined for mediocrity at best, and cannot fathom that they have the potential for greatness and success. This mindset must be completely erased, uprooted, wiped out, eradicated, deleted, (need I go on?) because, as long as it exists, the person will be firmly anchored to his/her current station in life. Excuses like these are among the dominant poisons.

I was once addressing members of a community in Europe, teaching them to lift their vision of what was possible for their lives. We had reached my favorite part of any lecture — open Q&A — when a man who had clearly been itching to ask a question jumped up and said, "Reb Naftali, I appreciate everything that you are saying BUT isn't it true that the world is designed to include people who have and people who don't have, people who give and people who take, people who succeed and people who fail? Won't there always be unfortunates in the world? Suppose I am destined to be one of them?"

I replied, "Yes, some of what you say is true. In fact, the *Chovos HaLevavos* speaks of the concept of a world in which some will be givers and some receivers. Nowhere, however, does it say that YOU have to be among the takers. Yes, there will always be people like that, but a person should never live with the belief that such was decreed upon HIM. Each person should have *bitachon* — the trust in G-d's love and care. A person should live with the trust that although there are people whose lives are a constant struggle, "that surely doesn't have to be me." A person would then direct his/her efforts toward avoiding this fate through proper *hishtadlus* and fervent *tefillos* and have trust that Hashem will bless his/her efforts.

☙ Why Not Me?

It is highly advantageous to live with the mindset, "If someone else can do it, then so can I." Imagine a room full of people who are accomplished, fulfilled, successful, and living a more inspired life, and then think to yourself, "There is surely place in that room for one more person to squeeze in — ME!"

I learned this life-altering lesson on a bus.

The year that my father (of blessed memory) passed away, I decided that it was time to take my first trip to Poland, so that I could pray at the graves of my holy ancestors and say Kaddish there. Since I am a great-grandson of the Rebbe Reb Elimelech of Lizhensk, I chose his yahrzeit for the pilgrimage. As I sat on the bus from Cracow to Lizhensk, I overheard two people behind me discussing how unbelievably crowded it was at the gravesite and how "impossible" it was to get close to the monument to pray. They both had long ago decided to stand outside and pray there.

Hearing their conversation, I became crestfallen. I made this trip and spent so much money just to stand outside? As if reading my mind, an elderly man sitting next to me turned to me and, in a deep European accent, said, "Don't listen to them. Don't be a quitter. I persistently but politely make my way up to the grave every year and place my hand on the headstone and stand there davening fervently for several moments." Surprised by his confidence, I asked, "How do you do it?" He said, "I tell myself that there will be those who will stand in that spot, so why shouldn't I be one of them? With this thought in mind, I inch closer and closer and don't stop until I am standing right up there."

If the bus had made a U-turn right then and there and headed back to the airport, the trip would have been worth it just to hear those few inspiring words. "If someone else will get there, then why not me?" Needless to say, I managed to get right up to the headstone, but I will note that people are far more accommodating to an elderly man, and so, my bus friend got there long before I did.

☙ Your *Neshamah* Is Your Ticket

Let's start with the premise that if you are reading this book, you are alive, and therefore you carry within you a lofty *neshamah*. That is the only qualification you need to be a member of the "potential for fulfillment and happiness club." When we underestimate ourselves and deny our ability to achieve our full potential, we are denying our essential self — the spark of our Creator that is our essence. We are negating the greatness that lies within every member of humanity and, even more so, within our great nation.

In the words of the *Nefesh HaChaim* (Gate 1, Ch. 3), the human was created *b'tzelem Elokim,* in the image of G-d, in that we have the power, through our thoughts, actions, and speech, to influence the entire creation for both good or bad. Hakadosh Baruch Hu calls the Jewish nation *b'ni bechori Yisrael,* my firstborn child (*Shemos* 4:23). This title was not intended to inflate our collective ego; rather, it conveys the deep responsibility that our Creator has placed upon us. Just like a firstborn is meant to set an example for the siblings who follow, we are here to set an example for the world, and sanctify Hashem's Name in the process. The truth of this concept is supported by the remarkably disproportionate number of contributions that our nation has made to the world in the areas of spirituality, science, philosophy, medicine, mathematics, economics, law, and so forth. We achieved all that because Hakadosh Baruch Hu knows that a beacon is more visible when it's situated high above the crowd. He therefore blesses our efforts and infuses us with a thirst for knowledge, greater resolve, and ironclad resiliency: traits that we need to thrive in a challenging world.

On a more personal level, Hakadosh Baruch Hu infused each of us with a *neshamah,* soul: a super-charged engine meant to take us, and the world around us, to loftier destinations. He didn't create us to be average or below average, and certainly not to be failures. As His children and partners in His creation, each of us, without exception, is charged with the task of maximizing potential; from that vantage point, we can emulate Him by elevating the world at large. Hakadosh Boruch Hu wants us to lead fulfilling lives and show the world the joys of a life of spirituality, morality, ethics, and kindness.

No person was ever destined to be average. If mediocrity is present among us, it is the consequence of someone's choice or the product of judging ourselves relative to others. Only if you see yourself as an individual and stop comparing yourself to others can you view yourself as a success irrespective of the success others may achieve. Too often we buy into the Satan's "put down" that we are nothing special.

In the words of the *Nefesh HaChaim* (Gate 1, Ch. 4):

> *No member of this nation, heaven forbid, should ever say. "What am I and what is my power that I should impact upon any aspect of the universe?" We should each understand and internalize how great and awesome are our actions such that each one rises up and impacts the highest heights in the supernal worlds.*

The *Nefesh HaChaim* doesn't single out the philanthropist, leader of multitudes, renowned scholar, highly intelligent… as those who impact the universe. He singles out you and me, because we each impact the universe by becoming the very best version of ourselves and teaching those around us how to do the same. We can acquire this achievement by standing at a podium lecturing to students, and equally well by changing diapers and doing laundry, painting someone's house or teaching third-grade children basic arithmetic. We can achieve it by being good parents, friends, and neighbors and by setting a good example for others. If we haven't yet achieved it, that doesn't mean that we cannot do so tomorrow.

Laminate it, hang it on the wall, and let it become your mantra — SINCE SOMEONE CAN, SO CAN I!

Satan says: ***"Who are you kidding? YOU are too old to change!"***

We respond: ***"It's never too late, because if it were, you wouldn't be so threatened by what I am about to do and you would finally leave me alone!"***

As young children, many of us had great aspirations. We were going to grow up to "be something, become someone special, and do great things," and life seemed to hold endless possibility. Somewhere along the way, however, those aspirations faded away and we grew tired and lost our ambition. People often wonder, "Is it too late to become the person that I once envisioned I would be? Can life still be fulfilling for me?" Sure, we have all heard the story of Rabbi Akiva who turned his life around at the age of 40 and became a notable *talmid chacham*, but what does that have to do with me?

The answer is that a life of fulfillment is within your reach; **it is not too late**.

A well-known adage says, "You can't teach an old dog new tricks." This means that at a certain age, you are who and what you are, and not much is going to change for the better. It's a futile expression, which is perhaps true of dogs and cats, but is definitely NOT true of humans. I have heard the words "I am too old to change" from people in their 20s, 30s, and 40s and have also seen 70 and 80 year-olds tackling new challenges for the very first time.

The *Sifsei Chaim* writes:

> *There are people whose primary thoughts, discussions, and daily occupation revolve around the past. This is especially prevalent among older people who have left the cycle of work and perceive their present and future state as weak and uncertain. As a result, they embrace the past — a time when they were young and vibrant and accomplished a lot. Living in the past becomes their primary source of pleasure and satisfaction and they believe that this provides them with meaning in the present. They repeat the feats of their youth, over and over, to anyone who will be kind enough to listen.*
>
> **They are, however, making a colossal mistake, because anyone who is alive must believe that every moment in life has its purpose and that purpose will be found in the present and not in the past.** *While people who are advanced in years aren't expected to exert themselves as they did when they were younger, they are expected to apply themselves according to their capabilities at every stage of life.*

These holy words are so true and so full of impact. Every moment in life has its purpose, and that is true at any age. Let us examine why this MUST be so.

Meet Mr. 48-Year-old

A man came to seek advice several years ago, because, let's just say, his life wasn't going as planned. It quickly became apparent that there were some real changes that he needed to undertake if his life were going to move forward instead of backward. His response after I shared my first idea for development was "You are so right, but I am too old to change. I am 'already' 48 years old."

I responded, "So in essence, you are calling the Ribono shel Olam a bad investor."

He gave me a perplexed look, and so I explained.

Imagine a banker who invests large sums of money in a company and initially watches it grow its revenues year after year. Naturally, he will continue to add to his investment. Now suppose that after a number of years the earnings begin to stagnate, or worse, they begin to decline. Well, now he isn't so sure if further investment is a good idea. His next step is to find out what's going on from the people inside the company. He quickly schedules a meeting with the CEO and at the meeting the CEO offers logical explanations as to what had transpired: Some mistakes were made but they are working to rectify them; new competitors entered the market and in response they are revamping their product offering; the economy was weak and is now improving. The investor, in this case, would be wise to keep investing.

What happens, however, if all the CEO can offer in response is, "Well, what can I say. It is what it is. We had some good years but this company has reached its potential and cannot grow any further," or "We made some serious mistakes but we are too set in our ways to do anything about them." As you can imagine, no right-minded investor would add another dime to this company, and in fact, would be wise to sell the stake already invested.

In the words of the Tanya, Nefesh HaChaim and many others, we are each alive right now only because at this very moment Hakadosh Baruch Hu is creating us anew, by blowing a neshamah (both breath and soul) into us. It is ***not*** *because being alive is the default option for everyone who was born into the world. There is no status quo of being alive, because we need the infusion of life each and every second or we would revert entirely back to a state of ayin, sheer nothingness. In fact, this is why change is possible in the first place — because our very essence is built on continuous renewal. We refer to this when we say each morning "Hamechadesh b'tuvo b'chol yom tamid maaseh bereishis" — in His goodness, He renews daily, perpetually, the work of creation.*

Mr. 48-year-old, can you imagine if Adam, the first man on earth, would have spoken your words at the ripe old age of 48! What would he have done with his life for the next 882 years? If growth were no longer possible at your age, then why would Hakadosh Baruch Hu continue to infuse you with life, given that we know Hashem to be the very wisest investor of all? Could it be that you, the CEO of your life, don't even know what your company is capable of?" Imagine if the CEO of a company had given up on any future potential for growth, and then one day Warren Buffett, one of today's greatest investors, visits the company and says "WOW! This company has real potential." Wouldn't the CEO want to try to figure out why a great investor like Mr. Buffett feels that way? Shouldn't we want to know what great potential lies in our future, given that the Creator of all is telling us that it exists?

Life is a gift and we are meant to use every single day to grow, whether we see the freshness of youth or wrinkles when we look in the mirror. Being old is a state of mind. A person is truly old only when he no longer believes he can make more of himself.

What Mr. 48-year-old was really saying was that he was set in his ways, perhaps tired of the struggle and lacking the motivation to change. In that case, there are many 23-year-olds who feel just as "old" as he does.

Some will surely argue that it is easier to change ourselves when we are younger and less set in our ways. This is true, but we can counter-argue that, on the other hand, at a younger age we do not yet have the skills to change; neither do we fully realize the importance of change. Without the skills and perspective, we lack the motivation. The perfect scenario would be to put the experience of someone older into the body of someone younger; this is something we try really hard to do with our children, but it rarely works. Every age group faces its own set of challenges that must be overcome, but change and growth is equally within the reach of all.

Satan says: ***"Who has the time and energy?"***

We respond: ***"We do, because this is our highest priority."***

Success and fulfillment may seem like lofty ideas to some. They feel that in today's world, just surviving is difficult enough. When they do find some time for themselves, they want to relax and take their mind off serious matters.

We can all empathize with such feelings; life can be utterly exhausting and we all need a break and time to recharge. Making survival our life's goal, however, means existing but not living. Imagine a man who is marooned on a deserted island, subsisting on berries and plants while spending his days evading a pack of hungry wolves that regard him as a tasty dinner. Ask him, "What is motivating you to survive?" and he would answer, "I need to stay alive long enough for someone to rescue me." The moment he realizes that no one is even searching for him, he will lose his energy to run, because he will think, "What is the point of surviving if I will never really live life?" Neither should we make survival our goal; we should strive to really live. This entails exalted ideals, because life is the loftiest of gifts, given to us by our Creator. Sure, we can spend some of our time relaxing and enjoying ourselves, and to some degree that is good for us, but it can't become life's mission. Getting through the day in order to relax, so we can get through another day, is not living.

In the coming chapters we will share Torah-based knowledge and techniques that will make "living" a real and achievable goal. The

Satan, however, wants you to remain in survival mode and will try to convince you that surviving is a viable alternative. Well, you have a very good reason to survive and ALSO to live, because many people are looking up to you and are eager to learn life skills from you. Your family, friends and all of Klal Yisrael need you as a role model, so we can't let the hungry wolf get his way.

Satan says: ***"You get to live life as you choose, so what's wrong with being satisfied with average?"***

We respond: ***"Taking the easy route may lead to short-term pleasure, but in the longer run I will be miserable."***

Why can't a person exercise free choice, opt for a life of mediocrity, and find happiness in that? Why opt for a struggle?

The reason is that as powerful as free choice is, it cannot alter the rules of reality. The Creator of everything taught us the realities of life through the holy Torah, and He alone makes the rules. A successful life entails accepting reality for what it is instead of trying to create an artificial one that better suits our whims. As an example, we might all wish that we could eat lots of chocolate cake and remain thin. Some people may choose to indulge in the cake while adopting the artificial reality that "a little cake here and there doesn't affect me." However, if their "little cake" is in reality more than a little, the size of their waist will ultimately prove them wrong. Reality always wins.

The reality of life is that we are each endowed with a lofty soul that is intrinsic to our existence. As a consequence of our soul's loftiness, we can't just squeak by. Ultimately, our destiny will catch up to us and we will grow disenchanted with life. Being average may suit us for now but one day it won't. Imagine a man who spends a few million dollars on a Lamborghini sports car and only uses it to drive to the corner bodega to buy milk. Each time he steps on the gas pedal, the engine will scream out in frustration, "Utilize me! I want to go 200 MPH on an open road. Why are you wasting me on this pot-hole infested side street?" Inside that body of ours is an engine that can soar faster and higher than any man-made machine. It is a force powerful enough to change the world. Our super-charged engines will only lie dormant for so long before we will begin to grow restless, frustrated, and depressed. This is a reality that none of us are able to escape, and the sooner we recognize this, the sooner we begin to live life in earnest.

In truth, no one wants to live an average life. Those who claim they do have merely given up because they are afraid to try for more and fail. Were someone to hand them an achievable roadmap to success, most would invest the time and energy needed to get there. The challenge is that some have bought into the idea that success is no longer in their future or that it should be achievable with a lot less toil.

Most importantly, we must understand that most everyone will feel uninspired at times. Life is a journey during which we sometimes seem to be moving forward and sometimes backward, and other times we feel stuck in neutral. We may watch others whizz by us and we may think, "Why can't that be me?" or despair and think, "What's the point of pushing myself if I don't see results?" While we would always hope to be moving in the right direction, in reality, even successful people falter at times. Everyone experiences ups and downs.

Satan says: ***"It's just too difficult. I am too strong. You will never succeed."***

We respond: ***"You want me to believe that, but it just isn't true."***

There is a famous parable about a man who sees a massive bull that is tied to a tree with a very flimsy rope. He turns to the farmer and says, "Seriously, do you expect that shoelace to keep that bull from charging?" The farmer says, "It works like a charm. I began using that thin rope when he was just a newborn calf, and he still hasn't realized that with one pull he can run free."

The *Chovos HaLevavos* (*Shaar Yichud HaMaaseh* Ch. 5) tells us that the most effective weapon we have against the Satan is our intellect. Even though it may seem that he is bigger and stronger than we are, through the power of intellect, the Satan quickly falls under our control and it becomes easy for us to mitigate the damage that he wants to bring upon us. The reason is that a bit of truth will dispel loads of falsehood, just as a bit of light dispels a lot of darkness.

He's weak; his strength is but a mirage, meant to scare us into submission. However, we may not realize this, because we are too intimidated to fight him.

The holy Piaseczna Rebbe (*Hachsharas Avreichim* Ch. 9) teaches:

> *I would like to mention that teachers and educators do wrong to discourage their students by painting the evil inclination as something powerful. It is human nature that if we hear about a mighty person of overwhelming strength, our hands and entire body will weaken and we will be incapable of withstanding him. Then our opponent will certainly overcome us — not because he is mighty, but because we are weak.*
>
> *The evil inclination is like a highway robber (based on Bereishis Rabbah 22) who is actually weak, and robs people only because they are afraid of him and think he is mighty. But a clever person sees that he is not mighty and so crushes and shatters him.*

The Satan is keeping us rooted where we are with nothing but a piece of thread. The moment we realize this, he will be revealed as the deceiver that he is.

Satan says: ***"You don't have mazel."***

We respond: ***"A person can rise above mazel, and no one knows what his mazel is."***

One evening at a lecture, a man asked me, "What about *mazel*? Isn't it true that some people don't have any *mazel*?"

My response began with a tangential, yet relevant, point. People often ask me how I deal with anti-Semitism in my profession, and my answer is always the same: I don't, because I have never experienced any. While working in corporate finance, I have traveled the country extensively and met with numerous executives at public companies in cities where Jews rarely step foot, and yet never once felt that I was being looked at differently — yarmulke and all. Some predicted that I would surely fail unless I removed my yarmulke, and they were all proven wrong.

For those who walk around looking for anti-Semitism, it will be everywhere, sometimes real and sometimes imagined. Those who live their lives as though it doesn't exist will rarely openly encounter it. Did a number of the people I met think thoughts of anti-Semitism? Likely. Did someone choose not to do business with me because I am Jewish? Probably. Did I ever give the matter a moment's thought? No.

When someone is not successful in business and blames it on not hiding his Jewishness, his troubles stem from his lack of *bitachon* and the resulting insecurity and lack of confidence he feels when he thinks, "The person across the desk from me is looking down at me." How can anyone effectively conduct business with thoughts like that swirling around in his head?

The Torah tells us that when the spies described their experiences as they entered Eretz Yisrael and encountered giants, they said (*Bamidbar* 13:33), "We were like grasshoppers in our eyes (compared to them) and so we were in their eyes." The Vilna Gaon tells us that the spies had no idea what the giants were thinking; they were merely projecting their own self-image onto them. They felt like insects and therefore assumed they were being regarded as such. Even if the giants were thinking that, it was only because the spies had those thoughts about themselves.

You are probably wondering what anti-Semitism has to do with *mazel*? The answer is: everything. They are two things that only have power over us to the degree that we give credence to them.

Not having *mazel* is one of the best cop-out excuses on which people can blame their mediocrity or failure. Many believe that *mazel* dictates their past, present, and future. They believe that, "It's destined that I not succeed," as though if they did succeed, they would be causing cosmic disorder in the upper worlds. We even coined a phrase for this attitude — *shlemazel*. May the worst sin we must answer for when we stand before the Heavenly court be, "Your *mazel* was to fail and you had the audacity to go and succeed!" The Gemara (*Chagiga* 15A) relates that Acher (Elisha ben Avuya, a scholar- turned-apostate) heard a Heavenly voice call, "Return, my children, return, except for Acher," and he therefore gave up trying to repent. He was faulted for this surrender, because we are not supposed to pay attention to proclamations that claim to pre-determine the outcome of our lives; they fly in the face of free will and obstruct our direct relationship with our Creator.

If someone walks around wearing a self-made label that says, "I have no *mazel*," it will prove to be a self-fulfilling prophecy. They will then live to say, "See, I told you I don't have *mazel*!"

The topic of *mazel*, which is the influence of the constellations/zodiac, is deep and spoken about extensively by Chazal. It is not necessary to delve into how and whether *mazel* impacts our lives. What is relevant is that (1) we each have the power to transcend *mazel*, and (2) despite what some may think, no one knows what their *mazel* is.

A *pasuk* in *Bereishis* (5-15:3) records Avraham telling Hashem that he has no benefit from all the goodness that he was given because he doesn't have a child who will inherit it from him. Hashem directs Avraham, "Go outside and try to see if you can count the stars. So too will be your offspring." The Gemara (*Yoma* 28b) teaches that Avraham was the most capable stargazer of his generation and that kings from afar would come and seek the predictions that he gleaned from the constellations. With this skill Avraham was able to see in the stars that he was not destined to have children. The Gemara (*Shabbos* 156a) teaches that when Hashem told him to "go outside," he was telling him to go out from under the influence of constellations.

Rav Yochanan, Shmuel, Rabbi Akiva, and Rav Nachman bar Yitzchak all conclude that *"ein mazel l'Yisrael,"* the Jewish nation is not dictated by *mazel*. The Ramban (*Bereishis* 17:1) writes: "A person should ingrain in his heart that Hashem is the only Power and He can bring goodness to everyone and anyone. Chazal tell us the reason that the Patriarchs and Matriarchs suffered with infertility was to demonstrate that we live above the natural order. In the natural order of the world, the Jewish people would not exist.

Unlike Avraham, none of us are stargazers and none of us have a clue as to what our *mazel* is or isn't. *Bitachon* means that we live with the belief that Hashem, irrespective of the constellations, runs the world. Our role is to think positively and trust that our Torah-guided efforts in all areas of life will bring success.

To summarize, the Satan will try his best to fill our minds with put-downs and thoughts of futility and despair, but these ideas are only as real as we allow them to be. Hakadosh Baruch Hu stands behind us as we strive toward our optimal growth, and He will aid in the process. We must learn to tune out the Satan, do our part, and take one step forward toward becoming the person we once envisioned we would be — a person who is successful.

We are now left with defining the word success, but before we do, we will first need to "un-define" it.

2

Defining Success

Any endeavor should begin with an understanding of what we are setting out to accomplish and how we will know when we've gotten there. Without this information, our efforts are bound to end in disappointment.

For example, imagine you are a husband who wants to give his wife a gift — usually a good idea — and so you buy something that you want her to have. As she unwraps the gift, the look on her face tells it all: she doesn't like it. Even worse, she asks if you would mind if she returns it. You are crushed and quite upset. How ungrateful can she be after all the effort and thought you put into buying it?

In retrospect, all this aggravation could have been avoided by asking yourself: (1) What am I trying to achieve with this gift? (2) How will success be defined? The answer to the first question is: to show my affection. The second answer, the marker of your success, is her delight upon receiving the gift. Well, if that's the case, the gift should have been something **she would want,** as opposed to something **you want her to have**. The lack of definition translated to a less than favorable outcome.

Okay, so she returns the gift; it's not the end of the world. But suppose it's not a gift we are talking about. Suppose it's the choice of a spouse. Imagine a person who didn't understand the objective of marriage and what constitutes a successful relationship. Is it likely that this person will choose the right partner and live in harmony?

If that sounds scary, let's imagine an even scarier one. Suppose a person never stops and asks, "What is the objective of life and what is the definition of successful living?" This person just lives, or worse, he lives with an erroneous definition. Is it likely that success will be his? Let's illustrate this using the game of chess.

Someone playing for the first time would be advised to read the instructions and learn the object of the game, which is to capture the opponent's king. Imagine that the person skipped the instructions, thinking, "Who needs instructions?" Instead, he played the game assuming that the goal was to lose fewer pieces than his opponent. This is quite a logical assumption, except that it's totally wrong. The player would therefore surely lose the match. In chess, a player who has lost many pieces can win even if the opponent hasn't lost any pieces at all.

Now let's imagine a person who thinks that the objective of life is to enjoy himself. What are the odds that he will succeed at meeting this objective, when the *Mesillas Yesharim* reminds us that the "years of man are filled with an abundance of pain, sickness, aches, and problems?"

Rav Shach once said that in the previous generations, the challenges we faced came from people becoming exposed to false *hashkafos* and opening their minds to heresy. Today's challenge is that we don't think at all, and therefore buy into the idea that we are here to enjoy ourselves as much as we can before our time runs out.

To recap: ***A clear and accurate definition of success will point us in the right direction.***

Furthermore, having a clear definition for life's objective and success will spare us the agony of realizing later in life that we adopted the flawed definitions of others around us. We are, after all, exposed to the word "success" every day, in what we read and hear in the workplace and see in advertisements. We are inundated with information about the presumably praiseworthy attributes that "successful people" possess. All this information inevitably seeps into our consciousness; it serves to influence our own opinions and ultimately the direction and aspirations for our own lives.

It is no secret; the world around us has adopted a warped definition for the term success. Society idolizes affluence and people line up for the autographs of those who are famous for something, no matter how trivial that something might be. Society also looks down upon people who are different, who don't quite fit in.

The Rambam writes (*Hilchos Dei'os* 6:1) that a person is naturally influenced by his surroundings. We must, therefore, remain highly vigilant and resilient if we want our lives to remain on the right track. The very air we breathe contains the ideology that fulfillment is to be found in worldly affairs, and that eternal pursuits were meant for the overly pious. It is therefore possible that the inaccurate definition of success is already ingrained in your mind. We must first dispel the myth so that we can embrace the truth — uproot some weeds in order to plant roses.

Let's start by acknowledging that while swimming against the tide of society is never easy, it is far from impossible. How fortunate we are that as Torah Jews we have truth embedded in our DNA. If we just open our eyes, the falsehood of these ideologies becomes apparent.

To recap: ***A clear and accurate definition of success will prevent us from adopting the falsehood of the world at large.***

Before we discuss the Torah's definition of success and life's objective, let us analyze what the Torah tells us they are not.

◆§ Wealth

Is there any one word that encompasses "success" more than wealth and the luxuries it brings? Most of us are guilty of having some deep-rooted notion that money and success are one and the same. I was once no different, but the years I spent on Wall Street, the realm of "ultimate success," served to cure me of this fallacy. While the stories are numerous, here is one that served as a real eye-opener.

Meet Sarah

**Sarah "had it all." She had never worked a day in her life; she had no need to do so. Her late brother, who never married,* *had left her hundreds of millions of dollars. She had six homes on four continents, an art collection worth tens of millions, and more money than a person could spend in many lifetimes.*

When Sarah was first referred to me, she was described as "uber successful," but I was warned, "She's impossible to work with and will eat you alive if you slip up even once."

Things worked out just fine and never once, in all the years she was a client, did a harsh word come between us. She was a Jewish woman, after all, and responded when someone spoke to her neshamah. She really liked when I spoke to her in Yiddish, her "mama-lashon," and doing so always magically calmed her.

One reason we got on so well is that I wanted nothing from her. Well, almost nothing. There was just one thing — that she part with some of her money and give charity while she was still alive. We discussed it many times and the answer she gave was always the same: "As soon as I return from Italy… France… my two weeks at the spa…" The last time we spoke was at her hospital bedside, where I said, "Sarah, you may be meeting 'your Hashem' (as she would so fondly refer to Hakadosh Baruch Hu) soon, and He will ask what you did with all of the abundance He gave you. What will you say? Why not put just 1 million dollars into a foundation, and when you are no longer here, we can name a school after you. We have seen you earn more money than that in just a single day."

She removed the oxygen mask from her face, smiled at me and said, "Just as soon as I get out of the hospital, dear."

Which, sadly, she never did.

Her funeral took place graveside, with just myself, my one Jewish associate, her grandson and seven Chabad boys that I managed to find in the cemetery who agreed to join us so that one Kaddish could be recited for her. There were no friends, other family members, neighbors or members of charitable organizations.

Even as I write this story many years later, I feel deep pain and sorrow at the tragedy of it all. Sarah had a *neshamah*, just like you and me. She would wait for me by the window when I would bring her a *lulav* and *esrog* to shake each year, and would remind me three times not to forget to send her "those round matzas." She loved "her Hashem" and spoke of Him often, so how could things have gone so terribly wrong? How can a person "have it all" yet leave this world with so little?

Is that the definition of a successful life? A life lived in such a manner that the person's passing causes almost no one to shed a tear? OK, you might be thinking, Sarah wasn't there to witness her sparse funeral, but surely life was pleasurable for her while she was alive. All that money — surely it bought her lots of happiness and pleasure.

I can attest that it didn't. She rarely smiled.

If you have heard this a million times before, yet still don't fully believe it, please listen to someone who is surrounded by extraordinary wealth all day long. Money does NOT buy happiness. While wealth may solve some of life's issues, it introduces many more. I have heard the sentence, "I was much happier when I had less," spoken many times in my years on Wall Street. Some wealthy people live happy and fulfilling lives and others do not, but the size of their bank accounts is NOT the determining factor.

☙ Disappointing Results

The Torah is clear as to why wealth and luxury don't buy happiness. It's because when wealth itself becomes life's goal, we never feel like we have enough, no matter how much we have. Shlomo HaMelech warned us that "a lover of money will never be satisfied with money" (*Koheles* 5:9). A life lived in a constant state of lack, needing that next dollar or "thing," is never a happy one. A person whose primary goal is to acquire more can never appreciate what he has; after the thrill of new acquisition fades, he is once again left empty.

I was once having lunch with a client and, during our conversation, I inquired about his friend David. His response: "David is doing really well. He earned 27 million dollars last year. I am hoping to get there one day, because, that's what I call REAL money." This came from a man who earned over 5 million dollars that year, but that was no longer REAL money to him.

◆§ Why Is It So? Why Don't We Ever Feel Like We Have Enough?

The *Haflaah* in *Panim Yafos* (*Parashas Re'eh* 14:22) teaches a profound lesson which opens our eyes as to why the pursuit of wealth is a never-ending chase. The *Midrash* (*Koheles* 1:34) tells us that someone who has one wants two, the one who has two wants four, and so it goes forever. Those who chase wealth are never satisfied. As the *Midrash* says, "A person will leave this world with less than half of his desires having been met." This is because up until the very end, he will want double of whatever he has.

The *Panim Yafos* asks, why does the *Midrash* speak of a progression from one to two, two to four… Why did it not simply say, "One who has $1 wants $200,000,000,000.00?"

The answer is that if a person realized upfront that he would never be happy, no matter how much wealth he had, he would become repulsed by the chase and would spend his life pursuing something more obtainable, meaningful, and fulfilling instead. He would stop and think, "If I won't be happy even with $200 billion, then what's the point of even trying? I may as well do something worthwhile with my time." The last thing the Satan wants is for us to realize the futility of the chase, and so he tries another tactic; he deceives us. He has us believe that the reason we don't feel satisfied is that we truly do not yet have enough, but once we reach 2, we will be satisfied. Then we can quit the chase and pursue that meaningful idea. However, once we reach 2, he says, "Oops, we made a mistake. Two wasn't enough, but that's only because of inflation. Without question, 4 will do the trick." And so it goes until the very end. As a wise person once said, "People can never have enough of things they don't need."

The Rambam writes (*Moreh Nevuchim* 3:12) that there are three kinds of troubles and pain that can potentially befall a person. The first kind is a result of natural circumstances such as birth defects and diseases that develop later in life. The second kind arises from people's acts of aggression against each other, which results in war, animosity, and hatred. The third category of troubles, which is by far the largest, is comprised of the troubles we each bring upon ourselves through our pursuit of excess and indulgences. As the Rambam explains:

> *These desires are without limit, while things that are necessary are few in number and restricted within certain limits. A person needs food, clothing, and shelter.* ***What is superfluous, however, is without end.*** *Those who are ignorant in their thought are constantly in pain because they cannot obtain the many superfluous things that others possess. The virtuous and wise, on the other hand, know their purpose in this world and seek only that which is necessary.*

The Satan dangles a carrot on a stick, luring people to chase an elusive goal for their entire lives. The Satan uses the same tactic to lure us into pursuing other worldly pleasures as well. Once we have obtained or experienced anything physically pleasurable, the law of diminishing returns kicks in and we need bigger and better. However, we think all the while that at some point, we will find the satisfaction and contentment we seek.

◆§ Honor

"Okay, money may not buy happiness, but being famous — name recognition — must account for something."

It does — indigestion.

> *Once, when Rav Boruch Ber came to America to collect money for his yeshivah in Kaminetz, a fundraising dinner was held on his behalf. His host, who had the honor of calling the Rav to the podium for his speech, introduced the Rav by enumerating all of his accolades. After the Rav addressed the crowd, the main course of fish was served. The host turned to the Rav and said, "The Rav may not want to eat the fish. It tastes a bit off." The Rav replied, "It tastes fine," and he ate it.*
>
> *Later that night, the host was awakened to the sound of Rav Boruch Ber heaving in the bathroom. When the Rav exited, the host said, "I told the Rav the fish was spoiled." Rav Boruch Ber*

replied, "The fish? I'm not sick from the fish. I'm sick from the exaggerated praise you gave me in your speech."

It is for good reason that the Mishnah in *Avos* lists *kavod*, honor, as one of the three pursuits that "remove a person from this world." Seeking honor can become an all-consuming endeavor, one that devours much time and energy, thereby leaving little mind-space for more important things.

Which aliyah did I get?
Was I seated at the right table?
Did they show me enough respect?
Was I noticed when I made my grand entrance?
Were any accolades omitted from my title?

The person who is obsessed with honor lives in a world of his own making, completely engulfed by his ego-driven pursuit and oblivious to the reality around him. He doesn't see that it's all a facade; it is rare for people to truly honor someone who expects to be honored.

We will never satisfy our hunger for recognition. Trying to do so is like drinking sea water when we are desperately thirsty; it only increases our thirst and makes us sick. The reason is that the more honor a person receives, the more his ego grows, which in turn stimulates an even greater hunger for honor. Each year on Purim, we mock Haman for his quick rise to power and even quicker downfall. The Vilna Gaon says that Haman's greatest character flaw can be found in the words: וְכָל זֶה אֵינֶנּוּ שֹׁוֶה לִי בְּכָל עֵת אֲשֶׁר אֲנִי רֹאֶה אֶת מָרְדֳּכַי הַיְּהוּדִי יוֹשֵׁב בְּשַׁעַר הַמֶּלֶךְ — *Yet all this is worth nothing to me as long as I see Mordechai the Jew sitting at the king's gate* (*Esther* 5:13). Despite "having it all," Haman was completely miserable because one Jewish sage refused to bow to him. His pathetic ego so desperately needed recognition that he couldn't function without it. The fifty-cubit gallows he erected in the hopes of reclaiming his honor ultimately became the instrument of his own demise.

My mechutan, Rav Ephraim Wachsman, tells a great story about a time when he traveled in the business-class section of a plane. Seated next to him was an Arab sheik. They conversed a bit during the flight and the sheik made sure to mention, numerous times throughout the conversation, that he normally didn't fly on a commercial plane, because he owned his own jet, but it was currently being repaired. Rabbi Wachsman thought, "Can you imagine, an Arab oil magnate wouldn't be able to live with himself if a Jewish rabbi from Monsey, who he will never see again, walked away thinking that he usually flies business class on a commercial airline. Is there anything more pathetic than a person who is so addicted to honor?"

☙ Social Standing

"Okay, the goal is not wealth and it's not honor, but we are surely successful if we fit in and win the approval of others."

Living a life focused on making a good impression and gaining the acceptance of others is an all-consuming and futile endeavor for several reasons. First, even if we bend ourselves into a pretzel, we will never meet with everyone's approval, and therefore, life will be fraught with disappointment. One of life's greatest ironies is that at the same time we are worrying about what others are thinking of us, they are trying to figure out what we think of them.

Secondly, does it even matter what most others think? There are people in our lives whose opinions truly matter, because it tells us something about our behaviors and areas of development, but these are rarely the ones from whom we crave approval. Instead we are focused on everyone else: acquaintances or complete strangers.

The need for mass acceptance is often a weakness in self-esteem — something we will address throughout this book. When people don't fully accept themselves, they often try to fill that void with other people's acceptance. In doing so, they live like chameleons, changing their opinions and mannerisms to suit those whose acceptance they are trying to win.

Some may feel that investing in a high-approval rating may lead to positive returns if and when they need something from someone. This seems to be a safety net for life: "I am so well liked that surely someone will be there for me should the need arise." Sadly, that is rarely the case, as too many have learned when they actually did need people and learned the lesson as to who their true friends were.

The *Chovos HaLevavos* writes (*Shaar HaBitachon* Ch. 3) that a fundamental aspect of *bitachon* is the belief that without the consent of Hakadosh Baruch Hu, no human can assist or harm us in any way, shape, or form. He writes that when a person internalizes this concept, he ceases to fear others and is no longer motivated to hope for their assistance or seek favor in their eyes. This is what we are meant to instill in ourselves when we recite the first *Ani Maamin* each day — that Hakadosh Baruch Hu alone creates and guides all creatures. Essentially, *bitachon* means letting go of fictitious safety nets and realizing that only Hakadosh Baruch Hu can help us.

Lastly, conforming to the masses will only serve to lead us off course, because to be successful, we must rise above the average people around us. Recently, at a lecture to a group of students from Berlin, a young man raised his hand and asked, "I have been on a path of self-growth for a number of years and have found that with each new thing I master, I have less in common with my peers and have fewer friends. What am I doing wrong?" The obvious answer was, "You are doing nothing wrong. Growth often means moving ahead of others and, therefore, having less in common with them. This is why growth-oriented people sometimes redefine their circle of friends at various stages in their life and may ultimately have fewer yet deeper and more dependable relationships."

The undeniable fact is that most often, what others think of us has absolutely no bearing or impact on our lives. There are those whose opinions do matter — parents, mentors, close friends. We will always want to consider their opinions because they have our best interests at heart. Beyond that, we would do ourselves a tremendous favor if the degree of attention we paid to what most everyone else thinks was highly discriminate. We weren't put here to win a popularity contest, and time spent gaining the approval of others only detracts from the important work on hand.

To recap: ***The three most common goals people view as a mark of success — wealth, honor, and acceptance — can never bring fulfillment.***

◆§ The *Neshamah* Knows Better

Did you notice the common theme between all three pursuits: materialism, honor, and acceptance? They lead to a disappointing life, spent chasing happiness that proves elusive, because the void we are feeling inside is not filled. That void is a good thing; it gets us off the couch and pushes us to make something of ourselves. The source of that void, however, is our *neshamah*. It knows what great potential this world possesses and is also only interested in pursuits that are of an eternal nature. The *neshamah* has absolutely no use for these mortal, transitory goals, and therefore it cannot be satiated with them. This can be illustrated by the story of the two kings.

The Two Kings

In *Chovos HaLevavos* (*Shaar Avodas Elokim,* Ch. 9), Rabbeinu Bachya tells a story of an island near India where the inhabitants came up with an extreme form of term limits: Each year, a foreigner would be appointed as their king, but, when the year was up, he would be banished from the island, taking with him nothing but the shirt on his back. Their first king was a foolish man. He never asked them how the system worked. Accordingly, he spent the entire year amassing wealth, building palaces and enhancing them. Not only that, but he imported to the island all the possessions he had in foreign lands. When the year was up, he was banished against his will and bereft of all of his possessions. He spent the remainder of his life deeply regretting his failure to learn the rules of the game up front so that he could have taken advantage of the opportunity that was given to him.

The Second King

The second king was a wise man. The first thing he did when he arrived at the island was to find someone who could tell him what had happened to the previous king. The mentor told him the whole story and stressed that the very same thing would be done to him.

Armed with this information, the second king did things differently. His efforts were focused on exporting all that he could off the island, while leaving in place the wealth he held elsewhere. He passed through the year experiencing a mix of pain and happiness intermingled. His pain was because his reign as king would soon end and he had not yet exported everything that he wanted to export. His happiness was because he knew that after he was banished, he would return to a place where great riches were waiting for him. When his year was up and the people escorted him off the island, he did not kick and scream like his predecessor; rather, the second king left with his head held high.

Lessons

Rabbeinu Bachya meant to convey several deep messages with this story. One king sought advice and learned the objective of his endeavor, and one did not. Our time here is very short and regret after the fact will not help us. Most importantly, there are things that we accumulate in this world that stay here after we leave, but there are also things that accrue for us in the world to which we are going. It is the latter kind of acquisitions on which the *neshamah* wants us to focus. If we do not, our *neshamah* will be ill at ease and we will not feel inner happiness.

Before we move on it is important to clarify: We are not suggesting that wealth, reputation, or acceptance by a community cannot be elements of successful living. They each have great benefits when acquired for the right reasons and used correctly. Were it not for philanthropists, many institutions and organizations would not survive. A person can accomplish worthwhile achievements with name recognition and so much can be gained when we display humility and are willing to conform to the standards of the good people around us. The pitfall we must guard against is pursuing these achievements for the wrong reasons and making these pursuits our life's mission. When we put our main focus on life's true objectives, these elements can prove complementary.

◆ But I Am Different

In the last chapter we discussed some of the Satan's tactics. We will now dispel one more.

Perhaps some of what we discussed seems obvious. After all, who doesn't know that money doesn't buy happiness? Don't we laugh to ourselves when we see people chasing honor, or pity those who thirst for approval? Of course, but that won't stop the Satan from trying to convince each of us that in *our* case, matters will be different. We will be the exception to the rule that "money can't buy happiness" or we WILL find fulfillment in acceptance and honor.

> *I recently sat across from a man at a wedding whose entire life was falling apart due to his unhealthy addictions and failing marriage. The lotto drawing the next day was for over 100 million dollars. When I asked him if he had purchased a ticket, he responded, "More than one." I said, "I am sure you realize that the very worst thing that could happen would be for you to win the lottery, since it would enable you to do ever more harmful things to yourself — things that you would readily do now but can't afford." He answered, "Not at all! If I win, I will use the money to turn my life around."*

Can't we all relate to this mindset? Don't we sometimes want things that we intuitively know are detrimental — things that we have seen ruin other people's lives? We still want them because we tell ourselves that we are somehow special and therefore, we are immune to that harm. If we stopped to think, it would be obvious that those things are damaging to our friends and neighbors, and yet we want them anyway. We think, "I will have the mansion, yet my children will remain humble and balanced. I will have power, fame, and influence, yet it won't affect my ego, marriage, and friendships. I will have great wealth, yet it won't distract me from life's purpose, nor disconnect me from Hashem."

With this fallacy of "I will be different," the Satan leads us down a path to nowhere, only allowing us to realize our mistake when it is too late. In the words of Rav Nachman of Breslov, the Satan is like someone running around a marketplace with his hands closed. The buyers think to themselves, "He surely has what I need," and so they chase after him. Only when the market closes does he open his hands and reveal that they were empty; he had nothing at all. In the days of Rav Nachman, this was the case. Today, I would argue, it is far worse. The Satan is running around with his hands wide open, clearly displaying the emptiness he is offering. We have only to open our eyes to see the reality happening all around us: depression, challenged children, broken families, addictions... yet some keep chasing after him and buying into his way of life.

> *A young man once sat in my office and revealed to me that he was drowning in an ocean of sin. I asked, "Are you aware that these types of behaviors are destroying your life?" He responded, "Of course I know that, but I still don't want to stop." (This story does have a happy ending. He did b"H turn his life around.)*

We actually *can* be different — by chasing loftier pursuits. When we live life as it should be lived, we don't squander wealth and name recognition on indulgence and self-promotion. We use them to further life's real purpose.

In summation: It is important to adopt a valid definition of success and life's objective. We can embrace the path of the first king or the second. As we begin our reign, we would be wise to seek direction, which is found in the holy Torah and in the *mesorah* that our Rabbanim, Rebbetzins, and mentors impart to us.

While wealth, materialism, reputation, and acceptance can play an important role in our lives, they will only do so when our lives are built on a foundation of purpose and meaning that transcend this world.

In this chapter we have underscored what success is not. We are now ready to define what it is.

3

Success: What It Is

With all the weeds gone, it's now time to plant some roses.

⌘ What Is Success?

When we reach the milestone of a *siyum mesechta* (completion of a tractate of Talmud), we recite the beautiful prayer that highlights the difference between our pursuits/toils and "theirs" — the secular world's pursuits. Although we and the rest of the world may work toward several of the same goals — raising and supporting children, helping others, obtaining knowledge — the outcome differs greatly because our intentions and motivations are different. How fortunate are we that at an early age we are handed a copy of life's instruction manual, the Torah, through which we learn the objective of life and the only real definition of success. This definition is to **understand and then to fulfill our purpose in being here**. As we will discuss, life has a universal purpose, each of our lives has a specific purpose, and the objective of life is to fulfill that purpose.

We wake each morning and thank Hakadosh Baruch Hu for giving us another day; we thereby recognize the day as a new opportunity, and hope to make the most of it. To fulfill the day's potential, we must start out by asking ourselves, "What is the reason that I was given this day? What purpose does it hold?" The answer to this question gives us direction — a mission for the next 24 hours. Living this way day after day is sure to lead to a successful life.

☙ Success in Every Situation

It may seem, then, that success depends on being able to check off a "mission accomplished" list at the end of each day. That would mean that when obstacles occur and we cannot carry out our intention, we have been unsuccessful. This is a mistake. We each have the power to choose success in every one of life's situations, because they all contain purpose.

The Torah illustrates this point. There is only one time it confers the exalted title *"ish matzliach,"* successful man, on anyone, and that is Yosef HaTzaddik, in *Parashas Vayeishev* (39:2). He alone is awarded this title despite the fact that from the standpoint of western society, he would appear to be anything but a success at that point in his life. He was a slave living in a foreign country, estranged from his brothers, without a friend in the world or a piastre (Egyptian penny) to his name, and he was about to be thrown into a dungeon for a crime he didn't commit.

The Torah crowns him with the title "successful" because rather than giving up, he rose to the top in whatever way was possible under the circumstances. He ran the affairs of Potiphar like clockwork, garnered his master's respect and trust and later did the same in prison. He remained an *ish*, which Chazal tell us is the highest status of a man, by retaining his stature and dignity even when his situation was about as bleak as it could get. He never lost hope, nor did he become bitter and blame others. There is not a single verse in the Torah that records Yosef bemoaning the injustices that were perpetrated upon him. He simply made the very best of every situation.

From Yosef HaTzaddik we can learn one of life's most important lessons: a person is in the position to choose success or failure in every one of life's situations. He can rise to the top of humanity while being either rich or poor, employed or unemployed, healthy or G-d forbid, the opposite. We have all met extremely successful poor people and wealthy failures. Some of the most fulfilled people live from paycheck to paycheck and some of the wealthiest people drive to their therapists in a Rolls Royce.

When successful people face a challenge, instead of complaining and blaming, they think, "How can I make the very best of this?" They realize that every encounter and situation — good or seemingly bad — is part of the bigger, purposeful, master plan for their life.

◆§ Purpose

We have defined success as understanding and fulfilling your purpose in being here.

So, why are YOU here?

Why should you care?

Here's why...

Imagine that one day, I decide to walk around my firm and pose the following questions to its employees: "What exactly do you do here each day and why do you do it?"

I begin my day in the mailroom where Jim responds, "I sort the mail so that Jack can deliver it."

Jack: "I deliver the mail so that employees can read it."

Bill, the trader, says, "I buy and sell securities because clients have placed orders."

David, the research analyst, says, "I delve into the earnings reports of companies so the portfolio managers can make better decisions."

Sean, the portfolio manager, says, "I build portfolios using the assets that clients invest with us."

And on it goes...

While each employee has technically answered my questions — what they do and why — I haven't yet heard anyone describe the ultimate purpose of what they each do — the overall purpose of the company's existence. To answer that question, I head up to where the really fancy offices are and ask the CEO, "What does this company do?" Imagine if he responds by saying, "We sort and deliver mail, we buy and sell securities, we research and trade stocks and bonds, we build portfolios and make a lot of money."

Probing further, I ask, "But why do you do all that?" He responds, "Because mail comes in, because clients place orders, because portfolio managers need information, because clients like to see their money grow."

"Is that all?"

"Umm, yes, did I miss something?"

Yes! He missed the fundamental purpose behind the company's existence.

Sure, the answer could simply be "to make lots of money," but we would never expect a response like that from the CEO of a truly great company. Reputable companies flourish and fade in accord with their mission statement, and the CEO's primary role is to uphold the objectives and ideals that are outlined in that document. Mission statements typically include lofty objectives such as delivering exceptional service, building communities, serving client's needs, providing peace of mind, creating jobs, employee advancement, and increasing value for shareholders. It may be unrealistic to expect that mindset from someone in the mailroom, but the CEO should certainly be thinking that way.

If a corporation needs a purpose to be in business, then, surely, we need one as well.

Ask your feet why they walk and they would say, "Because the brain told me that I need to cross that street." Ask your mouth why it chews and it would answer, "Because the hand just put food into me and the stomach is telling me that food can't be digested whole." Every other organ of your body would respond in similar fashion. But if you were to ask your brain why it spends its every waking moment running this massively complex operation called your body, you would hope to get a more meaningful answer than, "The body has to get places, has needs, is hungry, hot, tired…" Your brain needs a mission statement. As your personal CEO, its efforts should be directed to the purpose of life… YOUR life. Are you here simply to eat, digest, sleep, earn a living, and raise another generation?

This may sound a bit humorous, but is it really? Don't many of us go about our days, weeks, and years doing the things that we need to do without thinking about the purpose of it all? We work because we need money, eat because we are hungry, sleep because we are tired, *daven* because we must and raise children so they can grow up and raise children who will eat, sleep, *daven*, work... What is the purpose of all of this?

Of course, we all have some vague understanding about a spiritual world of eternal bliss, and perhaps we give this idea a fleeting thought every so often when we find the time to come up for air or matters don't go our way. If a person wants to live successfully, however, the purpose of life consistently needs to be at the forefront of his mind.

To recap: ***The tasks we perform every day, whether for work, pleasure, or to fulfill our Torah obligations, do not in themselves constitute a purpose in life.***

As we discussed, a Torah Jew's foundation is built on the first mitzvah listed in the Rambam's *Sefer HaMitzvos*, also described in *Tanya* (*Shaar HaYichud VeHaEmunah* Ch. 1) and *Nefesh HaChaim* (Gate 1, Ch. 2; Gate 3, Ch. 12), that Hashem created and continues to create the world, every second, *yesh mei'ayin* — something from nothing. Therefore, our existence is not the result of a default mechanism put in place at the beginning of creation. We exist at this moment because we were created anew at this moment. This belief opens our minds to the fact that this world and each of us has a higher purpose; we are alive **right now** for a reason. Therefore, we know that **everything** we do matters.

The bedrock on which our tradition stands is that world has a universal purpose and we each have our unique individual purpose. We are each here to run a franchise of Hashem that upholds our personal mission statement, that of our nation and of the world as a whole. To succeed, we must learn to ask ourselves questions like those mentioned by the Ramchal in his *sefer Derech Eitz Chaim*:

People spend most of their lives thinking about and evaluating their mundane and temporary affairs. Why shouldn't they also place their attention, if even for a short period of time, to thinking thoughts of true reality? *What am I, why did I come to this world, what does the King of kings, Hakadosh Baruch Hu, want from me? What will be the end result of my life?* This is the greatest and strongest cure to be found against the *yetzer hara*. It is relatively simple, accomplishes a great deal and bears many fruits. People should stop for some time each day, free themselves from all other thoughts and only focus on these questions... In summation, a person who doesn't give this matter thought will find it extremely difficult to achieve success, and the one who does will find that it is within their reach.

Western society would call these "philosophical questions," which is a fancy way of saying "not pertinent." In the Torah world, however, these are the most pertinent questions we can ask, and a day should never begin without a keen awareness of its purpose. The *yetzer hara* dislikes these types of questions and much prefers that we live in a perpetual slumber. He will only allow us to awaken much later on in life, when it is more difficult to do anything about the lost years, so that we can then spend our last days living in utter regret. As we have already said, we aren't going to let that happen.

⌘ An Elevator Pitch for Life

Anyone who goes through training for a career on Wall Street spends several days practicing his "elevator pitch," in essence, the answer he would give to someone important who asked him, "What do you do?" The responder has no more than 30 seconds to sum up his profession, and it has to follow what is called the three c's — clear, concise, and compelling. This type of exercise forces a person to think deeply about whatever it is that he is trying to convey, because, when you have 30 seconds, every word counts. What would we answer if we met the Chofetz Chaim in an elevator and he asked us, "*Nu*, so what do you do?" Would we answer by telling him what we do for a living? If that esteemed *tzaddik* asked, "What is the purpose of your life?" would we answer, "To raise and marry off my children?"

What I came to realize is that although I have yet to meet anyone in an elevator who has asked me what I do, the exercise was a most valuable one. It opened my eyes to the importance of having the right words to remind myself each day of why I do what I do. While I am a far cry from the Chofetz Chaim, I have asked the question, "What is the purpose of your life?" to many people and, in response, I usually get a blank stare or something like, "to be a good Jew." True, but that answer alone may not prove inspiring to most people.

◆§ Why Is Connecting With Purpose So Important?

Why does a corporation need a mission statement and why do you need a purpose for your life? Isn't doing what we are meant to be doing enough?

The reasons are numerous, but here are several.

1. If we don't grasp the purpose of life, how can we possibly hope to achieve any success at all? Success at what? Measured how? Success for the person in the mailroom means the envelopes get delivered, but the CEO has a deeper and broader definition of success, and his primary role is to benchmark the company's progress toward those lofty ideals. He is focused on whether or not the company is achieving the ultimate purpose for which it exists: "Are we providing our clients peace of mind? Do our employees enjoy coming to work each day? What do the communities in which we operate think of us?" We must ask ourselves similar questions. I am *davening* each day, but am I growing from the experience? Are the acts of *chesed* that I am performing transforming me and those around me? Am I applying what I am learning? Am I utilizing the abundance that Hakadosh Baruch Hu has given me to help others?

2. Have you ever gone shopping for something without having a clear definition of what you needed the item to accomplish? If you did, then one of three outcomes were likely to have occurred: In trying to save money, you purchased something that fell short of your actual need, or you overspent because the salesperson easily convinced you to add features you didn't need. Either outcome would have led to buyer's remorse. Or perhaps you experienced the third possible outcome: you didn't buy anything at all, because you couldn't make a decision.

The same three outcomes exist in a life lived without an understanding of purpose. We exert ourselves too little in important areas, we expend energy on purposeless pursuits because we were swayed by the actions and opinions of others, or we remain paralyzed by indecision when there is no clear answer to, "What should I do?"

Conversely, someone who walks into a store with a clear directive knows exactly what he came for and how much he intends to spend. He only buys when he finds what he needs at an affordable price. Similarly, a person who travels through life with a definition and understanding of his purpose does not waste energy pursuing detours to nowhere just because others are doing so, and rarely pursues something that he will later regret.

3. Purpose infuses us with vitality and energy; We go about each day fully alive and we are not easily knocked down. Even when we do experience setbacks, we get right back up because we know that there is important work to be done.

> *A man who is a web developer for a large company came to seek advice because he had lost his motivation to work hard. His issues began a year earlier when his manager asked him to spearhead the development of a website that would serve as an integral part of a new product launch. The website needed to offer entirely new functionality and innovation for it to serve its intended purpose. The man worked late nights and came in on Sunday due to time constraints. As the project neared completion, he was called into the manager's office and told to cease all work because the project was canceled. He expressed his deep disappointment, but the best consolation his manager could give was, "What's the problem? You were paid well, plus overtime, for your work. It's the company that took the loss."*
>
> *The boss's response was logical. However, since that time this man found himself coming in late, leaving early, and doing his work with little enthusiasm.*
>
> *I asked him why that incident had troubled him so, given that it seemed that his manager was right. He said, "Because all my work was for naught."*

"But weren't you paid well?"

"Yes, very well."

"Isn't that why you go to work each day — to support your family?"

"Yes, of course!"

"So, what's the issue?"

He thought a while and said, "No one will ever benefit from all the hours and thought that I put into the project. There was no purpose to it."

Aha! He said the magic word. I explained to him that this incident had taught him a valuable lesson about himself — that while money was important, it wasn't enough. He needed to feel a sense of purpose in his work, and robbed of that purpose, his motivation was lost.

4. Time becomes precious and isn't wasted. A purposeful mindset prevents us from becoming sidetracked with relationships and activities that serve little or no purpose. As an example, if an individual's personal mission statement is built around helping others and self-growth, then he will naturally gravitate to individuals and activities that support this purpose, and prune away the parts of his life that don't. Time is the most precious commodity we each have, and how we spend it defines the level of success we achieve.

5. Purpose enables us to set goals and motivates us to track our progress. Just as a company benchmarks itself vis-à-vis its ideals, a person who lives with purpose tends to set goals for himself and keep track of where he stands relative to those goals. Realizing that no one else has his purpose, he does not assess himself with the counter-productive question, "How successful am I relative to someone else?" Rather, he uses a much healthier evaluation: "How successful am I compared to my inherent potential and the goals that I set for myself?

Let's summarize: **Success is defined as living life in a manner that is true to its purpose.** Purposeful living begins by exploring the reason we were put here in the first place and what steps we were meant to take toward that purpose. When a person lives life without a definition of purpose and adopts the lifestyles and pursuits of others, the potential for success eludes his grasp.

I want to conclude this chapter with a story and lesson taught by Rav Avigdor Miller, *z"l*, which he learned during a visit to an old-age home:

> *I once visited an old age home and was looking at the people there. Old people, people who never thought about…why we are here. It was a pity on them. They were sitting around staring. Life had turned out to be a disappointment. "This hurts me and makes going to these places difficult," I thought. There was nothing but disappointment. Only complaints, that's all you could hear. These old people had all soured on life because they lived for this world and now it had all turned to nothing.*
>
> *But there was an old man with a white beard, sitting at a table with an open Gemara, and he was busy getting ready for the Next World. He was reviewing all that he had learned in his lifetime. And he was the happiest man in the place. He was busy because he knew he had a purpose and nothing had disappointed him. Everything was turning out exactly as expected! The arthritis, the false teeth, the nurses — they were all constant reminders of the great ballroom toward which he was heading. He was getting ready to cash in! He was counting now, counting all of his assets before he left, and making sure that he wouldn't leave anything behind. He was a happy man!*

A Jew who invests in the Next World knows that he is a visitor here, and therefore enjoys every minute, every pleasure [Hashem's gifts] that others disdain, but he also has the happiness of knowing he's living for a purpose and has prepared for that which Hakadosh Baruch Hu intended for him. He lives life flush with happiness of achievement in this world.

Now we have spoken about the purpose of having a purpose. In our next chapter, we'll talk about purpose itself.

4

The World's Purpose and My Mission

The CEO of a large Israeli corporation once reached out to me for financial advice, and we met for coffee in the upscale hotel at which he was staying. When we concluded our business discussion, he looked at me and said, "I see that you wear a *kippah.* I guess that means that you believe." (Can you imagine an American CEO saying that?)

"Believe in what?" I asked.

"In G-d."

"Naturally. Don't you?"

"No, of course not — I'm an atheist."

"What do you believe?"

"That we all come from apes and there is no Creator."

"So, I guess you lie and steal."

"No!"

"Even if no one would ever find out?"

"No, never!"

"Why not?"

"It's wrong!"

"Who says? Why shouldn't we have whatever we want?"

"It's just wrong!"

"Do you give charity?"

"Yes."

"Why?"

"It's the right thing to do."

"Who says?"

"My heart."

"As the CEO of a major corporation, you ought to know better than to follow your heart when it's leading you astray. The theory you believe in claims that only the fittest are meant to survive. Why then should your heart be motivated to help the less fit survive? Aren't you messing things up?"

"I guess I am."

"You can't explain why you don't lie, cheat, and steal or why you give charity because all of those things are based on the existence of morality, and in your world, morality doesn't exist. Don't you see? If there is no Creator, there is no right and wrong, and even if there seems to be, it is nothing more than an idea, fabricated by humans as a mechanism to keep the world from going amok. Who says that you have to follow 'their' rules, especially if you will never get caught? 'They' say it's immoral or wrong, but why can't you choose to disagree?"

Noticing his perplexed expression, I continued.

"Without a Creator, nothing at all has any purpose, and without purpose NOTHING *matters including* YOU*. In a world where nothing matters, right and wrong, good and bad, cannot exist. I, on the other hand, believe there is a Creator, and so, I believe in purposeful creation. I believe that* EVERYTHING *matters, and you do too, which is why you don't steal and do help the poor.* YOU *just don't yet realize that you believe, but your Jewish heart does."*

(I would love to end this story by telling you that he now davens and puts on tefillin each day, but I can't because I never saw him again.)

◆§ What Some Deny, We Accept as a Given

How fortunate we are that the truth of purposeful creation is ingrained in our hearts and minds. However, as the Ramchal stresses in his introduction to *Mesillas Yesharim*, the more obvious something is, the more we need to remind ourselves of it, lest it recede into the far recesses of our subconscious. Therefore, let us more closely examine these ingrained beliefs by focusing on both the universal purpose for creation and our individual missions.

◆§ Why the World?

The Ramchal (*Derech Hashem* 1:3), explains Hashem's purpose in creating the world. In summary:

1. Hashem, in His infinite goodness, wants to bestow goodness upon others in the greatest way possible. He created the world to be the recipient of this goodness.
2. The only true definition of absolute goodness is Hashem Himself. David HaMelech says (*Tehillim* 73:28), וַאֲנִי קִרְבַת אֱלֹקִים לִי טוֹב — "But for me, closeness to Hashem is good." All other good is transient. When we use the term "good" in our everyday speech, we are simply describing something in contrast to "bad." The only true, lasting goodness we can obtain comes through our connection to Hashem.
3. For someone to receive true good, he has to feel that he's earned it. Otherwise, he will be embarrassed to accept it. This is the principle of *nahama d'chisufa* — the embarrassment people feel when they accept charity.
4. If goodness only comes through our connection to Hashem, we have to know how to find that connection. There has to be some commonality, some point at which we resemble Hashem enough to relate to Him. We find this commonality when we apply our efforts to perfecting ourselves by emulating Him. The work we put into making ourselves more like Hashem is what provides us with a point of connection and earns the goodness

He wants to bestow on us.[1] The Gemara (*Shabbos* 133b) teaches: "Abba Shaul said, וְאַנְוֵהוּ, 'I will glorify Him,' meaning to be like Him. Just as He is merciful and compassionate, so should you be merciful and compassionate." The Rambam (*Hilchos Dei'os* 1:5,6) derives this idea from the *pasuk* in *Devarim* (28:9), וְהָלַכְתָּ בִּדְרָכָיו, "and you should go in His ways."

We climb toward a state of perfection, in which we're aligned with Hakadosh Baruch Hu's purpose, by using our power of free choice to grow and spiritually elevate ourselves. Whenever we choose perfection over imperfection, growth over stagnation, we are opening ourselves to more of His goodness.

To summarize, Hakadosh Baruch Hu created the world as a forum in which He allows us to experience His infinite goodness through the positive choices that we make. These are defined as the actions that emulate His goodness and perfection.

Is this a one-size-fits-all prescription? Far from it; Hashem also created a world in which you and I each have a unique mission, a set of challenges and skills. Therefore, each of us must follow a different route on this quest.

---

1 This idea of emulation can be beautifully illustrated through the selfless act of giving charity to someone from whom we don't expect to receive any benefit. It can be difficult to part with hard-earned money, especially when so many personal needs are beckoning. This act of giving charity, precisely because it is difficult, creates a deep connection to Hashem. Giving is why Hashem created the world, and is therefore inherent in the most exalted Name of Hakadosh Baruch Hu. The Holy Baal Shem Tov teaches (*Parashas Re'eh*) that hidden in the four letters of Hashem's Name, which brings forth creation constantly, is Hashem's relationship with His creations as the Giver of all. The first letter, *yud*, a small and simple letter, represents the coin; the second letter, *hei*, the numeric value of five, represents the hand of Hashem. The third letter, *vav*, represents the outstretched hand of Hashem; the fourth letter, *hei*, represents the hand of the receiver. To show our appreciation for the abundance we each have, which comes into being through the Name of Hakadosh Baruch Hu, we take our coin and extend it to the outstretched hand of someone in need. There is no greater expression of emulation than this, and therefore, giving charity enables us to deeply connect to HaKadosh Baruch Hu and infuses us with deep fulfillment and happiness.

☙ Why Me?

When someone wants to build an office building, he needs a large team of people, each with distinctly different abilities, to turn his idea into a steel, glass and concrete reality. The architect, the builder, the masons, the electricians, plumbers, construction workers, engineers — each has a job to do and none has the expertise to do the other's job. Each has challenges that the others don't have and each accomplishes something the others don't accomplish. In the end, together, they accomplish the overarching goal: a safe, sound, attractive, and functional building.

This idea offers a modern-day analogy for the teachings of the Ramchal in *Derech Hashem* (Part 2, Ch. 3): Like the servants of a king who are all standing in obedience and through all of them the work of his kingdom must be completed. Hakadosh Baruch Hu divided the tasks and challenges of the world among the individual members of humanity so that we can each strive to succeed according to our capabilities. Each is responsible to complete the portion of work that was apportioned to him, and based upon the work assigned, the king will reward him.

This directive empowers each of us to approach our purpose in a most individual way. It teaches us that although we all share the universal mission of developing ourselves and enhancing and rectifying the world around us, we each bring a unique set of skills and talents to the task. If we try to negate our individuality, we deprive the world of something it needs; if the electricians envied the masons and decided to lay bricks, the building would be a very dark place.

☙ Individuality

Chazal tell us (*Tosefta Berachos, Perek* 6) that just as people's faces are different, so too are their thoughts/ideas. No two humans share the same skills, talents, physical features, and emotional/intellectual composition.

Why is that? Why couldn't we all just be identical and face the same challenges?

While we will never understand Hashem's master plan, there are some reasons that seem apparent. First, we could ask the very same question about other things, such as food, for example. Humans could subsist on a single food source that supplies everything we need and nothing more. Hashem, in His infinite goodness, made life pleasurable through variety, and likewise, our uniqueness makes life interesting for all. Secondly, if we were all the same, nobody would ever get on our nerves and we would lack the *bein adam la'chaveiro* (interpersonal) challenges that spur us to strengthen and refine our character traits. We would have no incentive to work on becoming more patient and tolerant, to build our self-control and compassion. Lastly, uniformity would mean that we would not need others to compliment us, for no one would stand out in any way. As a result, the warmth and good will built by gratitude and praise would be missing, and relationships would be shallow at best.

These reasons, while inspiring, don't adequately answer the question. Because the Ramchal uses the metaphor of servants to a king, through whom the work of the kingdom (creation) is completed, it seems that our individuality is a fundamental element of the purpose of creation itself. However, it cannot be that the Almighty needs our individual contributions to make His creation operational. How can His kingdom lack painters, architects, and electricians? The Ramchal answers these questions in his introduction to *Sefer HaHigayon*.

> *When we behold the creations of the world, and the portion that has been given to each of them, we see that Hashem has given mankind the greatest portion of all. For mankind has the great role to refine and bring completion to the entire world. We can go so far as to say that the Six Days of Creation were merely a beginning and that the actual completion is given over to mankind in its entirety. Chazal have awakened us to this truth in saying (Bereishis Rabbah 11:16): "All that was created in the Six Days of Creation needs improvement. Wheat must be ground into flour and Turmusin beans must*

be sweetened." Additionally, we find (Tanchuma Tazria 6) that Turnus Rufus, the Roman governor, asked Rabbi Akiva, "What is finer, the handiwork of Hashem or that of human beings?" Rabbi Akiva answered, "The work of flesh and blood is finer." To prove his point, he brought him stalks of grain and loaves of bread and said to him, "Which of these is finer?"

In conclusion, the Creator, blessed is He, has left room for us to distinguish ourselves through our labor by perfecting that which has been given to us.

Think for a moment about what this *Midrash* says: **All that was created in the Six Days of Creation needs improvement.** The Ribono shel Olam left creation unfinished so that we would have an arena in which to emulate Him in the loftiest way: by creating. This is why we were given talents, creativity, skills, and individuality — because the world needs ALL of our skill sets to function, improve, and reach its ultimate rectification. The world needs every one of us and EVERY skill Hashem granted us.

In fact, it is impossible for any of us to be superfluous. Rav Yerucham Levovitz writes (*Daas Torah, Parashas Behaaloscha*) that everything that exists, in any shape or form, has a purpose and is necessary. Hashem does not create anything "extra." This is true for plants, organisms, each part of your body, and every aspect of who you are. If a person was endowed with attributes and talents, they were not meant for his benefit alone, but for a greater purpose — the very purpose for which he was created. Rav Yerucham asks: **"Were we unable to express our individuality through the use of our talents and skills, what purpose would there be for uniqueness? For self? For having been created?"**

Rav Shamshon Raphael Hirsch writes (*Tehillim* 25:6) that this individuality even extends to the unique family traditions that are passed down to each of us. These customs, he says, are "symbols of our special calling on earth."

⇜ The Role of Free Choice

In Hashem's design of the world, success is sometimes borne of necessity. For example, the cost of living creates a necessity for career success. Marrying and having children demand that we learn to be a competent spouse and parent. Living among people dictates that we refine our character traits so that we can get along with others. While we always retain the free choice to fail in any or all of these areas, the incentives to succeed are clear and obvious, as are the consequences for failure.

In most other areas, however, our mission is a deeply individual one, left to our free choice. As a result, we may each strive to be successful in a variety of ways such as:

- Positively impacting the lives of others;
- Making a difference in our communities;
- Changing the world at large;
- Obtaining and disseminating knowledge;
- Amassing wealth and using it to help the less fortunate;
- Perfecting our character and teaching others how to do the same.

This aspect of free choice translates to an experience that is highly personal and ever-more meaningful.

⇜ Convincing Your Heart

While all this may make logical sense, at times it can be difficult not to feel insignificant — just one in a world of billions. The Satan strives to plant the feeling of "you don't matter" into our hearts and minds, because this belief justifies our desire to take the easy route in life, and frees us of much guilt. Hakadosh Baruch Hu tells us otherwise: YOU MATTER. The world will not reach its intended purpose without YOU and everything with which Hashem has endowed YOU. For a person to achieve his life's mission, he must see himself as unique, significant, empowered, and relevant.

I once stood at the gravesite of my holy great-grandfather, Rav Naftali of Ropshitz, and contemplated the great person that he was — all that he had accomplished and done for Klal Yisrael. I began to feel like a flea in comparison and felt deep despair. Then, as though speaking to me from Gan Eden, the following words entered my mind: "Please don't despair. If I would have lived in your era and in the country in which you live, I wouldn't have become the holy Ropshitzer either. Your purpose is not to become me. It is to become YOU and fulfill your mission in life."

But it's not just the great ones who stir up those feelings of inferiority that are hidden within us. For some people, anyone at all who appears successful is a mortal threat to their sense of security. Once, I was hurrying to a meeting dressed in my business suit and carrying my attaché case, when a man walking toward me yelled, "You think you are so important!" I quickly replied, "I am, and so are you, but perhaps you don't realize it yet."

We should never marginalize ourselves by comparing ourselves to others who are alive today or who have lived in prior generations. The mission for which you were created is as important as that of anyone who has ever lived. An edifice of a building can be built by thousands of workers, but if the last worker doesn't install the doorknob on the front door, then nobody will be able to enter. In this generation of *Ikvesa d'Meshicha* (the footsteps that will herald the arrival of Mashiach), our every positive action has inestimable value and all of the prior generations are depending on us.[2] The world needs rectification today

---

2 I will share a thought that came to me when I was preparing to speak at my grandson's *pidyon haben* (redeeming of a first-born boy) a few years ago. We refer to lineage as a *shalsheles*, chain. Why a chain? The Mittler Rebbe of Chabad explains that when a person grabs the lowest link of a chain and shakes it, each link above it is displaced, but the highest link is displaced the most. The Rebbe says that we all stem from holy ancestors and may think, "What impact do my actions have on them? They are so lofty and distant." We therefore call our ancestry a chain to remind ourselves that the further away we are, the more our actions can move the highest links. As I thought about the Rebbe's words, I began to wonder why this was the case. Why do we have so great an impact at the top of the chain? The following thought came to me:

The Arizal (*Shaar HaGilgulim*) teaches that Hakadosh Baruch Hu created the world initially as a circle, and then introduced a *kav*, line. This system is called more than ever and if Hashem entrusted us with this great mission He also invested us with the capabilities to do so.

◆§ How Do I Determine My Mission?

The question now becomes, how does a person determine his unique mission, given that we aren't born with a job description in our hands? This is a question often posed by younger people who are seeking their path in life.

Our first step is to explore our given talents and inclinations. Our talents are our natural skills, as well as those skills which we have an aptitude to develop. Inclinations are activities and pursuits that "speak to us" and provide a sense of fulfillment.

By taking stock of our talents, and inclinations, we get an idea of what we are meant to accomplish. The Sifsei Chaim writes (*Menuchas Hanefesh, Vaad Alef*) that Hashem endowed each of us with the attributes, talents and skills that speak directly to our individual mission. This is what Hillel means when he says (*Avos* 1:14), "If I am not for me then who is for me?" If I don't fulfill my mission then there is no one else to do it. Others lack my combination of attributes and they have their own missions to fulfill.

Imagine a man is called before a king, who says, "I have a very important mission for you, but you cannot know what it is until you travel to a remote island called Earth. The cargo-hold of your ship will contain all that you will need to fulfill your mission." The man travels to Earth, descends into the cargo-hold of the ship and finds a chain

---

seder hishtalshilus, the chain-like descent of spiritual worlds between Hashem and Creation. This world, which exists in the realm of time and space, is linear — like a line or chain. However, the *olam hatikkun*, the rectified world, is an *iggul*, a circle, which has no beginning and end. The world began in a perfect state and became linear; we are here to rectify it — to restore it to perfection.

If a person wants to take a chain and create a circle, what must he do? He must connect the two ends of the chain — the last link to the first. Only the generation that is alive today has the power to bring the world (the line) to a state of rectification (the circle). When that happens, each of us will be connected to the ancestors that began the chain, and that is why we, at the end of the chain, have the capacity to move them the most.

saw, all kinds of tools, nails, and a sander. "Well," he concludes, "I was obviously meant to become a builder and not an accountant."

When we want to know what we're here on Earth to accomplish, we, too, have to take inventory of the supplies with which Hakadosh Baruch Hu dispatched us. The soul knows its purpose; it was given that knowledge before it journeyed here. YOU are tasked with revealing this purpose, and when you get it right, you feel fulfillment and contentment; this is the *neshamah's* way of letting you know that you are on the right path.

We also have the power to develop new skills, especially when they are essential to our success. This is a fundamental aspect of self-growth. The more we learn to do, the more we are able to accomplish. Our mission statement expands in tandem with our new skills and talents. Successful people often attest that they never could have envisioned the full extent of their potential when their journey initially began. They took their first steps using the talents Hashem enabled them to recognize in themselves, and then grew further by developing their latent talents. This is the toothpaste we spoke of in the introduction.

☙ No Makeover Needed

One of our greatest challenges in our quest for success at our special mission is to stop comparing ourselves to others and thinking that to achieve success, we need a major makeover or a new mission in life. It is crucial to understand that we were NOT meant to remake ourselves and we certainly shouldn't try to become someone else. If Hashem wanted a person to be completely different than he is, He would have made him that way. If He wanted two versions of the other person, He would have made two.

While other people may serve as role models of kindness, fairness, tolerance, benevolence, faith, humility, and honesty, we should not feel that we were meant to mimic them entirely as people. Just because Miriam's next-door neighbor, Leah, stays up until 3 a.m. cooking meals for those who are homebound, doesn't mean that Miriam is meant to do exactly the same, and she should never feel guilty about that. Leah's kindheartedness is surely exemplary, and by all means we ought to try to emulate her by utilizing the inspiration she provides to seek out our own path in life. Your path is the one that speaks to you as an individual and incorporates the wonderful traits with which Hashem has endowed YOU. Hashem created each person, that means you, exactly as He intended. He asks that you take advantage of the tools already on your belt and, if possible, try to add a few more.

The Rebbe Rav Bunim of P'shischa explains the *pasuk* (*Devarim* 30:12), *"Lo b'Shamayim hee leimor"* (It isn't in the heavens). He says that the people are searching for answers to their longings — how to grow, how to move forward — in the distance. They think that if they were like someone else, had someone else's money, strength, upbringing, intellect, or whatever asset they feel they lack, then their life would be more fulfilling. Instead of peering off into the horizon for the key to self-actualization, the Torah (*Devarim* 30:14) tells us, *"ki karov elecha hadavar me'od"* — this is very close to you. We need not and cannot, remake ourselves into someone else. Our goal is self-actualization; what you are seeking is right there, hiding inside you, waiting to be revealed.

To recap: ***There is no one else alive today, nor since the beginning of creation, who has the identical mission that YOU have. Only YOU are equipped to accomplish the specific rectification to the world that was assigned to YOU. We succeed by embracing our individuality instead of trying to be something other than ourselves.***

The Mission Statement

I've used the term mission statement several times in the last two chapters. Now, in view of what we've learned about the power of living with purpose, I'd like to share a vivid example of what a mission statement can do for a person's life.

I recently lectured to a group of secular college students who spent a week in Lakewood, N.J. being exposed to Torah observance through the remarkable work of the Lakewood Fellowship program. Since I was in the midst of writing this chapter, I decided to speak about mission and purpose. I encouraged the students to go home, think deeply about their lives, write a mission statement, and send it to me. Here is my favorite entry, submitted by Yigal.

> *"My mission in this world is to embrace a life defined by Torah values with a focus on self-improvement and helping others using the talents that Hashem gave me. Areas of self-development include, controlling anger, consistency, and resiliency in the face of failure. Talents include my intelligence, communication, and problem-solving skills. To marry a woman who is upbeat and modest and build a home of chesed together. The purpose of a life lived this way is to refine my animal instincts, ease the burden of others, and to bring joy to my Creator to Whom I owe everything that I have."*

Yigal followed the instructions to the T; he hit upon the two most important elements of a mission statement: what and why. Did you notice how short and concise it is? That's the point; it wasn't meant to be long. Rather, it was meant to define Yigal's mission and serve as a guide for him as choices arise in life. When options A and B are presented, Yigal will measure both against his mission statement. Yigal will have far greater clarity as he seeks his *bashert*. In addition, he will keep tabs on the progress he is making on the self-development goals he outlined.

Yigal does a wonderful job at identifying areas of development and articulating meaningful goals for his personal life. As Yigal matures, he would be encouraged to refine his mission statement further by identifying ways in which he can harness his skills to help and improve the lives of others.

In summary, successful living means purposeful living, which entails understanding both the universal purpose and our individual mission. A universal purpose is shared by all of us equally, but we will each take a unique road to get there. Hashem endowed each of us with talents and inclinations that serve as our guideposts along this road. Our goal in life is to become the very best version of ourselves possible, to strive for self-actualization, for that is the only standard by which we will be measured.

5

Meaning

There is no question about it; Moshe is very talented. He plays several instruments, sings beautifully, and has a way of lifting people's spirits. He is every Bikur Cholim organization's dream, and yet, no matter how many times he is asked to visit and play for patients in the hospital, he can't seem to bring himself to do it. "I don't feel comfortable. I'm shy among strangers and hate being the center of attention," he protests. While Moshe doesn't doubt that bringing joy to ill people is a meaningful purpose toward which to apply his talents, he can't seem to get past his discomfort. He wishes that he could.

Moshe knows what he should do, but somehow, he can't bring himself to do it. Examples like this are numerous:

- The doctor said to eat healthy; we know he's right, yet we don't change our eating habits.
- We know we ought to stop wasting time and focus on the work at hand, yet there just went another hour.
- We were told that a family is in dire straits. We can see the value of leaving our comfort zone and raising money for them, but we hesitate.
- We see others around us putting in the proper effort at work and achieving success, while we keep looking for shortcuts.

In all of these examples, the person fully understands the purpose of what he should be doing, but he still fails to act. Why? Where was the disconnect?

If you find yourself thinking, "What is he talking about? I always do what I know is right," then please close this book. You are hereby exempt from reading any further.

Still here? Happy to hear that.

The answer to the conundrum portrayed above is that while we may see the purpose in taking a certain action, we may not feel its meaning. Lack of meaning explains why we sometimes know that one course of action is right, and yet we find ourselves doing something else. Let's try to understand the meaning of "meaning."

☙ What Is Meaning?

We often hear the term "meaning" used synonymously with "purpose." Are those two words one and the same?

The answer is that while they might be similar, they are definitely not the same. The proof of this is that a purpose can exist even without meaning. Paying a parking ticket, for example, has a clear purpose; you will avoid penalties and your car won't be towed. There is nothing meaningful, however, about paying a parking ticket.

Meaning is built on a foundation of purpose, because something purposeless cannot have meaning. Many things in life have both purpose and meaning, such as remembering a spouse's birthday and buying a gift for him or her.

A key difference between purpose and meaning is that purpose speaks to the brain. It is "what" we are aiming to achieve. Meaning, however, speaks to the heart — it tells us "why" we are trying to achieve the purpose. We find meaning in something when it has more than a shallow purpose (parking ticket). Moreover, it has an ultimate purpose (birthday gift) and that purpose has become personal to us; it has been internalized. Put another way, when something has a purpose, we KNOW that we need to do it, but when it has meaning we WANT to do it. For example, someone can present us with a wonderful *chesed* project, and while our brain tells us that there is surely a purpose to what the person is proposing, the idea may not speak to us until we attach emotion to it. The purpose of the *chesed* project would be the answer to "what" we want to accomplish — in this case, to help the family get back on its feet after a recent tragedy. The meaning answers "why" we want to apply ourselves to this purpose — because seeing the family in this dire situation is heartbreaking.

Another difference is that purpose is often universal, while meaning is highly personal. Here's an example. Two women are standing side by side arranging flowers for an upcoming *tzedakah* event. They both share the same purpose – to help beautify this important evening while the meaning behind their volunteer work differs. For one it brings back fond memories of her as a young girl watching her late mother do the same while for the other it is an act of *hakaras hatov* for a cause that has been there for her family. We are encouraged to "find meaning" in what we do, because while meaning is often there, we are each seeking a meaning that is personal to us.

A further difference between meaning and purpose is that purpose is established at the outset and achieved at completion. During all the intervening steps between the inception and the result, however, purpose doesn't speak to us. Meaning, on the other hand, has the capacity to motivate us every step of the way. If the heart does not feel that an activity has meaning, it loses interest. That is when we get bogged down in laziness or derailed by fear of failure in the face of obstacles. In the case of the *chesed* project, the family won't be back on their feet until the money is raised. There may be a wide gap to traverse between the inception and the result, and our brain's understanding of our purpose will not have the power to keep us going. Only the meaning — the feeling of satisfaction we derive from helping someone — can motivate us to take the next step and the next step after that.

To recap: ***Meaning is a feeling of the heart. Purpose is a thought of the brain. Anything that has no purpose cannot have meaning. Meaning is personal while purpose can be universal. Our brains can perceive what needs to be accomplished, but for us to persist in the effort, our hearts need to feel the meaning behind the goal.***

◆§ Why Is Meaning So Important?

Meaning supplies us with the emotional energy to reach our full potential in our service to Hashem, personal and working lives. It is an essential element of willpower that strengthens our capacity to persevere against adversity. A person who finds meaning in what he is doing will stop at nothing until he sees it through to fruition. In the example of the person raising funds for a needy family, if the endeavor lacked meaning for him, then as soon as he was faced with a great challenge, he would immediately begin to think, "Well, I tried and it just didn't work out." In contrast, if he was driven by deep empathy, he would keep pushing forward despite any setbacks.

A human being is unstoppable when both mind and heart are fully behind an idea. Then all the person's strengths are pulling in the same direction. This can only happen when purpose and meaning are both present.

Connecting to the meaning of life and awakening our hearts as we engage in our daily actions also allows us to live with *hisragshus* — emotion. Ultimately, in some areas we can even achieve the exalted level of *hislahavus*, fiery passion. Our *neshamah* is energized through meaning; meaning gives us fervor. It awakens us.

The Piaseczna Rebbe writes in his *sefer, Hachsharas Avreichim* (Ch. 2):

> **"When the *nefesh* is hidden and the person is uninspired, he cannot overcome his physical desires. When we engage in most activities, we do not sense any part of our *neshamah,* whereas when we experience emotion, we have an awareness of the *neshamah.* Action is therefore lower than emotion. The power of emotion is so great that all of our other abilities become subservient to it. For example, when we are engulfed by love or fear, we do not even need to eat or sleep. That is the power of the *neshamah* revealed, before which everything else falls away. The greater our emotion and feeling, the more our abilities and senses fall away.**

And if this emotion grows until it rises and burns like fiery, flaming coals, then our entire being falls away. And that is called *hislahavus*, fiery passion."

The words of the holy *tzaddik* are profound. We have all experienced a time when we were so passionate about something that we were able to transcend both external and internal limitations. Unleashing this awesome power that resides inside of us will propel our lives forward and allow our potential to soar by freeing us of our physical limitations. People can endure great hardships or perform miraculous feats when they are fueled by passion.

Passion is a function of the heart — the *neshamah*. The more meaningful something is to us, the more passionate we can get about it.

◆§ Hashem Is Behind Everything

The foundation on which meaning is built is *Hashgachah Pratis*, Hashem's eternal and constant hand in every aspect of each of our lives. One of the foundations of *bitachon* is that Hashem is behind everything and therefore life not only has purpose, but a deep and personal meaning. Every event, encounter, or occurrence, whether positive or challenging, is individually prescribed for us, because it is precisely what we need in order to move forward toward our life's mission and to repair our flaws. When we know that our loving Father in Heaven stands behind everything, we connect to the wellspring of *bitachon* from which flows peace of mind and a life bursting with meaning.

◆§ Connecting to What and Why

All of the examples we cited at the beginning of the chapter portrayed people who might be aware of the purpose of a certain goal, but aren't connecting their hearts to the meaning. When there is a disconnect between the brain and the heart, the heart often wins. If the heart wants to eat fried chicken, then the doctor's orders fall on deaf ears.

How do we establish this vital connection? The road to meaning always begins by first analyzing **what** it is we are trying to achieve and then **why**. We bring purpose into the forefront and analyze it on a deeper level by uncovering all of the reasons that issue is important. In essence, even though meaning is a feeling of the heart, the feeling can only come after the mind grasps it and contemplates it. Then the mind can teach the heart how to feel.

Let's illustrate the point using the scenario with which we began the chapter. Moshe, the talented musician, was presented with the opportunity to make rounds in the hospital to cheer people up. In truth, if Moshe gave the matter more thought, he would realize that there is much more to this offer than first meets the eye. Contemplation might reveal that:

- Patients heal faster when they are upbeat and have hope. He will likely save a life one day, as the following story illustrates:

  Years ago, my friend's father had to undergo a serious heart surgery. However, he was drained due to the constant pain and had lost his will to live. The doctors told the family that the surgery would surely fail unless the patient's emotional state improved. Heartbroken my friend wandered away and soon found himself standing on the steps outside of the hospital crying. Suddenly he felt a hand on his shoulder. He looked up to find Shlomo Carlebach z"l smiling at him. "My holy brother, why are you crying?" he asked. After explaining the predicament, Reb Shlomo asked him for his father's room number. Fifteen minutes later, as my friend was returning to his father's room, he heard the sound of Shlomo Carlebach and his father singing loudly together. His father had the surgery and lived for many years after that.

- Showing that he cares will lift the spirits of the ill person's family. These people deserve and need that support.
- There is no greater *Kiddush Hashem* than when others see someone doing something that is uncomfortable for him, purely for the sake of another.
- This may be the very reason that Hakadosh Baruch Hu endowed him with his talents.

- Shyness will be overcome after one or two rounds, while the rewards will be eternal.
- If he can overcome his shyness in such a profound way, so many other areas of his life will be improved.
- He will be setting a great example for his children.

Before doing this exercise, Moshe's only connection to the proposed *chesed* was that he would be "cheering up the sick." This is a dry, abstract, factual, and unemotional statement that offers little for the heart to grab hold of. Rather, his heart feels threatened by the idea. It needs convincing; it needs to feel the "why," so that it will set aside its shyness and experience a desire to participate. The exercise introduces thoughts that awaken meaning, and when that happens, Moshe becomes passionate about the idea.

Much of life holds meaning for us, but we may not realize this until we stop and contemplate. How often do we give more than a fleeting thought to why we marry, have children, help others, take care of ourselves, and uphold the Torah? While the purpose may be obvious, uncovering and connecting to the meaning behind it all will awaken our hearts, bring a greater sense of passion, and renew our motivation. In the next chapter, we will analyze one area of life — work — and unearth the "why" that brings meaning to the seemingly mundane endeavor of earning a living.

6

Meaning at Work

Many people spend a significant portion of their waking hours earning a living. Those who succeed in their endeavors are those who are motivated and can persevere in the face of challenge. However, this level of engagement is only sustainable if our hearts are in the work we do. It is for this reason that the Gemara states (*Berachos* 32b) that earning a living is one of the four endeavors for which success requires "constant strengthening."

Many people are fortunate in that they find deep meaning in the work they do. They go about their business affairs or jobs knowing they are improving the lives of others and the world around them through the work they do. A doctor who saves lives, would be an easy example. Many in my profession find great meaning in advising organizations and wealthy families knowing that people rely upon them to help them make better decisions which, in turn, impacts the well-being of many. Others appreciate the meaningfulness of supporting their families, the highest form of *chesed*, and that acting in a moral, ethical and honest manner brings great Kiddush Hashem to the world. These heart-engaging thoughts infuse their days with vitality and enthusiasm. There are, however, those who struggle, consciously or sub-consciously, with identifying the meaning in their work efforts. They would much rather do other, perhaps in their eyes, more worthwhile things with their time. We will begin this chapter by addressing the latter group in order to follow the format of uprooting weeds before planting seeds.

◈ The Need to Earn Money

We can surely appreciate that working to support our families serves an important purpose. If we pay our mortgage, we keep our house. If we pay tuition, our children are allowed into school. The cause-and-effect relationship between earning a living and having the life we desire is quite obvious, but how much ultimate purpose and meaning do we ascribe to this entire process? Wouldn't life be better if we didn't need to work?

People often argue that working is a curse, "a *bedi'eved*" (an after-the-fact concession), not much different than paying a parking ticket. Working is something we would rather not do, and let's not kid ourselves; they say, we only work because we need the money. Adam and Chava partook of forbidden fruit and for thousands of years mankind is paying the price. With this mindset we go to work, slog through the day, and spend our week surviving until Shabbos, the only day of true meaning. We then wonder why, after x number of years, we grow tired of it all and burn out. Can we really keep our hearts motivated while fulfilling a curse?

The *bedi'eved* mindset is even more prevalent among yeshivah-educated men. Many sincerely desire to spend their days studying Torah, and only left the walls of yeshivah out of necessity. How can they give their all to something they see as second-rate? I faced this challenge personally, and I found myself drained of motivation as a result. I wished that each day at the office would be my last, and felt guilty that I wasn't living life as I was meant to live it. Matters only began to improve when I changed my perspective and began challenging myself by asking questions such as: Isn't everything we do a form of serving Hashem? Could work truly be a *bedi'eved* if life makes it necessary? Is it possible that Hakadosh Baruch Hu put me into a situation in which I must spend a large portion of my life doing something that I would have been better off not doing?

In truth, why should our hearts be in it; wouldn't life be so much better without bills? If everything were free? Think of all the time we could spend doing more meaningful things.

The answers that follow are meant to provide you with a new perspective which will lead to greater meaning and motivation at work.

◆ Life Without Bills

The late Richard Abramson, a man who took me under his wing when I first entered Wall Street, once taught me, "If you want to teach a lesson that people will remember, there is a very powerful way to do it. Make a big fat provocative statement and then back it up."

Ok, here goes.

Life without bills would be outright awful!

You should thank Hashem for every expense you have!

Don't close the book just yet. Please allow me to explain.

◆ The Power of Cause and Effect

In trying to understand the mindset of the typical person in the workforce, I once tried an experiment. I asked many people the same questions and always received the exact same answers, with perfect consistency.

Q - Why do we work?

A - To earn money.

Q - Why do we need money?

A- Because, in life, things cost money.

Pretty obvious, except the answers are false.

Chazal explain that Hakadosh Baruch Hu brings everything into existence through a process called עִילָּה וְעָלוּל, cause and effect. The Ramchal (*Sefer HaHigayon* 4:12) teaches that correctly identifying the cause of anything, as distinguished from the effect, is crucial to understanding any idea or reality. This is even more important when we are seeking a solution to a problem, for we can only reach an effective solution by addressing the problem's root cause. Rav Elchonon Wasserman amplifies this idea in his essay on the Great Depression

(*Kovetz Maamarim* v:1), in which he teaches that a person can throw one solution after another at any given problem and not achieve any success at all, until he correctly identifies the true cause. In fact, until we correctly identify cause and effect, we will often exacerbate the problem, because poor solutions will create even more problems. Imagine a doctor who skips the diagnosis stage and randomly prescribes medications for the patient.

Here's an example of mistaken cause and effect:

David, why did you get so angry? (effect)

Because Moshe, whom I once thought of as a friend, showed me great disrespect. (cause)

Accurately assessing cause and effect in this instance is crucial because the only way for David to prevent the effect from recurring would be to stop the cause. Given David's understanding of reality — that Moshe is the cause — his solution would be to add Moshe to his "ex-friend list" and avoid him. The problem is, it won't work

Well, of course it will work. If he never crosses paths with Moshe then how can Moshe possibly get him angry?

Valid point, but David is making a mistake nonetheless. You see, David reversed cause and effect. In reality, Moshe showed him disrespect (effect) **because** he has a tendency to lose his temper (cause) and Hashem (ultimate Cause) wanted him to see that he has work to do on his *middos*. David can avoid Moshe all day long, but it won't matter because "Hashem has many messengers" and tomorrow it will be Shlomie and then Chaim the day after. Someone will be sent to get him angry, and angry he will become, until he learns to improve his character traits. Since David misdiagnosed the cause, he will only make matters worse. Over time, the list of people he will need to avoid will grow longer and longer. He will become ever lonelier and consequently, ever angrier.

Back to our topic -

We asked,

Why do we work? (effect)

They answered…

We need money (cause).

This is the wrong answer. The truth is the exact reverse; we need money (effect) because Hashem wants us to go to work (cause). Things cost money so that we will need to work. Hashem could have easily created a world where all of our needs were met. Kids' shoes would grow on trees and we would each have an oil well in our backyards. That's how life was for Adam and Chava in Gan Eden. When they ate the forbidden fruit, Hashem didn't curse them; He gave the remedy to the challenges and inner battles that mankind would face now that the Satan no longer resided outside of us, but rather, within us. **He created the need to work by making the things that we need cost money.** Work is the cause, not the effect; needing money is the effect, not the cause. So let's try that again.

Why do we need money?

So that we will need to work.

Why do we need to work?

Because Hashem wants us to work and there is tremendous value to be derived from it. Work is a part of Hashem's master plan for the world, is a platform for self-rectification and a source of great meaning.

☙ Money Motivates

Given that our purpose in life is to emulate Hashem by developing our character traits and building the world at large, Hashem created a world in which we need money to exist. This situation in turn provides us a source of motivation to rectify our bad habits and character flaws. Here's a thought that highlights this idea: If a person parks at a bus stop in New York City, he can expect to find an orange ticket waiting for him on his windshield. Imagine a world in which, after ending a *Shemoneh Esrei*, we would find on our *siddur* a ticket marked with an X next to a box that reads, "lack of *kavannah* (focus) — $85.00." How much more *kavannah* would we have the next time we *daven*? LOTS more! Money is a motivator.

When we enter the workforce, a place where skills and human capital translate to greater earnings, we are motivated to work on ourselves because the bills keep mounting. If we were to analyze the elements that make us successful in the workplace, we would find that those same traits also make us successful people overall. Problem solving, communication and listening skills, honesty, diligence, motivation, teamwork, humility, tenacity, resiliency — these are skills that we are motivated to develop in the workplace because we seek advancement and a higher salary. These same skills also build character. The time-management skills we develop at the office are truly meant to be used at home and in the *beis medrash*. If we can effectively listen to our clients, then we are also able to listen to our spouse and children.

Work has deep meaning for us when we focus on the fact that it is an effective mechanism for growth that helps to promote the overall purpose of our lives. The money we earn is but a very temporary by-product of all that work, whereas, the true rewards will be eternal if we go about it with the right perspective.

> *I once received a call from a young man seeking career advice. He proceeded to give me three potential career options, and essentially asked me to play multiple choice with his life by picking one for him. Here is our conversation.*
>
> *How did you earn a living until now?*
>
> **I had a great job that paid very well.**
>
> *What happened?*
>
> **I was fired.**
>
> *Why?*
>
> **I haven't a clue.**
>
> *What reason were you given?*
>
> **I wasn't given a reason.**
>
> *Was there anything that you could have done that would have caused your termination?*
>
> **No, I brought in lots of business and earned lots of money for the company.**
>
> *That's odd — and they still fired you?*
>
> **I know. It is very strange. The only thing I can think of is that my boss was intimidated by my success. Perhaps he has low self-esteem.**
>
> *I was running out of time (read patience) and said, "I am*

sorry but I cannot help you. If you, who live with yourself all day long, have no reasonable idea as to why you were fired, then how can I possibly give you advice after knowing you for all of three minutes? Please call me back after you have had a long conversation with yourself and have more insights to share, other than, your boss, who hired you to be successful, felt threatened by your success."

We hung up. He called back a few minutes later and quietly said,

Ok, maybe I yelled at some customers.

Do you have anger issues?

NO!

What would your wife say if we called and asked her that question?

She would say that I have anger issues.

Imagine if I would have given him advice before knowing that!

I explained to him that whatever job he chose as his next one, he can be certain of one thing; that working on his anger will be the primary determining factor of his success. It is clearly Hashem's will, that despite being profitable for a business, a person should be fired as a result of his temper, because were that not the case, the person would never be motivated to take a good look at himself and realize that rectifying this flaw is why he is in the workplace in the first place. The primary purpose for this man coming to this world is to work on his temper, and the true meaning behind his job is to motivate him to do so.

☙ Other Meaningful Aspects of Work

The *Chovos HaLevavos* in *Shaar Habitachon* (Ch. 3) discusses two reasons that Hashem created a world in which people must work.

1. Pursuing our material needs subjects us to a great many tests. It challenges our *bitachon*, honesty, *kedushah*, ethics, and morality. It tests whether we will serve Hashem at the office, and whether we will avoid the trap of putting our work above all else. In passing these tests, we grow as people and reap great benefit in this world and the next.

2. Except for those who spend their time immersed in Torah learning, a person who was not gainfully employed would ultimately turn to sinful actions to keep himself busy. Not only would he stagnate; he would decay. Working was meant to keep us occupied and out of trouble. As someone who was financially stable and unemployed once said to me, "I must find a job. I am getting moldy!"

Furthermore, the Gemara (*Berachos* 43B) teaches that Hashem created the world in such a way that each person finds his profession appealing, thereby ensuring that the world will not lack for anything. Through our work, we help society function and thrive. The world needs teachers, accountants, and places to buy food. Nobody would be a garbage collector if he didn't need money. Without that incentive, we would be living in squalor.

Work also allows us to appreciate all that Hashem has given us because appreciation comes only with regard to something for which we toil. Moreover, we were meant to enter the workforce so that we can set an example of honesty and morality for the whole world to see, thereby making a Kiddush Hashem.

To recap: ***Chazal is telling us that if we didn't work, we would never be amply tested and would run the risk of deteriorating from idleness; we would never contribute to society, appreciate what we have, and make the large-scale Kiddush Hashem that results from our behavior in the work-world.***

☙ One Can Find Meaning in Nearly Any Job

As we began, some people are fortunate enough to have jobs that offer clear meaning, such as nurses, teachers, *rebbeim,* and coaches, but even people in those professions may tend to lose touch with meaning as the job grows monotonous and stressful. They too will need to remind themselves each day of the impact they are having on the lives of others, and how they are making the world a better place through the work they do. This challenge has been recounted to me many times by professionals who work with special needs children. After some time, they find it difficult to connect to the purpose and meaning behind the often-thankless work they do.

Here's one such story.

> *A young man once sought advice because he was struggling to earn a living as an insurance salesman. He was ready to throw in the towel because in his words, "Too many people were chasing too few clients." I asked him if, in his view, it was no longer possible for anyone to earn a respectable living in the insurance industry and he admitted that "it is surely possible." He realized that it was only impossible for him, because he had grown tired of hearing the word "no." I asked him why he entered the insurance field in the first place, given that rejection was a well-known factor. He replied, "I needed the money because I have a large family." I said, "Naturally, but why this field?" He thought for a moment and explained that he greatly enjoyed helping people and had heard too many stories of people passing away and leaving their widow and orphans in dire straits. He entered the insurance profession in order to prevent that from happening.*
>
> *This man goes to work every day to earn a living and in the forefront of his mind is the thought that, "I am doing this because I need the money and this job serves that purpose." What he forgot was the meaning behind his choice of profession. He was therefore being deterred by rejection, which as we know, can be overcome with perseverance.*
>
> *I advised him, "Every day when you go to work, verbally remind yourself of why you chose to work in the insurance industry. You are saving widows and orphans from starvation. On the path to doing so, many people will say no to you. Keep an image in your mind of a mother telling her young orphaned children, "Because a kind man hounded Tatty a"h, relentlessly for months, even after Tatty said no to him a million times, we B'H have a roof over our heads and money to send you to school." This man had pushed the meaning of the work he did*

way into the deep recesses of his mind, and it was time for him to bring it to the forefront. The man emailed several years later to state that he was B"H doing extremely well.

To those whose jobs do not offer apparent meaning, meet Wendy, the woman who brings my mail to my office each day. Wendy greets everyone by their name. She always has a pleasant "good morning" to share, which is followed by "Have a wonderful day." I once commented to her about her amazing attitude, and named her the most cheerful mail person in the entire planet. When I asked her how she manages to stay so upbeat in her job, she said, "I don't just see myself as someone who delivers mail. I see myself as someone who helps connect people in a meaningful way. Besides, your mail is important and so I am helping you to help your clients." What an amazing perspective! Whether she does it with or without her upbeat attitude, Wendy will be delivering the mail just the same. However, her attitude is what infuses her day with meaning instead of monotony.

If you recall, back in chapter 3 we introduced you to Sean the portfolio manager who sees their purpose only as someone that buys and sells securities in client portfolios. Not all that meaningful. Imagine you were employed in that position and were looking to infuse your day with meaning. How might you do so? You would start by connecting your position at the bank to the greater mission statement on which the greater company stands. Your contribution helps the bank and the clients succeed which in turn benefits the lives of so many.

I recently addressed an assembly of men who work as fundraisers for our nations yeshivos and *chesed* organizations. I was asked to inspire them because some were ashamed of being called a "fundraiser" and were therefore finding themselves sapped of motivation. I told them that I have never been in the presence of such profound greatness because the entire Klal Yisroel stood on the foundation of their efforts. Where would we be without Yeshivos, Kollelim and the myriad of *chesed* organizations that are there for us at every turn? Would any of these great institutions survive without funding? Is there a more noble and meaningful profession than fundraising?

Meaning at work can also be found in doing things for others that we aren't paid to do. If we look around our respective workplaces, we will see people doing things for others, quietly and unexpectedly. If you were to ask them why, they might not have ready answers, but the likely reason is that it feels good. Selflessness feels good and it satisfies the *neshamah* within us, which yearns to transcend our physical selves and honor the deeper meaning of our lives. The "it's not my job" or "not my problem" attitude, on the other hand, yells to the world that "the only value I see in this job is the money I earn."

We Jews are empowered to carry the idea of meaningful work much further. We are meant to use the workplace as a platform upon which to show the world the beauty and benefits of a life lived with faith, morality, and honesty. For example, last week we experienced a setback in my practice, which will cost one of my non-Jewish associates many extra hours of work. I was concerned about his reaction, because he sometimes doesn't let things roll off his back. I asked him how he was handling it and was pleasantly surprised when he said, "All good. It's *bashert*!"

We are also in the workforce to learn all that we can and then share that information with our brothers and sisters who are entering the workplace or seeking employment. Success can lead to so much more than just the paycheck we earn; it can serve as a meaningful way to help others.

To recap: ***If we misidentify the cause and effect in our careers, our daily routine will lack meaning and consequently our motivation level will be low. We can't go to work every day living a bedi'eved, a curse. We must develop a valid perspective on work as the will of Hashem and a platform for improving the world, self-improvement, skill development, and helping others.***

Work is but one area of life; in reality, to be living life to the fullest, we need to infuse meaning into all of the important activities in which we engage. Dealing with the everyday stresses of life can easily distract our focus away from the meaning in serving Hashem, parenthood, marriage, and the deeds we do for others. The more often we remind ourselves of the "why," the more motivated and fulfilled we will be.

7

Your Partners

From the day you came into the world, the sights and sounds around you began to make an impression on your mind. You didn't know what you were seeing; it was all just shapes and light and movement, voices and noises. Some pleased you and some frightened you. But as you developed, your parents were there to help you make sense of it all. You began to explore by touching and experiencing. Eventually, you gained proficiency in the language to ask questions. "What is that? What does it do?" You wanted to know about everything from the spoon in your hand to the airplane flying overhead. Then you began school, where you learned even more about the wondrous world around you.

Meanwhile, as you gained mastery of the external world, another world was developing as well. Your inner world began to awaken. Thoughts, emotions, feelings, inhibitions, fears, and ambitions began stirring within you, and by the age of about 18 months, you were already experiencing this mysterious inner world. Nevertheless, you couldn't obtain an explanation; you couldn't just point your little finger and ask, "What's this?" You lacked the words to describe feelings such as confusion, shame, desire, jealousy, anger. As time went on, instead of amassing information, you relied upon assumptions about yourself to explain where those feelings and emotions were coming from and what they meant. By the time your intellect was fully developed, self-awareness had become second nature to you and you had long ago labeled yourself in many ways. You may never have re-evaluated those early assumptions.

The *Chovos HaLevavos* (*Cheshbon Hanefesh* 3:24), recognizes that as we mature, we need to reconsider and improve our perspectives in all important areas of life. This is because we are no longer the same person we were in our youth. Our experiences sharpen our minds and deepen our power of understanding, enabling us to make better self-evaluations, decisions, and achieve greater growth.

If we want to fulfill our mission in life, it is imperative that we gain a deeper understanding of our inner world: our self. Delving inward allows us to identify, perhaps for the very first time, the source of the thoughts, feelings, and emotions we unthinkingly adopted in our formative years. Armed with that knowledge, we are in a better position to address these essential aspects of the identity we've formed.

Assumptions, labels, and in some cases, hours of therapy are not necessary to make sense of the inner turmoil and utter confusion many people experience. The Torah provides us with a blueprint of "self," which depicts, on a much deeper level, exactly what we are experiencing at any given moment. With this blueprint, we can discern what, if anything, we need to do about all that is transpiring inside us.

In the next two chapters, we are going to look at the concept of "self" and familiarize you with your inner world. In this chapter, we will discuss the two partners — body and soul — that accompany you throughout every moment of your life. In the next chapter we will discuss YOU.

Being Human

At birth, YOU were assigned a body and a *neshamah* — soul — two polar opposite entities to serve as your trusted partners on your 120-year journey in this world. Despite their disparate and often conflicting interests, they each play an integral role in your success. We cherish them both, because without either, we couldn't embody the exceptional potential inherent in being human.

Let's look briefly at the soul, the body, and the combination of the two.

Soul

Our *neshamah* comes from a place that is even higher than that of the angels, as the *Tanya,* after describing the *nefesh habehamis* or animal soul, states (Ch. 2):

> *The second, uniquely Jewish, soul is truly an emanation of G-d above, as it is written: "And He blew into his nostrils a soul of life," and (we say in our prayers) "You blew [that soul] into me." And it is written in the Zohar, "He who blows, blows from within," that is to say, from his inside and his innermost being.*

The *Baal HaTanya* elaborates (*Iggeres HaTeshuvah* Ch. 4):

> *Even though Hashem possesses no physical form, Heaven forbid, nonetheless the Torah speaks in the language of regular people...and the analogy here is that — unlike the angels who are described as coming from "the breath of His mouth" — the neshamah of a Jew comes from a deeper "place."*

That's where our soul comes from.

Body

Our physical body, animated by the life force that is called the *nefesh habehamis* (animal soul), is comprised of the four earthly elements: fire, wind, water, and earth. Rav Chaim Vital teaches (*Shaarei Kedushah* 1:2) that our traits, both positive and negative, are rooted in the four elements. **Fire** is the source of anger, arrogance, and hatred; **wind** is the source of idle chatter and forbidden speech; **water** is the source of desire for pleasure, and **earth** is the source of laziness and sadness. Each of these elements also has a positive "flip side" that includes humility, silence, and positive speech, disdain for indulgence, and happiness.

The *Tanya* teaches that the *nefesh habehamis* is therefore a mixture of both good and bad. By refining it we can distill the pure good.

As powerful as our physical nature seems to be, the *Chovos HaLevavos* (*Shaar Avodas Elokim,* Introduction) reminds us that the human body is physically tenuous and temperamental. Even in comparison to other living creatures, we humans are relatively weak. We are susceptible to heat, cold, and disease, and we require constant maintenance.

Furthermore, a human being's *emotional* equilibrium is highly sensitive. Even the slightest emotional misalignment can throw a person out of whack and leave him functioning below par. A more serious emotional imbalance can render a person helpless to the point where he doesn't function even at a basic level. He lacks the energy and motivation to eat, work, study, or control his unhealthy habits. When people are psychologically imbalanced, all of their worst enemies combined do not harm them as much as they harm themselves over the course of their lifetimes.

An animal, on the other hand, is much hardier. An animal survives in the wild, rarely gets sick, is productive no matter what mood it's in, and is rarely self-destructive.

The Combination

In *Tehillim* it states: אָחוֹר וָקֶדֶם צַרְתָּנִי, *Last and first You formed me* (139:5). Human beings are the bookends of creation. Why? Because we consist of both the loftiest and the most mundane elements of creation: a soul that is loftier than the angels and a physical component that is weaker than an animal. Not only are we the bookends, but we are also all the books in between them, because we encompass all of creation, are connected to all of creation, and are therefore able to impact all of creation.

Humans are capable of the greatest feats in Torah, medicine, philosophy, charity, and other worthwhile endeavors. Conversely, an unrefined body fueled by a sick and perverted mind is capable of causing more destruction and harm than even the worst of the so-called "acts of nature." The *Nefesh HaChaim* tells us that our positive actions fuel and bring light to the entire order of creation, while our negative actions cause vast, celestial darkness and destruction.

To recap: ***Each of us is a combination of polar opposites: a lofty soul and an earthly body, great strengths and great weaknesses, the potential for extreme good and the opposite. Furthermore, for a person to function at his peak level, he needs to be in a healthy emotional and psychological state.***

The Great Battle

On the surface, you would think that the partnership of body and soul would not be a harmonious one. And you would often be right. The *Tanya* describes this partnership as an ongoing battle between two armies fighting to conquer the same "city" — YOU. Their weapons are our thoughts, feelings, and impulses — all those things that baffle us. How do we identify which side is speaking to us? We feel hungry, so we eat. That's the body. We feel disconnected, so we pick up a *Tehillim*. That's the soul.

- The body entices us to stay in bed; the soul inspires us to get up and make something of ourselves.
- The body yearns for worldly things and wants to wallow in the physical pleasure they bring; the soul is repelled by this world and wants to separate itself from it. Instead, the soul desires the eternal: pursuits that connect it to Hakadosh Baruch Hu — its life force — and earn it a place in the World to Come.
- The body fears rejection and loss (we can literally feel that in our stomach), while the soul knows that there is nothing to fear other than its Creator.
- The soul knows why it is here and what it is meant to achieve, while the body rarely gives the matter any thought.
- The soul is focused on the future while the body enjoys the here and now.
- The soul craves toil while the body craves relaxation.

It is no wonder, therefore, that we often find ourselves bewildered and confused. Who wouldn't be with a constant war waging inside of them? When we become aware of this inner conflict, we experience an awakening. Then we are left with the task of grappling with it and trying to make sense of it all.

◈ The Body's Upper Hand

The challenge, the *Chovos HaLevavos* tells us (*Shaar Avodas Elokim,* Ch. 2), is that the body begins with the upper hand due to three advantages:

1. The intellect, an aspect of the soul, makes its appearance later in a person's life. In contrast, our bodily needs are satisfied from the day we are born and we become accustomed to this gratification.
2. The soul is a stranger in a strange land. It resides here without a friend in the world and is at a great disadvantage. The body, on the other hand, is created from the same four elements as all of creation and so it feels right at home. Additionally, the food that we eat and the pleasures that we enjoy all serve to strengthen the body while they weaken the soul (unless they are ingested with a loftier purpose in mind).

It is fair to say that if the soul was a stranger in this world in the days of the *Chovos HaLevavos*, today it must feel like an alien that has landed here from another planet. The world around us cherishes hedonism and to a great degree mocks the pursuit of spirituality. Materialism is all around us and the never-ending pursuit of more, bigger, better, fancier, and convenient is the loud, insistent religion of the masses. It reduces the voice of the soul to the barely audible whispers of the few.

3. We need our bodies in order to exist and the body has continual needs, day and night. In contrast, the soul is called upon only during those times of the day when we are learning, *davening,* and performing *mitzvos*. The more something is used, the stronger it becomes, and the less it is used, the weaker it becomes.

You might be wondering; how does the soul stand a chance?

◆ Torah — The Great Equalizer

The *Chovos HaLevavos* explains that, in order to bring a person into balance, Hakadosh Baruch Hu gave us the holy Torah, an unstoppable force that emanates from the same lofty place as the soul. When a person embraces the Torah, when he studies and practices it, the competing forces within him are brought into a state of equilibrium.

The Torah teaches us right from wrong and which pleasures are good for us and which are not. The Tanya (chapter 5) teaches, just as bread nourishes and gives life to the body, so too the Torah, when studied with concentration, becomes food for the soul. The Torah nourishes and strengthens the soul to the point where it can subdue the body and ultimately teach it what it knows: that the greatest pleasure in life is fulfilling our destiny and purpose. The Torah heals the damage inflicted on the soul by the detrimental choices we make and thereby amplifies the voice of the soul so that it can once again be heard. Without the Torah, the soul is overpowered by the body to the point where it is reduced to a mere ember.

Most of all, the Torah empowers us to discern what is actually transpiring inside of us. It helps us recognize which force — the soul or the body — is speaking to us at any given time. The Torah thereby turns inner confusion and murkiness into a more recognizable black-and-white set of choices. We will discuss this further in Chapter 9.

◆ Another Path

What we have delineated above clarifies why every Jew must strive to grasp every possible opportunity to imbue himself with Torah. While men have an obligation to actually toil in Torah, a woman has related obligations as well. She is required to master the laws of the many *mitzvos* that apply to her and to study the Torah and mussar that fosters personal growth, *emunah* and *bitachon*. This will strengthen her connection to Hashem and His *mitzvos*, inspire her in her service to Hashem, and imbue her with *emunah* and knowledge she can convey to all those whose lives she impacts. Additionally, she may voluntarily study many other areas of Torah. She may also achieve spiritual elevation and equilibrium while focusing on the support of Torah.

The *Maharal* writes (*Drush Al HaTorah*, p. 27) that since men and women have different spiritual natures, they have fundamentally different paths to self-rectification. Supporting Torah provides greater spiritual growth for a woman than that which a man attains by learning Torah. The reason, he explains, is that men in general tend to be more aggressive; they struggle to be calm and tranquil and are therefore further distanced from the World to Come, which is a place of tranquility. To balance this, a man must toil in Torah. Women are innately aligned with this place of tranquility. This form of spiritual toil is not a prerequisite to bringing her nature into balance.

The tranquility to which the *Maharal* refers is in essence a state of equilibrium. According to the *Maharal*, men enter the world with a body and soul that are more remote from one another; there is a fierce battle raging within. Because men struggle more with inner turmoil, the toil of Torah, which subdues physicality, is necessary to bring balance. In contrast, a woman's body and soul, by nature, are in less conflict with each other. Less effort is therefore required to bring her inner world into balance. Nonetheless, by extending herself in support of Torah learning, the *Maharal* says, her accomplishments may even surpass those a man achieves through his learning.

To recap: ***Body and soul are totally unlike each other, want completely different things in life, and are often at war with each other. Because the body starts out with enormous advantages, the soul would be crushed without the strength provided by the Torah.***

◆§ The Power of the Body

All this may leave you with the impression that the body is nothing more than a hindrance to the soul's purpose. That is not so; the soul needs the body as much as the body needs the soul. The beauty of the Torah is that both play an equal and integral role in the 613 *mitzvos*, since we need both physicality and spirituality in our service of Hashem. As we explained earlier, each element of the body has both a positive and negative aspect to it. Through the choices we make and the life we live, we have the opportunity to refine each element, diminishing the negative aspects and enabling the positive to flourish.

Our lower physical self is a challenge that yearns to be overcome. Like a child testing his parent's limits, its deepest desire is not to run rampant, but rather, to be reined in and pointed in a positive direction.

The body begs to be utilized and not ignored. Because it is designed to act and feel, it will drive a person toward action and feelings of any kind, just so that we take notice and make use of it. If we leave a child without anything constructive to do, he becomes destructive; if we give him a worthwhile project he will put his mind to it and accomplish wonders.

The body's physical drives and emotions also serve another vital purpose. *Hakadosh Baruch Hu* created the body to desire worldly things because this ensures the continuity and establishment of the world. Furthermore, the body's needs — for food, clothing, friendship, protection and so forth — force us to interact with people and contribute to society.

☙ Why Must They Be So Different?

Before we leave this chapter, let's address the question that sometimes makes us want to throw up our hands in frustration: Why the great battle? Why couldn't the body and soul just be more alike? The constant back and forth is exhausting!

The answer is that life would be utterly pointless if they were more alike.

The *Mesillas Yesharim* teaches us that the sole purpose of all creation is to create an environment of free will so that we will have the opportunity to make good choices within that environment. To make that possible, the body and soul must stand opposed to each other. Think about it: If the *neshamah* is loftier than an angel, then only an extreme opposite pull would present us with a set of choices that are less than obvious. If the body's advice was any less convincing than it is, choosing the advice of the *neshamah* would be a no-brainer. As an example, if ice cream's taste was similar to that of broccoli, would we ever opt for the calories of a chocolate sundae?

In the words of the Ramchal in *Derech Hashem* (Part 1, Ch. 3):

> *To achieve free choice, Divine Wisdom decreed that mankind be composed of two opposites: the pure, intellectual soul and the earthly, physical body. Each one is drawn toward its nature, that is, the body toward the materialistic and the soul toward the intellectual (spiritual). The two are therefore in constant battle.*
>
> *If the soul prevails, it will be elevated and the body elevated with it. The person thereby attains his destined perfection. If, however, the person allows his physical side to prevail, he will debase his body and also debase his soul. This individual will be unfit for perfection and cast away from it, Heaven forbid.*

The good news is that along with growth comes fewer battles. By learning to discern right from wrong — tuning into the voice of the soul and then making a habit of heeding its message — we tame our more mundane desires and, over time, we refine the body until it too becomes lofty. The manual for this task is our holy Torah and the *mesorah* that was passed down from our parents, rabbis, and teachers. Ultimately, with hard work, the body can learn to desire many of the same things that the soul does. When this occurs, life takes on a much higher meaning and the battles between the partners over petty things become fewer. With this accomplished, we now have two forces pulling toward the same goal instead of each pulling in a different direction. That is exactly what tranquility and equilibrium mean.

We can compare the body to a person who grew up in a poor neighborhood and is given his first glass of a fine Cabernet, or who sees a magnificent abstract painting for the very first time. His reaction may very well be something like, "This tastes disgusting," or "That looks like a child threw some paint onto a canvas." A more cultured person witnessing this scene would chuckle to himself and think, "This person is clearly uneducated and doesn't appreciate true taste and beauty."

This is analogous to the body before refinement. In this state, it cannot appreciate the soul's beauty and will firmly assert its own desires. However, as the body is refined, it begins to relish that which is lofty and eternal; it no longer desires emptiness and shallowness. That same body that once craved staying in bed now finds enjoyment in staying up late to visit sick people in a hospital, and is willing to do so even on an empty stomach.

Let's imagine that you were to show Rav Chaim Kanievsky *shlit'a* a million dollars in cash. He wouldn't so much as lift his head from the page of Gemara that he was learning to glance at it. However, if you were to show him a *Rashba* that clarified the page he was learning, he would beam with delight and thank you profusely. As the great Rav Aharon of Karlin once said "I have more physical pleasure when I recite *Nishmas Kol Chai* on *Shabbos* than the czar has from all of the delights his money can buy him."

To recap: ***The inner struggle and inconsistencies that plague us are normal. They tell us that we have a body and soul, which oppose each other right from our first day on earth. Our life's work is to establish shalom — to unify these opposing forces by refining the body and amplifying the voice of the soul and its presence within us. Hashem gave both men and women the Torah as an equalizing and soul-nourishing force through which we create this harmony.***

8

YOU

Twenty years ago, I had the distinct pleasure of hearing Rav Ezriel Tauber deliver a lecture in my neighborhood. He began by asking the audience, "Who are you?" Among the many perplexed faces in the crowd, one person spoke up and said, "I am me. Who else?"

He smiled and said, "Haven't you ever wondered who YOU are?"

I immediately sat upright and thought, "Maybe he is going to answer my question!"

As a young child, my Rebbe taught us that a person is a *neshamah* — soul. I raised my hand and asked, "But Rebbe, this morning we said the blessing that starts, '*Elokai, neshamah shenasata bi* (My G-d, the soul that You placed in me), You blew it into me.' If I am a *neshamah,* then who is the 'me' that is speaking?"

The question, unanswered at the time, was the topic of Rabbi Tauber's lecture. He explained that we cannot be our body because it will ultimately return to the ground, while "we" will transcend to a higher world. The body is a vehicle that takes us through life, and, if it performs its function diligently, it will merit resurrection at the end of time. We also know that our souls are on loan to us, as we say each morning in the aforementioned prayer, "... and You will take it from me and return it to me...". The prayer is intimating that "me" will exist for a time without the soul, until the *neshamah* is returned in the World to Come. In other words, "me" cannot mean the soul and must translate to something other than that.

In the last chapter we described YOU as having "partners," an idea mentioned in the *Maharal* (*Chiddushei Aggados Sanhedrin* 91b). Furthermore, the Gemara (*Taanis* 11a), commenting on the Final Judgment, states, "Rav Chidka said the *neshamah* of a person will bear witness on him." This supports the position that we are not identical with our *neshamah*, since a person cannot testify against/for himself.

There are many opinions[3] on how the body, the soul, and the "me" combine into our personal identities. For the remainder of this chapter, we will follow the opinion that we are neither body nor soul, but rather a third entity that is partnered with both.

What follows derives from Rabbi Tauber's teachings at that lecture, and insights from other sources that help shed light on who YOU are.

☙ "You" as Watcher

Without getting into deep Kabbalistic explanations, we will establish that there is a "you,"

> which, like a fulcrum on a scale, balances the polar opposites of body and soul,
> who has the ability to watch and listen to what the two opposing inner voices are communicating,
> who can completely silence the internal noise and enter into a state of quiet and solitude,
> who has free choice,
> who has the power to cling to Hakadosh Baruch Hu,
> who will receive reward in the World to Come.

The identification of self is important for more than philosophical reasons; it has practical applications, as well. First, it is crucial to remember that there is a YOU who is present in all of life's challenges

3 There are four possible answers to the question of who are YOU? The first, as we stated, that YOU are neither body nor soul but are rather partnered with them, a second, that YOU are both, a third that YOU are *neshamah* alone and a fourth, body alone. This is a complex idea and, in some aspect, each opinion is valid.

and that YOU are separate from all that is going on inside and outside of yourself at any given time. While all the noise and information swirling around may serve to influence you, draw you in, and prod you to take action, the fact remains that since YOU are separate from the thoughts and feelings buzzing around inside your head and stomach, YOU can always choose to detach yourself from them. For some, this revelation can be life-altering: "I am not my thoughts, feelings, and desires; I am me. I am in control and I can choose to ignore negative thoughts and even stop them altogether."

You are the guardian of your thoughts and desires but they are not you. YOU are a consciousness and self-awareness that is independent of the body in which YOU are contained.

Since the time that you first became self-aware, you may have believed that there was one unified component — you — and ascribed the inner conflict raging inside you to immaturity, confusion, or perhaps worse. When you begin to internalize that there are actually three components to the self, soul, body, and YOU, things start to make sense and you realize that there is nothing wrong with you.

◆ "You" as Chooser

From the writings of Rav Dessler, we can derive another practical definition of "you" — the "chooser." All growth in life involves making choices — good choices in the face of challenge and adversity — and "you" are the one who is choosing.

Rav Dessler (*Kuntress HaBechirah,* Part 1, Ch.1) illustrates this idea with an example: A man smokes a pack of cigarettes a day. Every night, he wakes up with chest pains and vows never to smoke another cigarette again. When he awakens in the morning, his addiction soon makes itself felt and he craves a smoke. At first, he resists, but, as the craving grows, he says to himself, "I will smoke just one cigarette. After all, one alone can't hurt me," and he lights up. Not long afterward, the urge returns and he uses the same rationalization for the second one ... and the third. That night, the pain returns and he repeats the vow. Were this man to experience acute pain immediately upon taking his first puff, he would surely give up smoking altogether. The fact that the pain is delayed allows the cycle of self-deception to continue as he tells himself that "one cigarette won't hurt me."

Rav Dessler asks: What causes a person to adopt the fallacious argument of "one cigarette won't harm me," and ignore the truth that "one cigarette will lead to another," which he knows from firsthand experience is the reality? Rav Dessler argues that it can't be that the man's will to smoke is perverting his reasoning process, leading him to conclude that the pleasure of smoking makes it worth the subsequent pain. If that were so, why the self-deception of "one cigarette won't harm me"? He should simply smoke with the full knowledge that it will hurt later.

He concludes that there is something other than the two competing wills that determines his choice. **That something else is the person himself.** HE is the one who chooses to deflect his mind from the truth and adopt the fallacy that one cigarette won't harm him. He could instead say to himself, "What is the point of pretending? If I smoke this one then I will wake up tonight with chest pains." Instead, HE deceives himself into believing that it will only be one.

Rav Dessler bestows the title of "fools" upon those who claim that the will to smoke is the true cause of this ridiculous daily routine. He argues that the will to live is surely greater than the will to smoke and a greater will should overpower a weaker one. The person himself, however, has the power to deliberately ignore the truth and accept falsehood in its place. The outcome of this is that when a person makes the claim, "I smoke because I am powerless to stop," the response should be, "No, you smoke because you choose to and you have no one to blame but yourself."

Rav Dessler teaches that choice lies completely in our hands and there are no forces that control us. People who have never challenged the pull of their harmful physical desires won't ever be able to understand this, because they are convinced that they are at the mercy of those compulsive needs. Such people have never made a free-choice decision and live under the illusion that human action is controlled by external or internal forces.

With his poignant words, Rav Dessler brings forth an axiom held by successful people and lacking in those who are unsuccessful: **"I am fully responsible for my actions because I alone am in control of my choices."** While there is a small subset of people who are choice-impaired due to various life circumstances, the majority of us are fully responsible for the choices we make.

People sometimes say things like, "I can't help myself. I am controlled by my anger/anxiety/fear/indecision/addiction/shortcomings," and the like. Blaming is a common theme in today's culture and it has perhaps even become socially incorrect to require that a person accept full responsibility for his actions. We may try to lay the blame on our society, upbringing, boss, weaknesses, addictions, or the "system," but we must realize that by doing so we are choking off any opportunity for growth. Successful people never hide behind excuses. We all make mistakes; the difference between success and failure is whether or not we take ownership of those mistakes. Even if in certain circumstances we may not be responsible for what happened to us, we do remain fully responsible for our responses and resulting actions.

☙ The Point of Free Choice

The additional aspect of self that can be learned from Rav Dessler's essay is that "you" are not static; rather, "you" are always in a state of movement, either up or down.

Rav Dessler explains that when two armies, A and B, are locked in battle, the actual fighting only takes place at the battlefront. (Recall that the *Tanya* called the body and soul as two armies locked in battle over YOU.) Territory that lies behind Army A's line is entirely under its control and there is little or no need to protect it from Army B. Territory that lies behind Army B's line is completely out of the reach of Army A at the moment and so Army A isn't focused on capturing it just yet. The battle is fought entirely at the place where the two armies engage each other, and in that one spot they are both equal; neither has control over it yet. As Army A advances, that territory which it conquers falls under its control and the battle is now fought at a further point that was formerly under Army B's control. The site of battle keeps advancing and retreating depending on who is winning at any given time.

According to Rav Dessler, the same is true in our battles with the *yetzer hara; right vs. wrong – truth vs. falsehood*. There is territory that is well under our control, such as *shemiras Shabbos, kashrus*, or wearing *tefillin*. For many of us, *Baruch Hashem*, the thought of *chillul Shabbos* or not eating kosher never enters our minds, and even if it does, in those situations truth will extinguish falsehood immediately. This means that our free choice isn't being exercised in these places. Our point of free choice may be in refraining from speaking lashon hora or being careful not to talk during *davening*. Then there are places where falsehood reigns because the person doesn't yet realize that what he is doing is wrong or because change is still beyond his reach. Free choice takes place where truth/falsehood, right/wrong meet each other head on and there is a real clash. Under that circumstance, making the right choice is a challenge.

This is what is meant by "Don't judge someone until you have reached his place." "His place" is his point of free choice. He may be winning more battles than you and capturing more territory, but he may have started somewhere far behind you when his war began.

The outcome of this is that "you" are not static. "You" are in a constant state of change, either advancing or retreating. Advancing means that the battles "you" are fighting and winning today will get easier and perhaps even disappear with time. Retreating, *chas v'shalom*, means that things that are well under "your" control today may not be so tomorrow if "you" allow the Satan to win battles and advance.

Another important lesson is that "you" are "you" and not someone else. Some people compare themselves to those who are way ahead of them; this causes them to feel down and question their self-worth. Others look at people they perceive as less than them and use that comparison to prop up their egos. Both are living a fallacy, because each individual himself is the only benchmark against which he or she can be measured. As I once heard Rabbi Akiva Tatz say, if an adult tennis player wins a match against a 9-year-old, neither has learned anything about himself because neither played a match. In some areas of life we are the 9-year-old, and in others we are the adult; the only way we can gauge our standing is by winning a battle where there is a genuine competition.

The *Mishnah* in *Rosh Hashanah* says that every year we pass through judgment *"k'vnei maron."* The Gemara offers an interpretation of a narrow mountain pass called "Beis Maron," which, Rashi says, was only wide enough to accommodate one person at a time. The Maharal explains that no two of us stand exactly side by side, and we are not judged on Rosh Hashanah according to how high or low we are relative to someone else. We are judged relative to how much we climbed in the past year. Our ultimate judgment will be based on how much we climbed in our respective lifetimes in light of the opportunities and skills we were given. We often waste precious time and energy evaluating ourselves relative to others, when an absolute evaluation is really all that matters.

Finally, Rav Dessler's words teach us an extremely valuable life lesson regarding growth. Growth only happens when we face a challenge and overcome it. However, there are two detrimental tendencies that tend to stymie our potential for growth:

1. We find something we are good at and do it over and over and over, refraining from further challenges in order to avoid failure. In essence, we evade battles and stay in our comfort zones. In doing so, we cannot win new territory and our point of free choice doesn't advance. Growth is only achieved outside of our comfort zones.
2. We attempt to capture territory that is far behind our enemy's lines by undertaking challenges for which we aren't yet ready. Then, when we don't succeed, we label ourselves as failures. Remember, if you play a tennis match against a professional, then you are guaranteed to lose. In truth, however, you didn't actually lose; you never even played. The person who plays the next match may be at the level to win, but if we spend our lives comparing ourselves to other players, we will suffer from an erroneously deflated ego. If there is an area of growth that lies beyond our reach, it's best to create a plan that starts with an

undertaking at which we can persevere and then move forward step by step, until we ultimately reach the objective on which we have set our sights.

To recap: ***Growth is defined by our movement up and down on the spectrum of choice. What may be a difficult choice to make today can become second nature over time. When that happens, YOU have grown. On the other hand, if you lose enough ground, an ideal you would never compromise on today can become permissible in your eyes over time. When that happens, you have fallen.***

So Far…

We have now provided a framework with which you can understand who YOU are: YOU watch, YOU listen, YOU make choices and grow through those choices. The territory that YOU conquer by making good choices leads to the refinement of the body with which YOU were paired. Through this effort, YOU reveal the body's inherent powers and potential for good, and channel the body toward a higher purpose.

We have defined success, learned the importance of purpose, meaning, and mission, demonstrated your potential, and introduced you to YOU and to your partners. We will now move forward and learn some ways to improve the choices YOU make.

9

Shedding Light on Choice

You have a dilemma, and the more you think about it, the deeper you sink into bewilderment. So, you go to discuss the matter with someone wise; perhaps a great *tzaddik* or mentor. He listens carefully, asks some probing questions, and gives you advice. But it's not just any advice; it's advice that causes something to click inside you. You have an "AHA!" moment. Your advisor has brought forth an answer that seems to have been inside you all along. So brilliant, yet so obvious! You just know it's the right answer. You can feel it in your bones.

Then you begin to wonder, "Now why couldn't I have thought of that? How much better would my life be if I could learn to find the answers on my own? After all, in most situations, I have to make decisions by myself."

In this chapter we will reveal some of the wisdom that enables someone to see a situation clearly and provide the appropriate advice. In a later chapter, we'll explore this concept at a deeper level. Soon, you will come to realize that you, too, can be the wise advisor for others, and perhaps even for yourself.

In the previous chapters, we introduced you to your partners — body and soul — and then to YOU. Now that you are acquainted with yourself and your two companions, life should be fairly simple from here. Just go make good choices; how difficult can that be?

Sometimes, quite difficult.

While we have laid some foundation, in reality, making good choices may still prove challenging. That is because we rarely perceive situations in life — especially what is transpiring inside of us — as black and white. If you mix black and white you get gray, a neutral color that lacks contrast. This is a deficit when we're trying to make choices, because we need contrast in order to bring clarity to a situation. It's much easier to choose between black and white. If there were a way to separate the gray into these two contrasting components, how much easier would it be to discern the right decision?

Wise people know this trick. What we see as shades of gray, they see as black and white. They see what is going on beneath the surface. In order to try to understand how they accomplish this, we will need to set some important groundwork in place.

◆§ Who Is Speaking?

As we explained, YOU are constantly receiving communications from one of your two partners: the unrefined body (lower self), or the refined soul (higher self). Discerning one voice from the other is a challenge, because the lower self often presents its ideas dressed up in the noblest intentions.

> *A very religious man came to me recently because his life was falling apart. His marriage was in shambles and his children were leaving the path one after the other. In his mind he was doing everything right by steadfastly adhering to his Mesorah and not tolerating even the slightest infraction. His home had become a battlefield with criticism, yelling and rebuke serving as the guns and tanks. I told the man, "I have the deepest sympathy for you. My yetzer hara comes to me dressed in a leather jacket, covered in tattoos, smelling of cigarettes, and driving a Harley. Shame on me if I listen to him. Yours comes dressed in tallis and tefillin holding a large sefer with a flowing*

white beard, so you invite him in and serve him cake and wine. Why wouldn't you?"

Here are some other examples as depicted by the brothers Reuvain, Shimon, Levi, and the rest of the family:

Reuvain can do *chesed* with the purest of intentions or as a means of self-promotion;
Shimon can fiercely defend a position to uphold the truth or to protect his ego;
Levi can amass wealth for either altruistic or selfish reasons:
Yehudah can choose a simpler life because he believes there is more to life than money, or because he is too lazy or afraid to strive for more;
Yissachar can give a client advice because it is in the client's best interests, or he can give self-serving advice while telling himself that the client will benefit;
Zevulun can rebuke his friend because it's a mitzvah, or because he feels threatened by his friend's success:
Dan can abstain from rebuking his friend because it won't help or is a one-time occurrence, or he can refrain because he is intimidated or doesn't want to be seen as overly righteous.

The *Chovos HaLevavos* warns us of this trap multiple times (*Shaar Yichud HaMaaseh* Ch. 5). Rabbeinu Bachya urges us to learn to recognize the voices inside of us and know who is saying what. Learn to discern your motives.

I was once at the Kosel on Friday night and there was a man talking loudly during Kabbalas Shabbos. One man finally spoke up and, shall we say, "really let him have it."

"This is the holiest time of the week and we are at the holiest place on earth, and all you have been doing is yapping endlessly," he said. For a moment I thought, "Wow! I sure wish I had the guts to speak up like him. I mean, that had to be one of the very best 'stop the talking in shul' speeches ever delivered."

He should have ended his speech right there, but he didn't. He continued, and proceeded to make his true motivations known by yelling, "I spent all this money to come to Eretz Yisrael in order to enjoy this Friday-night experience and you are ruining it for me!"

So, I ask you, how much did this person have Hakadosh Baruch Hu in mind as opposed to the cost of his vacation? He likely went home believing that he had heeded his neshamah and fulfilled the mitzvah of "Hoche'ach toche'ach" — "You shall surely rebuke" — when in reality, he should have asked the person for forgiveness. One's true intention during the act of rebuking another could spell the difference between fulfilling a positive commandment and the polar opposite, the sin of shaming another in public.

The common thread that runs through all the above situations is that the brothers are potentially heeding a lower will that is deceptively dressed in virtuous clothing. They have difficulty discerning which "partner" is advising them. The challenge this poses is obvious; when we decide on an action or inaction without recognizing the underlying source that motivates our decision, we often make improper choices. Furthermore, we will never see a need to consider re-evaluating those choices after the fact, because we believe we made a virtuous choice.

As a result of this, we sometimes confuse right and wrong. At times we remain unaware of what motivates our decisions; we may therefore spend years engaged in counterproductive activities, or do the right things for the wrong reasons. We feel confused, empty, and unfulfilled, and we cannot fathom why. The examples listed above are but a few, but ultimately the soundness of our decisions always revolves around the same question: Who is speaking to and motivating us, our higher or lower self?

◈ The Light of Discernment

To remedy this confusion, we will learn some methods that will help us to distinguish the lower voice from the higher voice. The answer always lies within us, and that is why the advice of the wise person so clearly resonates with us. What they have and we don't is the power of discernment. This is partially because we are in the dilemma and they are not, and partially because they have learned to focus on important variables that we may overlook.

While different situations may call for different methodologies, here are some ideas that may prove helpful.

Reveal the *Sheker* (Falsehood)

If we look closely, the truth is often right there staring us in the face. Looking closely means trying to find contradictions and inconsistencies in our reasoning, which are sure to be there if the lower self is speaking. Chazal tell us that falsehood does not have legs, which means that, upon closer examination, facts just won't add up and will topple over. Some point out that *sheker* does have a leg, the long one on the letter *kuf,* which causes the falsehood to stand out before it topples over.

To learn how to tease out the *sheker* from our thinking, let's go back to our earlier examples.

If **Reuvain** is motivated to do *chesed* for its own sake, then he should not mind someone else competing with him, as long as the other person isn't trying to undermine him. After all, if he is serving Hashem, then the more *chesed* and *Kiddush Hashem* in the world the better. If Reuvain's ego is behind all this, then he will be motivated to protect his turf. Another indicator of his underlying motivation would be whether his *chesed* is amenable to his wife and children, since true charity begins at home.

If **Shimon** seeks the truth, he should not feel threatened by the prospect of someone else being right. Truth is truth.

If **Levi** wants to amass wealth in order to help others, is he doing all he can to help others right now, with the resources he currently has available?

If **Yehudah** is choosing to live a simple life because he believes that his time can be utilized for higher purposes, how is he currently spending his free time? Is he learning Torah and helping others?

If **Yissachar** wants to do what is in the best interest of the client, then his advice should not change even if it means that he earns less money or even nothing at all.

If **Zevulun** is sharing rebuke with the right intention, then his words will be measured, soft, and delivered with humility.

If **Dan** is withholding rebuke for good reason, he should not feel cowardly afterward.

When ego is present, it rarely does a good job at hiding itself. If we pay close enough attention, we find the fallacy of reasoning and the personal bias that lies just beneath the surface. Someone recently told me that he has become more measured when rebuking his friends for their infractions because he realized that he was doing so with too much zest and fervor and wasn't performing any other mitzvos with that level of passion. This made him realize that it was partially his ego that was motivating him.

☙ Who Do We Want to Take Notice?

The *Chovos HaLevavos* (*Yichud HaMaaseh* Ch. 5) offers two ways in which a person can evaluate the purity of his choices and motivations.

A. He should clarify to himself from whom he hopes to receive reward and recognition for his actions: other people or Hakadosh Baruch Hu? The lower self serves itself, while the higher self serves its Creator.

B. He should clarify to himself whether or not he would perform the given action in the identical manner if he was all alone and no one would ever learn of it.

A person intuitively knows what he hopes to gain by any given action. If the person's ego is driving him, he tends to become frustrated when his intended outcome is slow in coming or doesn't come at all. "Hashem didn't keep His end of the bargain" or "Why isn't anyone taking notice of my good deeds?" are common ego-driven thoughts. Such a person slacks off or abandons a project entirely when he realizes that the recognition he desired will not be forthcoming.

In contrast, a person of noble character seeks nothing in return for his positive actions. The joy of performing his Creator's will by helping another person gives him a deep sense of fulfillment, which is reward enough.

By recognizing these two contrasting lines of thought, we give ourselves a reliable way to recognize the true source of our motivation in choosing a course of action. We can learn to ask ourselves, "What do I hope will happen if I choose A vs. B? What do 'I' expect to get out of either course of action?" If the answer is that we have ulterior motives then that's no reason to stop performing positive actions. We have however revealed to ourselves that we have work to do in directing our intentions toward a higher purpose.

ও Seek an Outside Perspective

The ability to question our own motives requires deep introspection, honesty and self-awareness. Therefore, we are sometimes better able to gain clarity by discussing the matter with someone wiser, rather than trying to sort it out ourselves. However, this route is only effective, if:

1. We are ready to be completely forthcoming with the person about all that is going on inside of us.
2. We are prepared to humble ourselves by admitting that we don't trust our instincts, and by asking the person questions like, "Am I fooling myself?" and "What am I not seeing?"
3. We expressly give him permission to be blatantly honest and reveal and say it like he sees it.

Many people claim they are seeking advice, when all they are really seeking is validation. The person's advisor may not know his true intentions, and as the saying goes, "The advice is only as good as the question that is asked." I have made it a practice to ask people seeking my advice for permission to be blatantly honest with them. I do this because my prior experience has shown me that people who ask me questions are not always prepared to hear my answers.

We all need an outside perspective from time to time, especially when we need help in seeing past our personal biases. Our goal is to separate black from white and uncover the falsehood, contradiction, or fallacy in our reasoning.

֍ Ask Yourself Revealing Questions

As we depicted at the beginning of this chapter, someone who needs help in clarifying matters can often gain clarity by answering one or two probing questions asked of him by a wise person. From this, the truth seems to magically spring forth. But there really is no magic. We can learn to ask ourselves these very same questions. Here are some examples:

- Which choice can I defend as being the will of Hashem?
- As the Piaseczna Rebbe writes, "Which choice would I make if today were my last day on earth?" We often use the fallacy of "I can make things right one day" as justification for ignoring the right choice in the present. When we remind ourselves that "there may not be another day," we make choices with far greater clarity.
- If someone I care about deeply were to ask me the very same question, what advice would I give him?
- Which choice would I make if recognition, money, or personal comfort were not a factor?
- What choice would I make if nobody could see?
- If my child were facing this very same decision, what decision would I want **him/her** to make?
- Which course of action will withstand the test of time? How might I feel about this decision when I look back at it one day in the future? A decision based on the desire of the lower self will always leave us with a case of buyer's remorse. As my Rebbe once taught me, it's easy to know whose advice we are heeding; following the lower self always feels good for the moment and rotten after the fact, while heeding the soul can be challenging for the moment but ultimately will be uplifting.
- Would I be prepared to share this decision, and all of its underlying reasoning, with someone whom I greatly respect? With someone whom I want to respect me? We can sometimes rationalize a bad decision to ourselves, but we intuitively know that someone unbiased will see right through us, and that Hashem is seeing right through us at this very moment.

☙ Deliberate and Don't Act Impulsively

Most mistakes and bad choices are the ones that were made impulsively, without thought. Chazal tell us in *Avos*, "Be deliberate in judgment." When trying to issue a ruling between two internal voices, we should realize that it's usually the voice of the lower self that wants us to act quickly. That voice is intimidated by time, lest the truth be revealed through thought or counsel. It's like a sneaky used-car salesman who knows that the minute you walk out the door, you will come to your senses and he will never see you again. He therefore says, "What do I have to do to get you into this car today?"

Take your time when you are truly unsure of your motives or can't differentiate white from black. Waiting and deliberating are not laziness or procrastination when they serve a real purpose. No matter how much it may seem that rushing into something is the right thing to do, most of the time, another day won't make or break a decision, while haste will often have unintended consequences.

In Conclusion

The better our choice-making skills, the more success we will merit and the more deeply fulfilling life will be. Shedding light on the source of the myriad choices before us will elevate our lives in unimaginable ways. We are each capable of making better choices using the power of objectivity and discernment. A bit of light removes great quantities of darkness.

In my profession, an inferior stock-picker has two options: he can improve his stock-selection skills by questioning his methodologies, reading books, taking courses, and seeking the guidance of successful portfolio managers. Or, he can leave finance and earn a livelihood elsewhere.

In contrast, there's no "career alternative" to living our lives. We can't run away from inept choice-making skills, because where would we go? Our only option is to get better at it, and then even better at it. We do this by,

Becoming more discerning and perceptive.

Learning *Mussar*, which teaches us the pitfalls of bad choices, the tactics of the *yetzer hara,* and how we become entrapped by the lower will.

Seeking out and attaching ourselves to spiritual mentors who will serve as our guiding lights.

Learning how to amplify the faint voice of the soul and to lower the volume of the lower self.

And above all, *davening* to Hashem to guide us along the proper path.

The roadmap is the Torah and the Rabbinic teachings that have been bequeathed to us by past generations. The more we study, the better equipped we are to identify the voice we should heed and the voice we should ignore.

To recap: ***Effective choice-making is challenging because right and wrong are often not clearly labeled as such. Instilling discipline, seeking advice, and working to clarify our true motives will lead to us making better choices and live more fulfilling lives.***

As I finished writing this chapter, Hashem sent me a messenger who opened my eyes as to what the next chapter should be.

10

Soul Nourishment

While writing the last chapter, a middle-aged man came to seek my advice. As he sat across from me, he broke down in tears and admitted that he has been struggling internally with his Torah observance for many years, while outwardly living as though all was well. This story inspired me to write about something that I wouldn't have otherwise discussed.

Many years ago, in order to help himself through emotional issues, this man began to study psychology. In doing so, he read certain books antithetical to Torah that instilled many unhealthy questions and ideas into his mind. While outwardly nothing had changed, inwardly he was crumbling. The look in his eye as he sat across from me was one of a man holding on to life by a thread. I asked him,

What Torah have you been learning all this time — Torah that would counter what you have been reading?

Only Gemara, which I don't particularly enjoy.

You mean you don't learn Chovos HaLevavos, Ramchal, or any other sefer that would heal the damage you are inflicting on your neshamah?

No, it is not the way of my Rebbe *zt"l*. (His Rebbe, a great *tzaddik*, passed away long ago.)

Did your Rebbe allow people to read heretical books?

Of course not!

I think it's fair to say that if your Rebbe were alive today, he would

surely prefer that you studied Torah that would heal the damage done by the books you have read. Gemara alone was prescribed to a healthy person. Today you are spiritually sick and need to be healed.

The man took the advice to heart and accepted an expanded learning regimen.

In light of this story, I want to underscore something we touched on in the last chapter: the study of Torah, for both men and women, as a means to successful living.

←§ Torah for Every Heart

The Torah is vast and there is an array of teachings from which to choose. Nevertheless, some people may pigeonhole themselves regarding what they study and never explore beyond that. They may be missing out on words that would speak to their hearts, bring them into balance, and accelerate their growth.

> *In a lecture I delivered to a community, I wanted to underscore a point with an idea that was beautifully illustrated in a sefer that, due to philosophical differences of many generations ago, was not accepted in this particular community. I therefore did something I rarely do; I shared the thought without naming the source lest it be discounted. The leader of the community, who was in attendance, came to me after the lecture and said, "I must know the source of that amazing Torah concept!" When I told him, he was astonished. I quickly added, "The great tzaddik who wrote this has a lot more to say that you would find amazing."*

If we aren't all learning *Mesillas Yesharim, Chovos HaLevavos,* and/or other works of *mussar*, then how can we hope to survive, let alone thrive, in the era in which we live? In today's challenging world, Torah that heals and uplifts us is oxygen for the soul.

אָמַר רֶבִּי, אֵין אָדָם לוֹמֵד אֶלָּא מִמָּקוֹם שֶׁלִּבּוֹ חָפֵץ (עבודה זרה יט). — *"Rebbe said, A person only learns where his heart desires" (Avodah Zarah 19a).*

We can, with proper guidance, seek out legitimate works of Torah that speak to us, and we will never know what they are until we seek advice and broaden the array of *sefarim* and books that we are willing to explore. Torah ideas, thoughts, and strategies to combat today's spiritual challenges can sometimes be found in *sefarim* that we have never opened; these are nuggets of gold that can elevate our mindset and improve the trajectory of our lives. We may learn something that will have a remarkable and penetrating effect, and it's difficult to predict from which *sefer* that inspiration will come.

Some may argue that people should adhere strictly to the path paved for them by their teachers and forefathers, with no deviation. I wholeheartedly agree; we are not speaking of deviation, but rather, of enhancement. The guidance we seek should come from the Torah leaders who follow our own traditions. We are also only speaking to those who seem to have stalled and are seeking Torah that can propel them forward. If what you are learning is working for you, then you are on the right track and should stay with it. If you find yourself lacking knowledge or inspiration, please don't turn to so-called "secular gurus" to fill that void. Seek out a learned mentor who can put a new work of Torah before you.

I fully admit that I spent too many years dismissing outright entire works of Torah because of a preconceived notion that turned out to be completely unfounded. When studying in Brisk, I would learn after hours in a shul near my apartment. Each night, in the same room where I studied, there was a *shiur* in *Sifrei Machshavah* which "of course" I never attended. One night, the elderly *tzaddik* who gave the *shiur* asked me, "Young man, why don't you join the *shiur* sometime?" to which I smugly replied, "I first need to finish *Shas* (the entirety of the Talmud) before I can even think of learning *Sifrei Machshavah*." The *tzaddik* retorted, "I have been around a lot longer than you, and can attest that if you learn *Sifrei Machshavah* once in a while, you will know *Shas* a lot better when you finish it." I didn't heed his advice then. After all, no respectable student of Brisk would deign to be caught learning *Sifrei Machshavah*. In retrospect, however, I really wish I had taken advantage of some of the opportunities that had been right there in front of me.

The benefit of the intermingling of Chassidish, Litvish, and Sefardic Jews that we have seen over the past fifty years is that our unique schools of Torah thought are now available to all of us. Back in Europe, where would a boy from the Chassidus of Belz ever be exposed to the Torah of Rav Elchonon Wasserman or a woman from Aleppo to the holy Kedushas Levi, or a young man in Warsaw to the Ben Ish Chai? Today, we *B'H* have an array of life-changing works of Torah lined up side by side on store bookshelves. All we need is Torah-true guidance and the willingness to learn.

◆§ Strategies

Aside from broadening our scope of Torah knowledge, we should also be open to adopting new strategies to combat the daily challenges that we face.

The holy Rav Hershel of Lisker, who was the Rebbe of Rav Shayele of Kerestir, quotes the *Shelah Hakadosh* in saying that the *yetzer hara* entered mankind when Adam and Chava ate from the Tree of Knowledge. The Gemara refers to his influence on us as the "venom of the snake." The *Shelah Hakadosh* teaches that the longer the venom of a snake remains inside of a person, the more damage is done, and the more medicine the person will need in order to heal. If a person arrives at the emergency room one day after being bitten rather than one hour after being bitten, he will require far greater intervention. The *Shelah* explains that this is the reason behind the concept of *niskatnu hadoros* — that each generation's spiritual level is weaker than the preceding one. The venom is traveling; it is harming us more and more, and we are growing weaker and weaker as a result.

Therefore, he says, each generation needs to seek out new remedies for that which ails them. They cannot rely solely on what worked for the prior generations. We should not say, "My grandfather didn't adhere to this stringency, so I won't either." As I tell my children, our grandparents, back in Galicia, didn't see in a lifetime the sordid, impure sights that we are unfortunately exposed to in one day's mail. What are we going to do about it?

While we never deviate from the path of our forefathers, and always follow our individual family customs, we must also realize that the *yetzer hara* is planning new schemes every day, and we may not be able to defend ourselves against his onslaught with a single lifetime strategy. Rav Hershel of Liska is teaching us that we need depth and breadth; we sometimes need innovation within our framework. This means that while we adhere closely to our individual *mesorah,* we remain open to proper enhancements.

The Chofetz Chaim offered the following parable:

> *A country had been at war, and a brilliant general led them to victory that ushered in decades of peace and tranquility.*
>
> *Suddenly, the country found itself once again under attack. The leaders brought the decorated general and hero out of retirement to lead the troops. He guided the troops with his previously successful tactics and armaments, only to be quickly and roundly defeated.*
>
> *The general had failed to take into account the new technologies and weapons being used by the enemy, so his decades-old approach was doomed to failure.*
>
> *The same is true, the Chofetz Chaim explained, when dealing with the Yetzer Hara. He is ever the innovator, and we must use the Torah to develop responses to his new methods and attacks.*

Another important idea can be found in the writings of the Baal Shem Tov, who teaches that when we devise a way to fight the Satan, we are opening a skylight to the heavens above. This opening brings us light, which allows us to see more clearly. The Satan, however, quickly works to close or obscure the skylight, and so, we must always be vigilant and active in seeking ways to open new ones.

In summation, each of us has our staple diet of Torah that supplies us with the basic nutrients we need. This might include a daily *Daf* of Gemara, chapters of *Tehillim, Chumash/Rashi, Chovos HaLevavos,* or *shiurim* that awaken us. However, people who seek greater growth and are realistically aware of the pitfalls of today's society open their minds and hearts to all that Torah has to offer. They learn Torah-based strategies others use successfully, and incorporate them into their lives.

11

Building Vessels

Who wouldn't want to win the lottery?

It's like a dream come true. So much money! You'd be set for life!

Who wouldn't want to win? Many of those who have already won. Here are real quotes from people who won big:

> *"Actually, the entire experience has been very depressing."*
> *"I wish it never happened. It was a total nightmare."*
> *"I was much happier when I was broke."*
> *"It's hard to believe that I filed for bankruptcy less than ten years after winning."*
> *"Life was so much easier before I won."*
> *"If I could turn back time, I would tear up that ticket."*

There's even a name for this sad phenomenon: "the lottery curse." This disappointing outcome is not limited to lottery winners; it is also prevalent among those who are thrust into the public spotlight or achieve instant fame and recognition. Their lives often fall apart. How can seemingly positive occurrences cause so much destruction?

In this chapter we will discuss an extremely important aspect of success; building ourselves, through refinement of our character traits, into worthy and reliable vessels that can contain the blessings that Hakadosh Baruch Hu wants to bestow upon us. In the absence of this refinement, one reason that you may not receive what you so deeply want is simply because you aren't ready for it and at this point it may not be in your best interests.

The Breaking of the Vessels

The Arizal teaches that this world came into being through a process called *Shviras HaKeilim* — the breaking of the vessels. This is a profoundly deep yet accessible concept that underpins the fabric of all of creation.

The Arizal teaches that Hakadosh Baruch Hu began creation by creating *keilim*, vessels, to hold His emanation. He then infused them with a spiritual light that was so powerful that the vessels couldn't contain it and they burst. Built into creation is the following law: If the content of a vessel exceeds its capacity, the vessel will shatter. Growth involves building ourself into a worthy vessel.

Let's examine this concept.

Hashem created the world in order to emanate His light — His goodness — to us. For a person to receive light, he needs to first build himself into the vessel with the capacity to contain it. Were Hakadosh Baruch Hu to infuse us with goodness before we prepared ourselves to receive it, we would burst. As we learned from the Ramchal in an earlier chapter, we can only be recipients of Hashem's goodness when we teach ourselves to emulate Him. This is how we become vessels; otherwise the good wouldn't be good at all.[4]

Shviras HaKeilim, in the case of the unhappy lottery winners, is the result of people receiving a large money infusion for which they had not built the capacity. Their lives, therefore, literally blow up. Starting a business and building it brick by brick takes discipline, perseverance, and a lot of internal work. It takes many years and many *tefillos*. Therefore, when the entrepreneur achieves success with Hashem's help, he has already built the *keilim* for it and will know how to treat the

4. Tears are a form of *Shviras HaKeilim*, because when we hear unexpected good news, or the opposite, the information is too much to contain inside.

abundance with discipline. Allowing a lottery computer to pick some numbers takes a split second; it does nothing to build the character traits necessary for the winners to wisely handle the infusion of money. Therefore, the winnings often break apart the people who suddenly strike it rich. They splurge on things they always envied and often lose their spouses, friends, and family in the process. Ultimately, without discipline, all the money in the world isn't enough and they end up broke and depressed.

While this may sound irrelevant, since I am guessing you did not win the lottery lately, it nevertheless may explain why some people are not as financially successful, or as famous, as they would like to be.

Rav Tzvi Hersh of Lisker, in his *sefer Ach Pri Tevuah* (*Bamidbar*), writes that the reason Hakadosh Baruch Hu created the world through *Shviras HaKeilim* is to provide a lesson to anyone who feels that he isn't receiving enough. Hashem wants us to know that He wants to give us so much more in all areas of life, spiritual and material, but we aren't ready for it yet. An analogy comes to mind of a baby who is frustrated by the small hole in the nipple of the bottle. The baby doesn't realize that his life would be in grave danger if that hole was any bigger.

Why Some Are Given Abundance

The *Chovos HaLevavos* says in *Shaar Hachniyah,* "Gate of Submission," that Hakadosh Baruch Hu gives a person abundance for one of three reasons; as a reward, as a punishment, or as a test. While the *Chovos HaLevavos* uses wealth as an example, the same holds true for all of the gifts Hashem bestows upon us.

The Reliable Vessel

When Hashem grants a person wealth as a reward, He does so because it will benefit the person and those who rely on him. Since he has already built himself into a vessel to receive abundance, when the benefit comes to him, he sees it as an undeserved blessing and it does not inflate his ego. He does not lose his mind and drown in materialism, lust, and wastefulness. On the contrary, abundance motivates him to help others and serve Hashem with greater fervor, out of a deep sense of appreciation and gratitude.

The Defective Vessel

When wealth is a punishment, success destroys the recipient's life and sometimes the lives of his children as well. Because he did not work to become an adequate vessel, the wealth causes great damage. He is still materialistic, selfish, and greedy; he is a flimsy container that bursts when filled. We need not look very far in today's world to see the casualties of wealth.

The Vessel in Progress

For those in the third category, Hashem uses success and wealth as a test, just as He uses poverty as a test. In the case of wealth, Hashem causes the person to face difficult choices as to how to relate to the abundance he has received. It is for good reason that Chazal tell us that wealth is one of the most difficult challenges to overcome. If the recipient prevails by working on his *middos*, the wealth becomes a reward. If he fails, it proves to be a punishment.

Why Would We Want to Be Punished?

Hakadosh Baruch Hu knows where each of us stands in life. Because His purpose is to bestow goodness on us, He takes our capacity into account when choosing to give or withhold. He knows what wealth, success, honor, and fame will do to us if we aren't ready for it, and so, He sometimes withholds what we want until we start to build ourselves into worthy vessels. He doesn't want to punish us with abundance. That is because He loves us.

For example, if a 12-year-old boy asked his parents for a million dollars, would they give it to him, even if they had far more than that in the bank? Of course not! The parents love him, and giving him what he requested would completely destroy him. The boy would surely think his parents were mean and stingy, but that's because he has some growing up to do. Likewise, sometimes Hakadosh Baruch Hu withholds abundance from us until we build the *keilim* for the blessing. We may not like that at all. We want it now and on our terms. However, we are meant to trust that Hashem knows what is best for us, far more than we do. The only constructive action we can take is to *daven* for what we want and grow in those areas that will make us vessels worthy of containing it. Throwing a tantrum won't get us anywhere.

Polishing Facets

My father *a"h* was a diamond cutter. As a child, I would occasionally accompany him to 47th Street in Manhattan to watch him work. It was fascinating to watch something that looks like an ordinary stone, something we would kick aside if we came across it on the street, turn into a brilliant and valuable object. The stone is held down on a whirling cutting wheel and carefully ground and polished until the brilliance is revealed and a facet is born. The stone is then turned slightly and the process repeats itself. When completed, we behold a sparkling gem.

This is life. We are here to constantly hone our rough surfaces to reveal new facets that bring a new light of abundance into our lives. Rav Ahron of Strashela, in his *sefer, Shaarei Avodah,* teaches that many of the most valuable items in this world are found deep underground, encrusted in rock. Think oil, gold, platinum, and gemstones. This is because it is Hashem's will that the most valuable items should require the greatest effort to reveal. The same is true with us. The untapped strengths that lie inside of us, buried under our negative traits, will one day shine bright. Just as my father *a"h* was able to look at a rock and see a beautiful gem, we too must look at ourselves as a diamond in the rough and never discard the potential that lies within. We are here to cut away rock — jealousy, selfishness, anger, low self-esteem, greed. Each facet that we polish adds a dimension to our status as a vessel and allows new blessing to enter our lives. Improving our *middos* is the way to fortify ourselves as vessels. Abundance placed into a humble, disciplined, appreciative, empathetic, spiritual, selfless, and altruistic vessel will translate to great blessing to both the recipient and the world at large. Hashem waits for us to present ourselves to Him as such vessels.

> *It was Friday afternoon in the home of Rav Nochum of Chernobyl, the holy Meor Einayim, and his saintly wife was facing a dilemma. She had only three coins with which to purchase food for Shabbos. Her issue was that she didn't have a*

pot, and if she purchased one, there would be no money left for food. When she arrived at the marketplace, she decided to buy the pot, but when she arrived home, she starting questioning her decision. What good is a pot if you don't have any food? When the tzaddik saw what she did, he said to her, "Git hust du gituhn — you did right. Our job in this world is to prepare the utensil; Hashem Yisbarach will surely fill it up."

Strategy

Middos, character traits, fall into two categories — those with which we were born and those that are still encrusted in rock. If someone is born humble or selfless, then he is indeed fortunate, and he will surely earn reward if he uses those *middos* in positive ways. However, that isn't the primary reason we are here in this world, says Rav Tzadok HaKohen (*Tzidkas Tzaddik* 49). Rather, our purpose is to perfect the *middos* that present us with the greatest struggle. We can be sure that our mission lies in those areas. Those are the facets that build us into vessels.

You can begin the process by working on something that will impact your life in a positive way; something that is preventing you from moving forward in life. As my Rebbe once taught me, we go to shul on Yom Kippur, undertake a long list of resolutions and find that a year later we are no further in life than we were the previous year. The reason is that we tried to achieve too much. To remedy this, he taught me to pick one thing, and only work on perfecting it for an entire year. Then pick something else the year after. If we change one small thing about ourselves each year, then 10 years later we are completely different people. It might not even take that long.

Think about it: Can you compare a person who embodies

- Self-esteem
- Confidence
- Trustworthiness
- Reliability
- Patience

- Humility
- Empathy
- Honesty
- Consistency
- Resiliency

to someone who does not?

Imagine the positive impact that an improvement in any one of those traits would have on the life of someone who was lacking in that area. Notice we used the word "improvement." We do not seek perfection, but only that the trait reaches a higher stage of development. Burnishing facets is time consuming but the end product makes it all worthwhile.

Success in any area of life is motivating. More than just changing that one thing, it changes our perspective of what we believe is possible for ourselves; it sets our sights on loftier undertakings.

To recap: ***Hakadosh Baruch Hu wants to give you abundance, but He won't do so if it will cause you harm. Knowing what is ultimately best for you, He withholds only out of pure love. To earn the abundance we strive for, we can daven and create a vessel that allows abundance to enter. We accomplish this by working on our middos and revealing our hidden capabilities and spiritual strength.***

12

Higher Will

We will begin this chapter by briefly recapping what we have learned thus far.

- We discussed common arguments advanced by the Satan to undermine your progress and how best to respond.
- We underscored what success is not, and then we defined it as fulfilling life's purpose.
- We defined our ultimate purpose as earning closeness to Hashem and His goodness through self-actualization. We do this by choosing actions that emulate Hashem, foster our growth, refine our *middos,* and enable us to achieve our full potential.
- We demonstrated that we are each here to achieve a specific mission, which we fulfill through our free-choice decisions.
- We introduced you to your partners — body and soul — and to YOU, the entity whose task is to heed the voice of the higher self and refine the lower, physical self.
- We learned that in order to receive and benefit from Hashem's goodness, we have to build ourselves into vessels that are strong enough to contain it.
- We defined YOU as the watcher and chooser.
- We encouraged you to nourish your soul according to its needs.

Now we are ready to explore a deeper aspect of self — one which is the driving force behind everything that you do. When you are driven to succeed, grow, give, and so forth, what is driving you? In this chapter we will define the energy source that powers your entire system, explore why you may lack a full supply of this energy, and learn how you can fix that. Before we answer this question we will lay some important foundations.

◈ The Ten *Sefiros*

In the early 1950s, the world of biology and medicine experienced a breakthrough with the discovery of the double helix; the twisted-ladder structure of DNA. This discovery enabled scientists to take a much deeper and practical look at life. While this discovery was certainly of great significance, the Jewish people have possessed a far deeper and more foundational knowledge since the day we stood at Sinai. We have knowledge of the code on which not only life, but all of reality, is based: the *Sefiros*. As a comparison, if DNA were Mount Everest, the *Sefiros* would be the sub-atomic components from which the mountain is composed.

We are exposed to the concept of *Sefiros* in our daily prayers and throughout the Jewish calendar. They are a key feature in *Sefiras HaOmer* and seven of them are represented by the seven guests who visit the succah. Nevertheless, many people lack even a basic understanding of what they are and the important role they play.

What are *Sefiros,* and can people like you and me comprehend them?

While the topic of *Sefiros* is quite deep and discussed extensively throughout Kabbalah, we need not be Kabbalists to understand the topic at a level that has a high degree of impact on us. Most importantly, an understanding of the *Sefiros* will help shed light on what lies behind everything around us, including what is transpiring in our personal lives.

◈ What Are *Sefiros*?

There are ten *Sefiros*. They are *Keser, Chachmah, Binah, Chesed, Gevurah, Tiferes, Netzach, Hod, Yesod,* and *Malchus*. Let's begin our discussion by sharing a few of the many translations for the word *Sefirah*.

1. "To tell" as in the word *l'saper* (as "to tell" a story), or *sefer*, book, since the story behind everything lies within the *Sefiros* (*Ramak Pardes* 8:2).
2. "To count" *lispor* as in *Sefiras HaOmer*. "Just as numbers stretch to infinity, so too there are infinite ways in which Hakadosh Baruch Hu's light impacts reality through the *Sefiros*" (*Gr"a, Sefer Yetzirah*).
3. "That which emits a radiant light," sharing its root with the word *sapir,* sapphire. Hashem's emanation shines into all of existence through the *Sefiros,* and through them the world is constantly being created and impacted (*Sefer Chareidim, Ramak*).

Let us now explore the various roles that *Sefiros* play in creation.

☙ Sefiros as Prisms

Hashem is infinite and all-encompassing, and as Hashem told Moshe, "No one can see me and live." Just as we cannot look directly at the sun without protective eyewear, neither can we come in direct contact with Hashem's emanation, because, if we did, we would cease to exist. The ten *Sefiros* are necessary to serve as filters.

In addition, *Sefiros* help to explain a very integral part of our *emunah,* which is *Yichud Hashem,* the absolute Oneness and consistency of Hashem. Unlike mortals who have their moods, Hashem isn't one way today and another way tomorrow. Thus, when we say that Hashem is being merciful or that Hashem is judging, we are in essence saying that at this point in time, we perceive Hashem's emanation through that given *Sefirah* (*Chesed* or *Gevurah*).

You can think of *Sefiros* as colored glass through which Hashem's emanation shines forth. As an analogy, if light radiating from the sun passes through blue glass, the light will appear as blue. If it passes through green, it will appear as green. The sun's rays have not changed; the difference is in the filter through which the rays pass. As a verse (*Malachi* 3:6) says, "I, Hashem, never change."[5] Therefore, even though in a certain situation we might experience Hashem's *Chesed* and in another situation, we might feel the impact of His *Gevurah*, the difference is only from our perspective. Hashem is everything always and His emanations contain everything always.

We might understand this from a human perspective by thinking of times when we consciously show different aspects of ourselves to the world with which we interact. Sometimes we seek to conquer (*Netzach*) and sometimes we are submissive (*Hod*). Sometimes we give (*Chesed*) and sometimes we withhold (*Gevurah*). This doesn't apply to times when our *middos* have actually changed, but rather, to times when we are consistently maintaining our *middos* but applying different expressions of them to accomplish different, worthy goals. For instance, someone might exhibit *Netzach* when trying to convince a potential donor to support a good cause, or *Gevurah* when trying to prevent a child from doing something dangerous.

✥ *Sefiros* as a Process

Chassidic writings focus on the *Sefiros* as the step-by-step process that Hakadosh Baruch Hu uses to bring about all of creation. As an example, light is brought into existence when Hashem says, "*Yehi ohr*" — Let there be light. However, that step is preceded by ten steps that begin with *Keser*, the will to create light, and end with *Malchus*, the actual words, "*Yehi ohr*." The Baal Shem Tov teaches that this ten-step process is not something that Hashem keeps to Himself. Rather, since all of creation, and especially Mankind, is an emanation of Hashem's light, anything accomplished on this world comes about through this ten-step process.

On a practical level, the *Sefiros* can be viewed as the pipeline through which Hashem infuses you with life-energy and powers all of your thoughts and actions. They are also the pipeline through which all of your thoughts are brought into action. It follows, therefore, that if you want to see greater success in life, you want to make sure that

---

5. אֲנִי הַשֵּׁם לֹא שָׁנִיתִי

your pipeline and processes are functioning at peak level, without obstruction or misalignment.

◆§ *Keser*

With this understanding of the *Sefiros*, we are ready to learn about the energy source that powers your every action and decision. This is *Keser* (crown), the first of the *Sefiros*. *Keser* is revealed in the physical world as ***ratzon — will***.

As the highest of the *Sefiros*, *Keser* is the first link in the chain. It is the closest to Hakadosh Baruch Hu and is therefore directly connected to the Source. The Arizal teaches that *Keser* is composed of two aspects — an internal aspect called *taanug* (pleasure), which we will discuss in a future chapter, and an external aspect called *ratzon*.

Rav Ahron of Strashela, a *talmid* of the Baal HaTanya, writes that *ratzon* — will — is the genesis of and the motivation behind everything. Every word we speak, thought we think, and action we take is driven by a *ratzon*. Even inaction is the result of will. We all know that the decision to do nothing at all can sometimes require the greatest will; for instance, it takes great strength to remain silent in the face of insult.

◆§ *Keser* Powers Everything

The *Sefirah* of *Keser* and its expression as *ratzon* infuses the *Sefiros* below it with life, vitality, and energy. Just as a crown that sits on the head of a king empowers him to take action, so, too, *Keser* energizes all the *Sefiros* beneath. We can see this clearly in a practical example: Without the will to help and to bring happiness to another, no act of *chesed* would ever take place. The Sfas Emes writes that the root of the word *ratzon* is *ratz* — to run — because *ratzon* is what causes a person to run to pursue goals in life. This is the trait of *zerizus*, alacrity.

Keser is like the light that fills your room. It is everywhere, even though it isn't physically part of the room in the way that the walls, ceiling, and furniture are. You can also think of it as the electricity that is powering everything in your home right now. You can't see it, yet you know it is there because the lights are on and your appliances are running. *Ratzon* is the energy of life, the electricity that fuels your entire system.

Given that *ratzon* lies behind everything and as the saying goes, "nothing can stand in its way," how much better would life be if we better understood it and even learned ways to create it?

Will vs. Motivation

One of life's greatest challenges is finding the energy and impetus to undertake and complete important tasks and growth-oriented initiatives. Motivation, drive, and ambition are among the key attributes found in successful people. However, for those who are lacking in these areas, finding a method through which to access them can prove elusive and frustrating.

How do we motivate ourselves? Can we? Many people believe that drive is something that is either built into a person's nature or is not. They believe that inherently motivated people become successful, unmotivated people are destined to struggle, and there is not much that can be done about it. We will do our best to prove them wrong, because while it may be true that there are so-called "go-getters" among us, we can each develop the motivation that lies behind successful living.

Before we begin, we will need to better understand these two important words: will and motivation. Are they one and the same?

The answer is that they are similar but definitely not the same. *Ratzon* describes what we want to accomplish, and motivation is the drive to carry it out. *Ratzon* is the cause, and motivation the effect. We have a *ratzon* that gives us motivation; we then use that motivation to bring our will to fruition. As an example, because someone has the will to live, he is motivated to listen to his doctor and eat healthily. This may seem like an irrelevant nuance, but it isn't, because to cure anything we need to get to the root of the problem. Most often, when a person lacks motivation to do something, he actually lacks something deeper; he lacks the will for it. He may understand the purpose but not connect to the meaning. In our example, the person who lacks the motivation to take care of himself may never find it until he learns to fully appreciate the gift of life. Therefore, before we can discuss ways of finding motivation, we need to address weakness in *ratzon*. Can a person create *ratzon* in an area of life in which it is lacking?

❧ *Ratzon* Comes in Two Flavors

As we explained, everything in life requires *ratzon*. Therefore, it is never true to say that we lack *ratzon* because we are always doing something. We may lack *ratzon* that is beneficial, but we surely have *ratzon* of some kind. In our example, if someone decides to keep on eating in an unhealthy fashion, he doesn't lack *ratzon*; he has a will to eat what he wants and lacks the higher will to preserve his health. Success in life is the result of choosing to allow a higher will to fuel our system more often than not.

Let us now explore some ways by which we can bring forth higher will.

1. Praying for it

Like life itself, higher will, or *ratzon* Hashem, is received as a gift from above when we *daven* for it. Three times a day we can ask for will in *Ashrei* when we say, "Open Your hand and satiate every living being with *ratzon*." *Chazal* tell us that we are obligated to concentrate on those words or they must be repeated. When you say those words, it is a great *segulah* to bring to mind those areas of your life in which your will is lacking. Rav Nachman of Breslov was known to have said that if you don't have a will for something, yet have the will to have a will — you want to want — that too amounts to a lot. When we submit ourselves to Hakadosh Baruch Hu in prayer, we can say, "I know that I need to improve, and yet I lack the will to do so. Please infuse me with that will because only You have the power to create something that doesn't exist."[6]

6. The simple translation of the verse, *Posei'ach es Yadecha u'masbia l'chol chai ratzon* is, *"Open Your hand and satisfy the desire of every living being."* The explanation above addresses a deeper understanding of the verse, since the word *ratzon* connotes will, which is what lies behind desire. People of Sephardic descent have a tradition to open and hold out their hands when reciting these words as a form

When a Jewish male says the words *"Posei'ach es Yadecha"* — Open Your Hands — in the prayer of *Ashrei*, a right-handed male touches the *tefillin* on his left hand with his right hand and then kisses it while a left-handed male will do the opposite. When he says *"U'masbia l'chol chai ratzon"* — and satiate all livings things with will — he touches the *tefillin* on his head and then kisses his hand. As a young boy, I wondered why we touch the *tefillin* on the head while saying the word *"ratzon."* I then learned that the Arizal says that *Keser / Ratzon* enters a person through the fontanel, the place on the head where the skull of a newborn baby is soft. That is precisely where the *tefillin shel rosh* — which Chazal refer to as a *"keser"* — are worn. When we utter these words, we can ask Hashem to infuse us with higher will. [7]

2. Connect to purpose and meaning

Internalizing a deeper understanding of the purpose and meaning behind that which you wish to achieve can often bring forth *ratzon*. In an earlier chapter, we met the very talented Moshe who had a lower-self will to stay in his comfort zone. He lacked the higher will to cheer up the sick because it put him in an uncomfortable position. Once Moshe understood the deeper purpose and meaning of using his talents for *chesed*, the discomfort was outweighed by the will to do something profoundly meaningful. Sometimes thinking a matter through and highlighting its meaningful benefits is enough to energize us with *ratzon*.

---

of submission and acceptance that Hashem is the Source of all will and satisfaction of desires.

7. There is a song that we sing before *Bircas HaMazon* of *Seudah Shelishis*, the third Shabbos meal, called *"Kel Mistater."* This magnificent song was written by Rav Avraham Maimon, who was a disciple of Rav Moshe Cordovero. It is a deeply mystical song that offers profound insights into the ten *Sefiros*. The words it uses to describe *Chachmah*, the *Sefirah* directly below *Keser*, are *"mei'ayin timatzei...* — from nothingness it comes into being." *Chachmah* is revealed from nothingness, meaning that *Keser* is referred to as *ayin*, nothingness. Every great thing that was ever accomplished by a human being since the creation of the world began with an initial thought. Through an initial thought, *Chachmah*, we first become aware of our higher *will*. To us, it appears as a *yesh mei'ayin* — something from nothing — a gift from Hashem Who has the power to create something from nothing. This explains why people often say, "an idea popped into my head..." — and they truthfully cannot tell you where the idea came from.

3. Start a chain reaction

Try to recall the last time you took a meaningful project from its inception all the way to the finish line. You thought to do something, planned it, motivated yourself, persevered through countless obstacles, and brought the idea to fruition. What you did was take a higher will — *Keser* — and bring it all the way down through the lower *Sefiros* to *Malchus*, the realm of completion.

Now, try to recall the first thought that came to mind upon experiencing the sense of accomplishment and fulfillment that washed over you as you crossed the finish line. Most likely it was something like, "Now what? … What is my next project? … I need to do more!"

Why is that? Why does climbing a mountain to the top spur us to seek an even higher mountain to climb? The *Mishnah* states that one good deed begets another good deed. Why?

The answer lies in the elegant connection between *Malchus* and *Keser*; I am sure the royal commonality didn't escape you. The *Nefesh HaChaim* tells us that life is a continuous series of chains made up of ten links; the completion of one chain begins a new chain, and so on. Every *Keser* is born from the *Malchus* above it. In fact, the *Malchus* itself becomes the *Keser* of the new chain: i.e. it serves as the last link of the previous chain and the first link of the subsequent one. This connecting link is analogous to standing in a room on the upper story of a multistory building. If you look down at the surface beneath your feet, you see a floor, while if the people on the floor beneath look up at the same surface, they see a ceiling. What you perceive as a floor is their ceiling, because it is both, depending on where you are standing.

This is why the completion of one action immediately becomes the spark for a new one. Completion becomes higher will, and that new will wants to initiate another completion.

And so, while it is true that *Keser* is a gift from Hashem, it is a gift that comes after we do our part in its creation by carrying our prior will through to *Malchus*. Internalizing and building strategies around this phenomenon can literally change your life.

To internalize this idea further, let us try to understand how this works on a practical level. Why does completion give birth to a new will?

The answer lies in the fact that there are some essential ingredients that need to be present in order for higher will to take hold. The first one is the belief that what you are setting out to accomplish is doable and that "YOU" can do it. The Gaon of Vilna calls our capability to do something the vessel that contains the will. You can never will yourself to do what you deem impossible or beyond your capabilities because if you did, your life would be an endless series of disappointments. You may want the impossible, as in "I want to be a multibillionaire." You may even dream about it — but wanting, dreaming, and willing are very different things. Are you willing to actually do something consistently to make it happen? If not, then it's just a dream.

People with low confidence and self-esteem lack willpower because they lack will. They may say, "I know I need to…" or, "I really want to…" But knowing something and having the will and motivation to do it are very different things. Because they don't believe they can do it, they don't will themselves to do it. In their estimation, they lack the vessel for higher will — capability — and so they adopt the will of the lower self instead and do nothing.

Malchus gives birth to *Keser* because it introduces the belief that "I am able to accomplish." The thought that quickly follows is, "If I am able to do that, then perhaps I am also able to do something even greater." This is the definition of confidence; we can therefore conclude that the tried and true remedy for the absence of will, which is the result of lack of confidence, is to DO SOMETHING and start the process of building chains. Building confidence is like climbing a mountain; we go higher and higher one step at a time: *Malchus* to *Keser*, *Keser* to *Malchus*. With each completed chain and increase in confidence, the tasks we are able to will ourselves to tackle become more challenging.

Meet Duvi

> *Duvi is in a difficult state because he is disorganized and irresponsible. Important matters keep falling through the cracks and he has developed a reputation as being unreliable. He hasn't been able to hold down a steady job, his finances are a mess, and his wife carries the brunt of the household responsibilities. All this has naturally caused Duvi's self-esteem to plummet.*

Despite having been lectured to a million times by nearly as many people, he has resigned himself to the way things are, meaning that he lacks the will to do something about it. Duvi often deflects criticism by saying, "If Hashem intended for me to be more responsible, He would have created me that way," or, "I am the creative type, and people like me tend to be all over the place" (although, upon further reflection, he may admit to knowing creative people who are highly organized and responsible).

How would we help Duvi? We would find one area of his life where he could roll up his sleeves, set firm goals, and be held fully accountable for his actions. It could be one aspect of his job, daily routine, or responsibility at home, and all his efforts at self-improvement will now be directed in that one area. We need to lay a foundation on which to build; we need Duvi to achieve just one *Malchus*.

Standing in opposition is Mr. Satan who knows exactly what Duvi is trying to achieve, and has several tactics to stop him from climbing rung by rung.

He convinces Duvi that things are fine as they are and no work is needed. (Denial)

He has Duvi blame his shortcomings on his upbringing, circumstances… (Excuses)

He convinces Duvi that he is hopeless, so why bother? (*Yiush* — despair)

He gets Duvi all excited so he tries to do too much and therefore he fails and experiences despair.

He allows Duvi to start as many initiatives as he wants but will work overtime to make sure that he doesn't finish any of them. Chassidim often say that one of the names of the Satan is an acronym for *Siyum Mesechta Ein La'asos* — never finish a tractate of Talmud, because the completion of one tractate will prompt the drive to start the next one.

Malchus is the Satan's greatest enemy; therefore, the way to beat the Satan is by setting goals and achieving them. These need to be realistic, measurable goals that take us up just one rung at a time: goals that push us out of our comfort zone, but within a range that we still believe we can reach. Remember, we are seeking to conquer territory that is just behind the enemy lines. We need to achieve *Malchus* — and then repeat.[8]

4. Outside Inspiration

A life infused with higher will begins with the will to learn Torah. Learning subdues our lower-self desires and prepares us to embrace the higher will. When we appreciate the transformative powers of Torah wisdom, maintain a regimen of daily study and inspiration, and then incorporate that wisdom into our lives, we have found a clear path toward a life that is built on *ratzon Hashem*. By learning what Hashem wants for us and how our lives improve by accepting His will, we develop the motivation to live by it. Beyond keeping the 613 mitzvos, successful living means adopting and embracing Hashem's will in all areas of our lives, including work, family, and recreation. In all of life, free choice is always present — our lower self sometimes stands in opposition to what Hashem wants for us. By studying Torah that is geared to our particular challenges, and attending classes that strengthen us in those areas, we tap into resources that enlighten us and create the *ratzon* to grow.

Another important source of inspiration may be our rabbi, teacher, or a mentor who can instill in us the confidence we need so that the higher will can take hold. We call this *chizuk*, strengthening, because a stronger vessel can hold more will. It is an undeniable and universal truth that those who adhere to the advice of the *Mishnah* (*Avos* 1:6), which says, "Make for yourself a teacher," live more successful and fulfilling lives. In this world of great uncertainty and darkness, it is difficult to imagine how a person can navigate the daily challenges of life without availing himself of people who can inspire and guide him.

Here too, the Satan uses the egotistical argument of, "I am fine and I am quite capable of making my own decisions in life," to prevent us from humbling ourselves and admitting that we need help. If that

8. Sometimes, despite our best efforts, we are unable to bring a will to completion. It is important to consider whether anything might have been done differently, learn from the experience, and then quickly move on. We sometimes derive false conclusions about ourselves after a failed venture, when the only real message is that it wasn't meant to be and that we now are being tested on whether we can rise above the disappointment and move forward.

doesn't work, he will resort to my all-time favorite: "There is no one out there worth speaking to."

5. Become a Receptacle

As we said, higher will must have a reliable vessel into which it is received; otherwise, it won't come forth. The Baal Shem Tov describes a three-part process of submission, separation, and sweetening[9] as a means of achieving the self-rectification that strengthens this vessel. This process can be applied to many situations, but we will apply it to the discussion at hand.

Submission

In order to receive higher will, we must be a receptacle for it. The Talmud teaches us that Hashem says of the arrogant person, "I and he cannot reside in the same place." Where our egos reside there is darkness, and where we are humble, Hashem's light enters. The process of making room for this light is called *hachnaah*, submission; we humble ourselves to Hashem and admit that we desperately need Him and His inspiration. As long as people believe they can live a fulfilling life while being driven by their lower-self will, they are in essence denying the role that Hakadosh Baruch Hu plays in everything. When we internalize that we desperately need a connection to Hakadosh Baruch Hu, we surrender our lower will and ask Hashem to guide us utilizing His Will. This is what King David requests with the words (*Tehillim* 27:11), "Teach me Your way, Hashem, and lead me on the path of integrity."[10]

The *Mishnah* (*Avos* 2:4) teaches, "Nullify your will before His will,"[11] because as long as we hold on to what "we want," we will not be shown what Hashem wants. In the example of our disorganized and irresponsible friend Duvi, his lower will has one desire: to protect his ego. It wants to believe that he is fine as is and no improvement is needed. That mindset would serve to keep Duvi rooted in a world of self-deception and living in a state of utter darkness. To receive the

---

9. הַכְנָעָה, הַבְדָּלָה, הַמְתָּקָה

10. הוֹרֵנִי הַשֵּׁם דַּרְכֶּךָ, וּנְחֵנִי בְּאוֹרַח מִישׁוֹר

11. בַּטֵּל רְצוֹנְךָ מִפְּנֵי רְצוֹנוֹ

light, he would need to surrender the desire to protect his ego and realize that the only thing that brings us true success and fulfillment is embracing what Hakadosh Baruch Hu wants. [12]

Separation

In this stage, Duvi would make an earnest effort to separate himself from the behaviors of the past by first admitting that, through his actions, he brought about untold damage and pain to himself and his family. He would also admit to the fact that he has been fabricating excuses for himself, understand why he has been doing so, and concede that these excuses have translated into many lost years that could have been used for progress and growth. He would become disgusted at his actions (but not at himself) and, as we will discuss in a later chapter, become angry at the source of those actions to the point where he wants to do battle. He would express remorse for what he did to Hashem as well as to his spouse and others who have been negatively impacted by his actions. By separating his essential self from his prior actions, Duvi is preparing himself to be a receptacle for higher will.

This may sound straightforward, but it isn't easy; the person may need some coaching to pull it off. I once shared this idea with someone who had serious life issues and we went so far as to write up a list of the people to whom he would make amends and what he would say. Five years later, he still hadn't made the first phone call and sadly his life is exactly where it was when we first spoke: stuck in neutral with time passing him by.

Sweetening

This last stage involves turning our past mistakes into a positive. In doing so, we sweeten them. By learning from the past through an

---

12. There is a profound idea attributed to the holy Baal Shem Tov that trying to draw down holiness from above by desperately trying to make it happen is like tugging on a rope that spans to the heavens. It doesn't work because the rope disengages at its upper point. The reason is that "needing" something and trying in desperation to "make it happen'" is in itself an expression of ego. Therefore this approach pushes the *kedushah* we are seeking further away. Only through submission can holiness be attained — no pulling or pushing required.

understanding of how and why things went awry, we are motivated to create strategies that ensure that we don't fall back into the Satan's snare. In essence, the energy we spent on protecting the ego will now be used for good. We will direct it toward protecting our connection to Hashem. In our example, Duvi would develop effective strategies and disciplines that would serve to keep him on track going forward. He would also incorporate periodic self-evaluations that would ensure he is living up to the improvement goals he set for himself. In doing so, he would become a reliable vessel for Hashem's Will instead of one that cracks at the first sign of adversity. Duvi will achieve the ultimate sweetening of his past mistakes when he shares them with others who suffer from those issues and teaches them the way out and forward. All this growth would have never been possible were it not for Duvi's years of setbacks, which turned something bitter into something sweet.

6. Awakening Through Action

There is a profound idea that can be found throughout the writings of the *Zohar* and Arizal that "an awakening from below leads to an awakening above."[13] "Said Rav Elazar, I have seen that an awakening from above only comes after there is an awakening below, because an awakening from above is dependent on a desire from below" (*Zohar* 86b). Hashem created the world so that nothing meaningful happens until we first awaken it down here. The reason, says the *Meor Einayim* (*Parashas Noach*) is so that we can play a role in creation. If everything came from above, then what role would we play? The outcome of this principle is that often, when we muster the will to act on any level, we draw down a more powerful will from above.

7. Higher Will May Be Present, But Is Being Eclipsed

A man named Shalom once came to seek my advice. Shalom needed to work much harder in order to support his family, yet he was not motivated to do so. He was at a loss as to why finding that motivation was proving so elusive. After we had spoken a while, it became apparent that Shalom's issue wasn't motivation; it was will. You are surely wondering how a man can lack the will to support

---

13. אִתְעֲרוּתָא דִלְתַתָּא leads to אִתְעֲרוּתָא דִלְעֵילָא

his family. The answer is he didn't lack it. He just couldn't access it because it was buried under a much stronger lower-self will — the will to stay in his comfort zone and not take a risk that may lead to failure. Shalom wanted to protect his ego more than he wanted to support his family, but he didn't realize that and thought that he needed increased motivation. He had plenty of motivation, only it was driving him to do nothing because he was afraid of failure. As long as Shalom didn't let go of his lower will, 1000 mgs of motivational pills a day would do nothing for him.

Uncovering a lower will and revealing it for what it is often allows a higher will to descend and energize our system. As we explained earlier, where ego exists, Hashem's emanation will not enter. We can think of Shalom like the bottom half of an hourglass that is filled to the half-point with black sand. Right above him sits the upper half of the hourglass, filled with white sand, which won't enter until the black sand is removed. As the black sand spills out from the bottom, white sand will flow down and take its place.

As we will learn from the Piaseczna Rebbe in a later chapter, Hashem's emanation is everywhere, but it conceals itself when our ego is present. We don't need to work to add light; removing the darkness alone will allow the light to shine forth.

Shalom was encouraged to spend time understanding where his fear of failure was coming from, what was motivating him to protect his ego so strongly, and how to strengthen his *bitachon*. It was not surprising that within a relatively short period of time, he was filled with higher will and motivation.

To recap: ***We have glimpsed the profound world of Sefiros and explored Keser — will — and Malchus — completion. We defined capability and confidence as the vessels in which will is contained, and learned seven techniques that can help to generate or reveal higher will. In the coming chapter we will delve into the workings of motivation.***

13

Motivation

In the prior chapter, we met Shalom, a person who initially thought that he lacked motivation, but came to realize that he actually lacked will. In many cases, creating *ratzon* leads to motivation, but what happens when it doesn't? Furthermore, what about those instances in which we begin a project with great motivation, but it peters out as time goes by and the initial excitement wears off? What went wrong and what can we do about it?

We have each experienced a time when our supply of motivation was plentiful enough to take us through the obstacles and bring our idea to successful completion. At times, our will was so powerful that we didn't seem to encounter any obstacles at all. We decided to do something and we acted with *zerizus* — alacrity — which means that we faced almost no internal opposition. If only that were the rule instead of the exception! More often, our initial motivation somehow fizzles out before we complete the task. We may surrender in the face of obstacles, or the passage of time alone may cause our motivation to dissipate. It would seem that as long as our supply of motivation is deficient, higher will alone may not guarantee that we will prevail in our endeavors.

What exactly is this all-important fuel called motivation? As we did when exploring the idea of will, we begin our inquiry by defining our terms. What is motivation, and how is it created?

Will and motivation are two separate entities that flow from two completely different sources; will flows from the mind, while motivation flows from the heart. In other words, when our mind grasps the purpose of something, this can trigger will; when we internalize the meaning of it in our heart, this can lead to motivation. Will, when energized by the heart, becomes motivation or willpower — will with power.

As we explained earlier, will originates in *Keser,* which energizes all the *Sefiros* beneath it. From its inception in *Keser*, will descends and enters *Chachmah* and *Binah*. These *Sefiros* are the realm of the intellect. Then, it descends into the lower seven *Sefiros*, the first of which is *Chesed*. This is the point at which will enters the realm of the heart, where enthusiasm, excitement, and motivation are born.

In the *Sefiros* of *Chachmah* and *Binah* thoughts are generated. This is where we create the idea to do something to effectuate the urging of the will. Our intellect tells us that there is a purpose or need we must fulfill. However, we don't yet have the desire to do so. We lack motivation, and therefore, will must delve deeper into *Chesed, Gevurah,* and the other *Sefiros,* which will supply the needed motivation.

Let's try an analogy. Think of will as an electrical current. It leaves the intellect as a 10 amp current, which is not powerful enough to overcome the obstacles ahead and travel all the way to *Malchus*. It needs enthusiasm to boost its strength to 20 amps. That boost will come from the heart, which is where *Chesed, Gevurah,* and *Tiferes* reside.

To recap: ***When we lack motivation for something that we already have the will to do, the deficiency is in the heart — the emotional component that supplies the energy to follow through.***

Why is this important? Because only when we identify the root cause can we find the remedy to a lack of motivation. We must seek strategies to energize our will by awakening our heart.

◆§ Strategy 1: Retrain Your Focus on Will

To gain awareness of anything, as we will discuss in a later chapter, we must focus our mind on it; in doing so, we energize our connection.

For example, we may love our children, but when we are not thinking about them, that love resides in the back of our mind. When we begin to think about them, feelings of love emerge. The more we think about them, see photos of them, recall stories of them when they were little and cute, the stronger those feelings become. We don't love them more as a result of focusing our minds on them; we have simply brought memories to the forefront of our consciousness and, in doing so, awakened existing feelings of love. This is the faculty of *Daas*, which Chazal teach, is represented by the neck, which connects our head to our torso. Likewise, *Daas* connects the intellectual *Sefiros* of *Keser, Chachmah,* and *Binah* to the lower *Sefiros* where emotion and action reside. *Daas* brings awareness to the heart and in doing so, elicits feelings. It tells the heart, "This is what your mind is thinking."

Activating our *Daas* can carry us through when our higher will is not sufficient to supply us with enough motivation. Sometimes our higher will is buried in the recesses of our minds by the daily routine that captures most of our attention. Higher will may be so inaccessible that we barely remember it is there. This leads to a life that lacks passion, enthusiasm, and motivation. In that state, will weakens and lacks the energy to withstand obstacles and the test of time. Only by purposefully turning our focus toward our higher will can we access its power.

As an example, we often begin our *tefillos* with the will to remain focused throughout, yet somehow, we find ourselves distracted along the way. Chazal teach us to spend a few moments thinking about before Whom we are about to pray and how much we need Him. Doing so motivates us and draws our heart into the process, which strengthens the will so that it can withstand distractions.

On a practical level, the purpose of people keeping a picture of their family on their desk is to remind them of why they are at that desk in the first place. It helps them to get through a challenging day, since they have a tangible reminder of the people about whom they care most, and for whose benefit they are working.

To recap: ***The more often we stop to remind ourselves why we are doing the things we do, the more motivated we will be to do them.***

◆ Strategy 2: Don't Bypass Binah

Binah is the *Sefirah* that follows *Chachmah* — the first spark of a thought. Rashi defines *Binah* as contemplation, understanding, and comprehension; the ability to take an idea apart and understand it in a deeper sense. *Binah* also serves to amplify will, so that it has the power to motivate us. In our electricity example, *Chachmah* delivers a 5-amp current to *Binah,* which intensifies it into a 10-amp current and then sends it onward, through *Daas,* to *Chesed,* and so forth.

The three higher *Sefiros* are intellectual, because their realm is thought and decision-making. Once the decision is reached, *Binah* must pass the decision on to the lower *Sefiros,* where the heart resides. Because the plan needs to go into action, we need feeling and emotion. Otherwise, we won't have the motivation to carry the idea through to completion.

It is interesting to note that *Chachmah* is referred to as *Abba,* father, *Binah* is referred to as *Eim Habanim,* the mother of the children, and the lower *Sefiros* are referred to as "the children." This is like a typical morning in my house. I wake up my wife who then wakes up the kids and urges them to get ready for school. It is the parents role, to educate the lower level of the family hierarchy on the how and why of a decision. You can see how this works in your own mind and heart: As you spend time in the realm of *Binah* — contemplating your idea and how to actualize it — you begin to get excited about it. *Binah* — the mother — has begun to awaken the children — the lower *Sefiros* — which are tied to the heart.

Let's use an example in order to illustrate how *Chachmah* and *Binah* interact, and the benefits of allowing each its full expression:

Avraham wants to show appreciation to his wife on her birthday. The idea first appears to him as a thought: "I want to make Sarah happy on her birthday." Avraham's thought, to "make Sarah happy," is his underlying will. It makes its first appearance in *Chachmah,* which then passes the idea to *Binah,* which says, "Well, there are a few ways to accomplish this. You can plan a surprise party, buy her a gift, plan a vacation..." *Chachmah* says, "I like the gift idea," and so *Binah* presents the various categories of gifts that can be purchased — jewelry, clothing, practical items. *Chachmah* says Sarah likes spiritual things, so *Binah* presents options that meet that criteria: a new candelabra, a leather *Tehillim*, a set of *Machzorim*. *Chachmah* and *Binah* will bounce this idea back and forth until they come to a decision on exactly what will be bought, how much money will be spent, and other details. Essentially, *Chachmah* and *Binah* are engaged in sorting out the game plan for accomplishing Keser's will. While all this back and forth is going on, Avraham's *Chesed* awakens, and begins to emotionally connect to the idea being contemplated. Therefore, enthusiasm makes its appearance.

You will notice that the more thought that goes into an idea, the more enthusiastic you will be when you set out to accomplish it and the more success you will achieve. Spending adequate time in *Binah* serves two important functions; first, it allows us to adequately plan, which raises the odds of success, which in turn gives us confidence. Secondly, it energizes the will with motivation so that it has the power to break through obstacles. Those who are quick to flare up and act without adequate thought and planning are also quick to burn out and quit. Adequate thought and planning, prior to putting a plan into action, generates the motivation and enthusiasm needed for the journey.

To recap: ***The more we plan the things we do, the more motivated we will be to do them.***

◆§ Strategy 3: Know Whose Will You're Hearing

Often, we think that we are fueling our system with a will that is our own, that speaks to our essential purpose for being in this world, but in actuality, that isn't the case. Instead, we are trying to run our systems on someone else's will, and that is why we lack motivation. As we explained, we need purpose and meaning in our lives to fuel us, and these won't be present when we use will in our engines that isn't self-generated.

Imagine three people who are running — Reuvain and Shimon because they are being chased by a grizzly bear, and Levi, who doesn't see the bear, but sees his friends running. Reuvain and Shimon are running for their lives, while Levi is running because he wants "to be just like them." Who do you think will run faster and for longer, or should I say, who will be the bear's lunch?

Some people are motivated in certain areas because it speaks to their mission in life, while others try to motivate themselves because the message they pick up from others is that this endeavor is important. Those in the latter group, in most cases, find their motivation petering out over time.

As we discussed, someone who has not written a personal mission statement and is out of touch with his individual purpose in life tends to look around him and adopt someone else's mission. He thinks, "My neighbor has a desire for nice things, so I should have it too." "My friends are all doing... so I need to as well."

This may work at first, but as time goes on, or as obstacles set in, the person may notice that his motivation begins to wane. Subconsciously, he asks himself, "Why am I doing this exactly?" Some people go on like this for 20 or 30 years until one day they wake up and ask themselves, "Where am I and how did I get here? This is not the life that I envisioned for myself." This is commonly the root cause of a mid-life crisis. The person's soul knows the truth and, with the sand in the hourglass dwindling, it cannot allow the person to remain motivated toward something that was never "him" in the first place.

As an example, there are perfectly healthy people who think that there is "something wrong" with them because they are not motivated to work like maniacs to try to earn even more money so they can make purchases that they don't need. When they look around and see others running, they think that is what they ought to be doing. Therefore, they run as well, at first with gusto, and then over time with little or no motivation.

Let's be honest with ourselves in each area of our lives and ask, "What is the reason I want to succeed at _______?"

So my friends will think highly of me?

Because others are?

Or,

Life holds so much potential.

This is consistent with my mission.
There is so much good that I can do.
I owe Hakadosh Baruch Hu so much.

To recap: ***The more we do things that <u>we</u> believe in, the more motivated we will be to do them.***

☙ Strategy 4: Divide the Will Into Reachable Goals

Sometimes, what we are trying to achieve seems impossible to our emotional self. We "think" we can succeed but we don't "feel" that we can, and motivation is therefore not forthcoming.

In my Wall Street practice, I am fortunate to meet some of the most remarkable people alive, and no one fits that description more than my beloved friend, Mr. Andrew Burian. His story of surviving the Auschwitz-Birkenau and Mauthausen concentration camps, as well as the infamous death-march evacuations of each camp, has been memorialized in a book called *A Boy from Bustina*. Andy, as we fondly call him, has inspired tens of thousands, young and old, with his unwavering faith and ironclad endurance. I once witnessed him in action as he kept a room of several hundred young Jewish students spellbound for two hours. Here is a life-altering story that he told me.

> *It was January 18, 1945, when we began the infamous death march, marching out of Birkenau to the Gleiwitz railroad station more than 30 miles away. We marched five abreast on a road that only held 2-3, which meant that many of us had to walk on the side of the road, deep in snow. I witnessed people falling to the ground and subsequently being shot by the SS, may their memory be obliterated. The retreating German army was heading alongside us as they returned from the front lines, having suffered defeat. The wounded soldiers, who were lying in the back of the trucks, were using their last ounces of strength to take target practice by shooting into our midst. Overhead, Russian fighter planes attacked, killing Germans and Jews alike.*
>
> *I was malnourished, had rags on my feet in the place of*

shoes, and was freezing to death. Although I knew all too well that stumbling or not keeping pace meant instant death, by day three I could not motivate myself to march any longer. And so, I began to give up and slow down. Despite my will to live, all I wanted to do at that point was sleep. The Jewish man marching next to me noticed me weakening and said, "Don't give up, young man. Look up ahead. Do you see the steeple up ahead? That's where we need to get to and we will then be at our destination." I thought, "I can hold out until that steeple. I can see it up ahead."

When we reached the steeple and didn't stop, I turned to him and he quickly said, "No not this one, the one just up ahead," and this scene kept repeating itself until I understood the message — that a person can motivate himself to do anything so long as there's a goal in sight. With this thought, I motivated myself to walk, mile after mile, from steeple to steeple."

He ended the story by adding, with his classic youthful twinkle in his eyes, "Now you know why Poland has to have so many steeples — so that I would have a way to stay alive."

Andy never lost his will to live; he had merely lost his motivation to carry out his will because he no longer felt it was possible to achieve. With each steeple that he reached, his heart experienced a triumph and enthusiasm and hope returned.

Find a steeple, an achievable goal, and head toward it. Take a task, and break it down into parts, and don't give up until you succeed. Then repeat.

To recap: ***The more we feel things are possible and within reach, the more motivated we will be to do them.***

◆ Strategy 5: Draw Motivation From the People in Your Life

In life, there are people who infuse us with hope, optimism, and enthusiasm, and then there are those who drain us of these much-needed feelings. People who desire to live to their fullest potential would do well to be mindful of the amount of time they spend with negative and cynical people — those who are always apathetic, cynical or look at the dark side of things. They should try to spend more time with enthusiastic, positive, and motivated people and allow their positive energy to rub off on them.

It cannot be stressed enough how radioactive negative people are to us and how much damage they can inflict. Negativity and pessimism are highly contagious emotional diseases for which no vaccine has been invented. We may even find ourselves drawn to these types of people because they mirror the way we may feel at the time, because we pity them or because of some sense of obligation. They may be family members, neighbors, or co-workers. No matter, we need to recognize how detrimental their attitude can be and reinforce ourselves so it does not penetrate our psyche especially when we find ourselves low on motivation. We can learn strategies that will help us become impervious to the negativity we may be exposed to, such as constantly reminding ourselves of how detrimental their mindset is and telling ourselves that, "I choose to have a more positive and optimistic outlook on life."

To recap: ***The more motivation in the environment surrounding us, the more motivation we will absorb through osmosis. People who are down bring us down and those who are up lift us up.***

To summarize what we've learned in this chapter, motivation is will, powered by feeling and emotion. The heart is awakened through planning and contemplation. We've discussed five methods to awaken the heart through both internal and external stimuli: retrain our focus on our purpose; contemplate our ideas; set achievable goals; make sure our own will is setting our direction; and surround ourselves with positive people and sources of inspiration.

14

Pleasure

In life, we all want the same things. Driven by our will, we seek success, fulfillment, tranquility, respect, knowledge, validation, happiness, money, friendship, freedom…

Have you ever asked yourself, Why?

Why do you want those things?

What lies at the root of your drive to achieve these things?

Deep down, what is it that you are yearning for?

We must correctly identify our ultimate goal, because if we don't, we may accept a cheap imitation, instead of the real thing, as a reward for our toils. The reason for our quest, Chazal tells us, is that we all seek pleasure. In this chapter, we will discuss the definition of pleasure; what it is, why we seek it, and what role it plays in successful living.

Pleasure

As we discussed earlier, the Arizal (*Eitz Chaim: Shaar* 12,13), teaches that the beginning of everything, *Keser*, is comprised of two elements: an internal aspect of *taanug* — pleasure — and an external aspect of *ratzon* — will. Because *ratzon* and *taanug* originate in the same place, they are bound to each other. Therefore, we will ourselves to do things that bring us pleasure, and carrying out our will brings us great pleasure. Every action, inaction, exertion, and acquisition, therefore, is a means to an end, which is to experience pleasure. Hakadosh Baruch Hu designed us so that the pursuit of pleasure motivates us to get out of bed each day and make something of ourselves.

☙ What Is Pleasure?

Rav Dessler *zt"l* teaches in *Michtav M'Eliyahu* (Vol. 3, p. 180) that pleasure, both physical and spiritual, is the result of a need being fulfilled. A person lives in a constant state of lack, and is therefore always looking to fill a void so that he/she can feel whole again. When we are hungry, we eat; tired, we sleep; cold, hot, restless, bored — we do something about it. We may face many obstacles along the way to filling our needs, but the greater the need, the more effort we are willing to expend to overcome those obstacles.

Rav Dessler further points out that the greater those obstacles, the greater the pleasure we will feel when the need is met. When a need is easy to fulfill, then the resulting pleasure is small because the person did not feel a great lack in the first place. For example, if there's bread right in front of you, and you are hungry, then eating the bread will be less pleasurable than if you have to walk three blocks to the bakery in the rain to buy it. Think of the last time you saved up to buy something you wanted and how that felt in comparison to buying something you could readily afford.

Here's an interesting example of the connection between effort and pleasure: In the 1940s, General Mills brought the novel idea of Betty Crocker instant cake mix to market. When it wasn't the hit they thought it would be, the company's marketers began investigating to find the problem. Their first thought was that people didn't like the taste of the cakes the mixes produced, but that wasn't it; people actually loved the taste.

Upon further research, they realized that these instant cakes were too easy to make. People didn't enjoy the results as much because they couldn't experience the pleasure of eating or serving home-made cake. There was too little exertion, time, and effort required, and therefore baking these cakes rendered too little pleasure. The end product lacked a sense of ownership. So, what did the company do? It removed the eggs from the mix so that people now had to crack a few eggs and mix it into the batter. The new "improved" formula sold like hotcakes.

How counterintuitive is that? People would rather buy something requiring more work than something easier. This concept, called the "subtraction technique," is the secret behind Ikea's success — furniture of marginal quality that delivers great pleasure because the customer feels, "I built it."

Why is pleasure directly correlated to how much we toil to obtain it?

Chazal tell us that there is a fundamental difference between this world and the next. This world is a world of "becoming" and the next is a world of "being." In this world, there is no pleasure in simply being. Therefore, no matter what we are, what we have, and what we've already achieved, we grow restless if matters remain status quo. *"Adam l'amal yulad"* (*Iyov* 5:7) — man was born to toil and become more than he is. Therefore, pleasure only comes from work — from acts of creation.

The next world is a realm of being. This is a state of existence whose meaning we can't fathom because in our current state, we can't comprehend feeling pleasure in just being, unless it is for a very short period of time. Try going on a dream vacation and staying there for a month, a year, forever. That's not vacation; it's prison. Deriving pleasure from "being" is reserved for the next world, where pleasure is everlasting.

This is why Shabbos is called *"oneg."* It is the culmination of six days of work — the peace and tranquility that follows a week of "becoming." On Shabbos, both the body and soul are able to partake in pleasures because Shabbos offers both. There's good food, wine, and physical rest for the body, as well as a slower *davening*, extra time for learning, spiritual growth, and quality time with the family to satisfy the soul. Shabbos is called *"Mei'ein Olam Haba,"* a taste of the world to come, because it is the time of the week when we are the closest to just "being." If every day were Shabbos, however, it wouldn't be pleasurable at all.

To recap: ***Pleasure is the uplifting feeling that arises when a need is met. The greater the lack, the greater the pleasure; the greater the exertion required to fill the need, the greater the resulting pleasure. This is the principle of — לְפוּם צַעֲרָא אַגְרָא — reward is commensurate with the work we put in.***

✤ Spiritual Pleasures

This phenomenon is even more relevant with regard to spiritual pleasure, because the lack people feel in their spirituality far exceeds their lack in the material sphere. Rav Chaim Vital (*Shaarei Kedushah* 1) teaches that like the body, the soul has 613 parts, and the 613 *mitzvos* nourish them. Here too, the greater the toil, the greater the pleasure. This explains why there is no greater pleasure than struggling and persevering to perform a *mitzvah*. When a person fills the spiritual needs of the *neshamah,* he experiences pleasure that is far deeper and longer-lasting than that which he derives by meeting a bodily need. In fact, physical pleasures, with their shallow and finite nature, pale in comparison to the eternal pleasures of the *neshamah*.

The drive to experience pleasure is what propels us forward to acquire, build, and create. What we pursue is left to our free choice. We can spend our time pursuing shallow pleasures or we can pursue pleasures of an eternal kind — pleasures that never wear off and have far deeper and life-changing effects on us. Some examples of these pleasures are:

- Helping someone get back on his feet;
- Being honest when doing so proves difficult;
- Becoming knowledgeable in a significant area;
- Encouraging someone who is about to give up;
- Overcoming a negative character trait;
- Giving with no expectation for reciprocation or recognition.
- The sasifaction of a difficult task well done.

The pleasure that washes over the person in such instances is the pleasure of the *neshamah* when it feels its need — to fulfill its mission — being satisfied. The feeling of fulfillment and pleasure a person experiences when answering the *neshamah's* need is so profound that he will be able to relive it years later.

☙ Meet the Satan

Hashem put us on this world to partake of many pleasures — both spiritual and material. Living an elevated life requires that we choose more of the spiritual kind and less of the other. It also entails elevating the material pleasures in which we partake to the level of spiritual. This pertains to the way we enjoy Shabbos and many other experiences.

The Satan's job is to have you forgo real pleasure and spend your life chasing empty pleasures instead. The Satan wants you to give priority to the experiences that deliver faux temporary pleasure over those that bring real, lasting pleasure. (Remember what Rav Nachman taught us in Chapter 2 about the Satan running around the marketplace with his hands closed and the buyers chasing after him?)

If we think about it, it's quite astonishing that the Satan ever succeeds at all. Seriously, can we compare:

- The satisfaction of visiting someone in the hospital and cheering them up, to the fleeting pleasure of a gourmet meal?
- Teaching someone the beauty of Torah, to spending a day bungee jumping?
- The deep joy of successfully soliciting funds so that an orphan bride can go to the *chuppah*, to the excitement of purchasing a new watch?
- The incredible *nachas* of seeing a child make his first *siyum*, to the pleasure of buying the latest gadget?
- Looking back at years of growth and toil, to looking back on relaxing at the seashore?
- A life of selfless giving, to a life dedicated to amassing wealth?

Can we even use the same vocabulary to describe the two experiences? So how does the Satan manage to persuade us to exchange eternal pleasures for shallow and temporary ones? Well, never one at loss for cunning tactics, he does several things:

- He causes us to misinterpret the lack that we are feeling inside and has us think, "I need something material to make me whole."
- He greatly magnifies, in our eyes, the pleasure that we will feel when we obtain a material "need."
- He exaggerates the sense of lack that we feel right now so that we become fixated on the pursuit of the object that we "need" to the point that we "can't live without it." He convinces us that life will be glorious with it and utterly miserable without it.
- He fabricates a need when one doesn't exist at all, and has us confuse the word "need" with the word "want."
- He hides the fact that actual pleasure doesn't come as much from the object itself as from the toil that was required to obtain it. This leads us to seek shortcuts in life, especially in our spiritual endeavors.
- He has us forget the most obvious of facts; that pleasure resulting from material pursuits has little if any lasting effect.
- He has us marginalize and even negate that which we already have so that we are motivated to pursue that which we don't.

The Gemara (*Chullin* 139b) asks, "*Haman min haTorah minayin?"* — Where does Haman appear in the Torah? It answers that after Adam ate from the forbidden fruit of the *Eitz Hadaas,* Hashem asked him *"Hamin ha'eitz?"* — Did you eat from the tree from which I commanded you not to eat?" The word *Hamin* is comprised of the letters *Hey, Mem,* and *Nun,* which also spell Haman.

The Vilna Gaon reveals the connection:

Megillas Esther tells us that Haman was driven to annihilate the Jews because Mordechai refused to bow to him. His wife and friends tried to reason with him by highlighting his great wealth and stature. They argued that, in the grand scheme of things, was it really a big deal if one Jewish sage refused to bow to him? Haman's response was, "All of this is worthless to me as long as Mordechai sits at the palace gate and doesn't bow to me." The lack that he felt as a result of something so trivial caused him to negate everything that he had. His life was void of pleasure.

The Satan used the very same tactic on Chava. We can't even fathom how wonderful and splendid Gan Eden is, and Hashem allowed Adam and Chava to enjoy it all, except for one tree. They were given countless pleasures and only one small restriction. The Satan, in the form of the serpent, convinced Chava that she had absolutely nothing pleasurable as long as she lacked the fruit of that one forbidden tree. He enticed her to the point that she could almost taste the fruit before she actually bit into it, as the Torah states, "And the woman perceived that the tree was good for eating and that it was a delight to the eyes…" (*Bereishis* 3:6) The fabrication of a fictitious need; the negation of that which Chava already had; and an exaggerated promise of pleasure were the illusions through which the Satan brought about mankind's first sin. He has been using that same tactic on humans ever since.

As an aside, it is worthwhile to note that the Satan today speaks to us through the advertisements with which we are bombarded every single day. One moment we feel complete and the very next moment we feel incomplete, because we saw an ad for something that we didn't even know existed a minute ago. We were made to feel lacking, and now we "must have it!"

To recap: ***The drive to experience pleasure is at the root of everything for which we strive. Buying new things or experiencing new thrills delivers pleasure that quickly wears off. Meaningful, spiritual experiences, on the other hand, bring about deep, all-encompassing and eternal pleasures.***

To keep us growing, Hashem created a feeling of lack in each of us and gave us the inclination to fill that void. Each time we reach into ourselves and bring forth a hidden talent or strength, accomplish a goal, or help another do the same, we experience great pleasure. We have emulated Hashem and become partners in creation. Our job is to become pleasure *connoisseurs* and never fall for cheap imitations.

15

The Essential YOU

Human beings are fascinating. Really. What other creation is capable of such incredibly altruistic and intellectual feats, while at the same time, can say things like,

"I don't know what I was thinking!"

"What in the world came over me?"

"That was so not me."

"I must have been having a bad day."

"I am not feeling like myself lately."

We would laugh if not for the fact that it is normal for us to say such words and hear them from others.

What *did* come over us? What *were* we thinking? If we can sometimes feel or act in strange ways, then how do we know who we really are? Are we inconsistent? We certainly are, but that's the symptom and not the cause. What are we when we are ourselves, and what are we when we are not? If we only knew the answer, we could spend more time being the people we really are.

Daas — the YOU Inside of You

The Gemara (*Berachos* 33A) teaches that *daas* is so great that it appears between two mentions of Hashem's Name *Ki Keil Dei'os Hashem (Shmuel I* 2:3). It is so essential that it is our first request in our weekday *Shemoneh Esrei.* The Gemara also states that it is forbidden to show compassion to someone who lacks *daas.* The reason is that the compassion will be wasted on the recipient; he is incapable of utilizing it because "he" isn't present. Rav Shlomo Wolbe in *Alei Shur* (Vol. 2, p. 249) calls *daas* the very essence of the person — **"the person inside the person."**

When you are *b'daas* YOU are present, when you are not, then to varying degrees, YOU are not.

Before we delve into *daas*, let us review some important sources that speak of its importance in achieving success in life.

The Gemara states (*Nedarim* 41a):

> *"One who lacks everything" (Devarim 28:48), Rav Nachman taught that lacking "everything" refers to someone who lacks daas. Says Abaye, we have a tradition that there is no truly destitute person except one who is impoverished in his daas. In the West (Eretz Yisrael) they said, he who has this (daas) within him has everything within him, he who lacks this within him, what is within him? If he acquires this, what does he lack, and if he does not acquire this, then what has he acquired?*

Rav Shlomo Wolbe writes that from this Gemara we learn that *daas* is the most essential and fundamental trait of a person. The Baal Shem Tov writes (*Parashas Vayeira*) that during a spiritual challenge, a person's *daas* is taken from him; the resulting confusion is itself the test. When the person recovers his *daas,* he can see the situation with clarity, which leads to overcoming the challenge at hand.

The *Nesivos Shalom* (Vol. 1, Ch. 1) begins his *sefer* by explaining the faculty of *daas.* He undoubtedly chose this as his opening essay because without *daas,* a person cannot hope to learn anything else from his writings. He, too, speaks of *daas* as a human being's foundation:

> *Therefore, the main thrust of the Satan's work is in this area; to constrict and confuse the daas of a person seeking to serve Hashem, and through this to minimize, diminish, and limit the supreme spiritual level of his service to Hashem. Even more than his temptations and effort to overcome a person in the*

areas of refraining from sin, desires, bad traits or stopping a person from performing mitzvos, the Satan digs his nails into the mind and heart of a Jew to burden and confuse him in the area of daas, in order to constrict and minimize his spiritual perception to the point where all of his service is done in a state of smallness of daas.

◆ What Is *Daas*?

While a comprehensive answer would fill volumes, there are essential aspects of *daas* that are easily understood and accessible to anyone. In this chapter we will delve into two — **awareness** and **connection**.

◆ Awareness

Daas is YOU in a state of awareness and presence, where nothing is constricting YOU or pulling YOU elsewhere. It is YOU as your essential self, in a state of watching and choosing. When a person is in a state of *daas*, his internal and external perceptions come from the vantage point of his true self. His internal eyes and ears are wide open. He is watching and discerning while unconfused, unbiased, calm, rational, dispassionate, and able to interpret information in an effective manner. He is in a state of equilibrium. He can discern right from wrong and view his experiences and the events transpiring around him as they truly are.

Rav Shlomo Wolbe writes (*Pirkei Kinyan Daas* Ch.3) that the reason we recite words of *havdalah on Motzei Shabbos* in the fourth blessing of *Shemoneh Esrei*, the blessing of *daas*, is because just as Hakadosh Baruch Hu separates between holy and mundane, and between light and darkness, likewise we use our *daas* to become aware of the changing circumstances of our lives and what our response should be. Someone who lacks *daas* remains oblivious as circumstances change; dangers and pitfalls appear, and yet he does nothing about it. Furthermore, our inner and outer world is replete with opposites — arrogance/humility, upheaval/tranquility, good/evil. We must develop our faculty of *daas* to be able to discern one from the other, so that we can choose and act accordingly.

◆§ States of *Daas*

There are several states of *daas* in which we can find ourselves. Let's take a look at each.

A. *Daas B'galus* — This is when a person is said to have completely "lost himself," as occurs with anger, great panic, anxiety, or overwhelming fear. When he returns to some level of *daas,* he may wonder what had come over him. His words and actions while in that state may not reflect his true values and beliefs because "he" was nowhere to be found in the midst of the situation.

The Baal Shem Tov refers to this state as *daas b'galus* — *daas* in exile; the essential self is tied up and gagged, locked somewhere inside of a closet. The *Sefer Chareidim* writes that a person who loses himself in anger causes his *neshamah* to leave his body. This means that his essential self is left alone in a spiritual vacuum, without his voice of reason. A person in that state is capable of doing and saying nearly anything. This is why losing ourselves in anger is the most destructive way to lose *daas,* and necessitates the longest recovery period. The person has to literally invite his *neshamah* to return.

B. ***Bilbul/Katnus HaDaas* — confused or constricted** *daas*. In this state, the essential person is present, but is in a state of confusion, irrationality, or distraction. This is caused by internal or external chaos, apathy, despair, bias, desires, or information overload. As the *Nesivos Shalom* teaches, this is the state in which the Satan wants us to spend the majority of our lives; he promotes this state even more than that of no *daas* at all. The reason is that when a person has experienced a state of no *daas,* he becomes keenly aware, once he gets back to himself, that something went terribly wrong. He knows that he has to work to ensure that it doesn't happen again. Because people can't function with no *daas,* their lack alarms them and forces them to respond.

With *katnus* of *daas,* on the other hand, a person can go about his day and function at a reasonable level. He can *daven,* eat, work, do homework with his kids, and even study Torah. He does all that, but "he" is barely there. He does things in a rote fashion, with little or no passion; his thoughts are elsewhere. Ask him if he *davened* that morning and he will say, "Sure." Ask him if he has any recollection of saying any specific words of *davening* and he will respond with a blank stare. There are very few outward signs that trouble is brewing, and so no alarm bells go off. Of all of the areas of our lives in which technology and overall information overload has diminished and damaged us, this is the area. As the Gemara says, if we lack *daas* we have nothing. The *Nesivos Shalom* teaches that the Satan prefers that we go through life like zombies, without ever realizing that anything is wrong.

It is frightening to think that a person can go through life, doing what he does each day, without ever realizing that he is living in a state of smallness and constriction. In fact, we sometimes become so accustomed to this state that we have come to believe that this is the way things were meant to be. We believe that moments of keen awareness and calm are states of mind that are unrealistic and lofty and surely can't last for very long. We see those moments much as we view going on vacation; it's nice, but it isn't real life. Real life is the state of confusion and overload that we experience the rest of the time. How wrong we are.

> *A close friend of mine went for a routine cardiovascular exam at the age of 57, and learned that he was born with his main heart arteries connected in the wrong fashion. Instead of two connected to one side and two connected to the other, he had three on one side and only one on the other. He called me, quite shaken, because he needed a serious surgery to correct this. He told me, "The craziest part is that while my heart has been defective since birth, I have always felt fine." I went to see him right after his surgery. He looked at me and said, "I never knew what feeling fine actually meant, until now." His definition of "feeling fine" had always been relative to his own experience and expectations. He never knew how others were feeling when they felt fine.*

Some of us walk around with a low hum of distracting anxiety inside us, and we don't even realize it is there. It's like sitting in a room with a noisy air conditioner all day. We don't even realize how noisy it is until someone turns it off. Likewise, we are often oblivious to the thought-deafening noise inside of us — noise that crowds out our essential self — until we learn how to lower the volume or even turn it off completely.

C. ***Yishuv HaDaas*** — This is a settled *daas*, a state of calm and equilibrium in which we are able to listen to what we are hearing both internally and externally, and discern who is saying what and why. In this state, we have sharper focus and amazing recall. We see things more clearly because our emotions and biases are in check. We are ourselves, unclouded by any confusion, anxiousness, or unsettledness. This state goes hand in hand with *menuchas hanefesh*, because *Kabbalah* tell us that the *nefesh*, the lowest aspect of soul, is closely connected to our body, which is the source of the needs and desires that pull at us. When the *nefesh* is in a state of rest, we can experience *yishuv hadaas*.

In this state we can:

- Think thoughts of *bitachon* and *hakaras hatov*, because we have the presence of mind to focus on what we have and Who has given it to us. When in a constricted state, all we can think about is what we don't have and what we still want to obtain.
- Make rational, unbiased, decisions based on information and intellect instead of emotion and feelings.
- Truly listen to what others are telling us because the internal ego-generated noise isn't occupying our thoughts.

D. ***Ha'aras HaDaas*** — This is an elevated and enlightened *daas*. When a person utilizes his state of *yishuv hadaas* to think lofty and holy thoughts, his *daas* becomes a conduit for supernal connection. In the words of the Nesivos Shalom, *ha'aras hadaas* is the state described in the *pasuk*, אַתָּה הָרְאֵתָ לָדַעַת כִּי ה׳ הוּא הָאֱלֹקִים אֵין עוֹד מִלְּבַדּוֹ — "You have been shown in order to know that Hashem, He is the G-d, there is none beside Him." He switches the order of the *aleph* and the *reish* in, הָרְאֵתָ to read הַאֹרַת which means illuminated. A person reaches the state of illuminated *daas* when he connects his essence to the knowledge that there is nothing but Hashem. In doing so, He lifts himself to a higher state of mind. This elevated state, says the Baal Shem Tov, is the definition of *dveikus* — total cleaving to Hashem. We can achieve this level when we *daven* or at any time during the day when we want to fulfill the positive commandment of וּלְדָבְקָה בוֹ, to cleave to Him.

◈ Connection

Another aspect of *daas*, built upon awareness, is the power to connect. When we focus our attention on something, and thereby connect to it, then we have placed our *daas* on it.

The *Tanya* states (*Likutei Amarim*, Ch. 3),

> *Daas is understood from its use in the following verse: "And Adam knew Chava," which is a term of attachment and union. Daas, knowing Hashem, thus involves binding one's daas with a very firm and strong bond, and fixing and immersing one's thoughts on the greatness of the blessed Ein Sof, without diverting one's daas from Him.*

We connect to things through our faculty of *daas*. Therefore, the more *daas* we have at any given time, the deeper that connection will be and the greater the impact it will have.

As you may recall, when we discussed the ten *Sefiros*, we separated them into intellect (upper three) and *middos* (lower seven). *Daas* is likened to the neck in that it connects the upper to the lower — knowledge to emotion and action. This is why *Chachmah*, *Binah*, and *Daas* are often mentioned as a group. Without *daas*, there would be all sorts of disconnection such as:

- We may know a lot and do absolutely nothing about it. Knowledge remains purely theoretical.
- We may know something — for example, that there is nothing to worry about in a given situation — but that knowledge won't change the way we feel. If *daas* does not transmit that knowledge, our lower self will continue to cause knots in our stomach.

- We may do things without thinking about what we are doing.
- We may feel things, both physically and emotionally, but have no idea why.

With *daas*, knowledge translates to action and action is done with thought, feeling, and awareness. Knowledge dictates our feelings instead of the other way around, and we understand what we are feeling and why we feel it.

Daas also allows us to connect to things transpiring outside of us, as we will illustrate with this simple example: You are reading this book right now and hopefully it has caught your attention. The more interesting the book, the more it pulls you in, which means that your *daas* becomes completely fixated on it to the exclusion of almost all else. You may be holding this book in your hands as you read it, but do you actually feel the book itself? Well, now you do. Are you sitting on a chair? Do you feel it pressing against you? Now you do. Can you feel your feet on the ground just now?

Isn't it odd that all these sensations were available to you while you were reading this book, and yet you didn't feel any of them until I mentioned them? That's because you weren't putting your *daas* on these other sensations. Your *daas* was on the words on this page. And this is only a book. Think of some other potential implications:

- Our spouses may speak to us, but we miss many cues because our attention is elsewhere.
- Someone shares personal information with us in the hopes of receiving some empathy or advice, but all we do is nod and walk away because we failed to connect.
- We say something hurtful or offensive. The other person cringes or turns pale, but we don't notice.
- A person blows a great business opportunity during a sales presentation and has no idea why. He missed many cues that could have alerted him to alter his strategy, but he was too consumed with thinking, "I really need this deal," to connect to what was transpiring around him.

◆§ *Daas* — Eyes Wide Open

The greatest benefit our awareness and connection can give us is that which we achieve when we use our *daas* to recognize Hashem's presence and delight in His wondrous world. The Chazon Ish, in his *sefer Emunah and Bitachon* (Ch. 1) teaches in beautifully poetic fashion:

> *Emunah is a refined tendency of the soul that is accessible to a person only when he is in a state of equilibrium and free of any bodily desires. In this calm state, he looks up to the sky in wonder, and down to the depths of the earth. He is moved and astounded. The world seems to him as an impenetrable, wondrous mystery, one that engulfs his heart and mind to the point that he almost loses his senses and no breath of life is left in him; all he can think about is the mystery; he longs to know the solution.*

The Chazon Ish is teaching us that accessing *emunah* and appreciating the world around us are only possible if we free our *daas* from the shackles of constriction and enter into a state of *yishuv hadaas*. We can see the wonders of the world before our eyes all day long, yet it won't penetrate if we aren't in a state of *yishuv hadaas*. Can't we all relate to this? Don't we often find ourselves oblivious to the beauty around us until our child points it out to us? From the state of *yishuv hadaas,* we can go further and achieve illuminated *daas* by pondering the Creator and the wondrous world He created, to the point where we "lose our senses."

To recap: ***Yishuv hadaas and the power of awareness and connection are foundational in life's work. When a person is in a state of settled daas, he is capable of connection and making a rational, informed, free-choice decision to embrace right and reject wrong. In a state of confusion, we are barely able to think, and therefore our ability to choose is impaired.***

As an important side-note, throughout this book, I often use the term "awareness," because it is the first step in any exercise of self-rectification and problem-solving in general. All growth must begin with an awareness of our present state: what is right, what is wrong, what should be improved, and what our purpose is in the world. We can only ask ourselves these questions when we are in a state of *yishuv hadaas,* because when our desires, emotions, fears, and biases are yelling at us on top of their lungs, we cannot possibly provide the correct answers.

We often *daven* for *yishuv hadaas* and its close relative, *menuchas hanefesh,* and *davening* surely helps. However, there is a lot that we can be doing, here and now, no matter the circumstance, to achieve that desirable state. There are ways for us to grab hold of ourselves when we seem to be drowning in stress and confusion — techniques that free the real YOU from prison and unleash the great power that awareness and connection can bring. We will explore these in the next chapter.

16

Yishuv Hadaas

I once brought a high-powered businessman to meet my Rebbe, z"l. When we left the room, he turned to me and said, "I want whatever he has and I'd give away half of my fortune to get some. The holy man I just met is the epitome of calm and tranquility. With everything that is clearly going on in his life (he noticed the pile of kvittlach on the Rebbe's table), he was completely present in the moment. I can't focus on anything for more than 30 seconds." I told him that he need not give away even a penny of his fortune, because that which he sought was already inside of him.

The really good news is that *yishuv hadaas* is not some lofty state of mind that can only be achieved while we sit high atop a mountain, meditating with our eyes closed. To the contrary, the Piaseczna Rebbe tells us that *yishuv hadaas* is our default state of mind when no internal noise is eclipsing it. There are, however, many everyday issues that tend to rob us of this desirable state and it is worthwhile to learn how to avoid falling victim to them.

In this chapter we will explore techniques that will help us restore our inner peace. We will begin by outlining common mindsets that cause us to become confused and unsettled in the first place.

☙ Materialism and Honor

As we discussed, some people are fixated on the pursuit of materialism and honor. Their focus is on acquiring whatever they do not yet have. These two pursuits — material gain and honor (social acceptance) — are alike in two ways. First, both are motivated by a need for something external to fill an internal void. Second, they keep the person living in an illusory future due to his inability to find satisfaction in the present: "Life would be so much better if only..."

As we will learn, this mindset is the opposite of *yishuv hadaas*. Those who acquire a settled state of mind can only do so by accepting that life is as it should be in the present.

(Please note: The next examples are not referring to people with medical conditions who require professional help. They refer to the everyday challenges that many of us face.)

Worry, Fear, Anxiety

"How will I pay my bills?" "What will tomorrow bring in this world of uncertainty?" "Will my family be safe from harm?" "Will I become ill?" "Will I succeed at...?" "What will happen if...? "Things may be fine now but will they always be?"

Thoughts like these sometimes race around in our minds like runners doing laps, going over and over the same turf. They keep us confused and distracted, and worst of all, they drain us of our *simchas hachaim*, our zest for life. These all-consuming emotional thoughts occupy the mind to the point where rational thinking and perspective become impossible to sustain for more than an occasional fleeting moment.

Depression, Despair, Bitterness

"Where has my life gone?" "Things are hopeless." "Others have it so much easier than I do." "Life is so unfair."

When we are down in the dumps, it is often because we are looking backward, reliving and regretting the past, and then using our "track record" to predict a bleak future: "I have always failed and will always fail." In this state of mind, we are drained of all optimism, which leads to despair and bitterness. In this state of mind, constructive and settled thought become impossible.

Anger, Frustration

Anger, resentment and frustration are all-consuming states of mind that obstruct *daas*. For some people, thoughts like these may linger for a very long time. I have unfortunately met people who have allowed their anger and frustration over something that transpired 10, 20, and even 50 years ago to dictate how they lived the rest of their lives. It's as though time stopped at some point in the past and all future time held no value to them. Like a broken record, they play the injustice over and over in their minds, making it their solemn duty to never let go. I once met someone who writes down every wrong that has ever been done to him, lest he forget any of the details. A person who carries around anger and resentment will alternate between states of no *daas* or constricted *daas*, but never experience the full power of his *daas*. This is why others are able to clearly see how finally letting go of his grievances would be the best thing for him, but he can't see it himself. Without *daas* there is no objective rationality.

Unsettled Affairs

It is human nature to put off or ignore uncomfortable matters. It may be a difficult conversation that we know we need to have, an important task left unfinished, anger that needs to be cleared, a worry spoken over with a friend, an apology we owe, or a wrong that needs to be righted. We mistakenly think we can put these things on the back burner and they will somehow go away or get easier to address with time. What we may not realize is that life's issues are not biodegradable. At best, we can temporarily suppress them, but they will only resurface the moment we stop thinking about other matters. When these unfinished circumstances pile up, they eat away at our *yishuv hadaas*. Allowing these matters to remain open is like never closing software programs on your computer. Then you wonder why it is running at a snail's pace. The reason is that the open items in the background are draining your computing power. Likewise, unsettled affairs drain us of our decision-making and awareness power — our *daas*.

We will now move on to solutions — remedies that restore our natural state of *yishuv hadaas*.

◆ 1. *Yishuv Hadaas* Is Found in the Present

The aforementioned states of mind have one thing in common — they keep the person rooted in the past and/or future and disconnected from the present, which is the ONLY place where *yishuv hadaas* is found. The most effective remedy for constricted *daas,* therefore, is learning to live in the present.

I always remind my children that life was meant to be a current-events class. While it's good to read history once in a while in order to learn important life lessons or try to plan for a better future, we should always remember that life is lived right now. In fact, all of the techniques that follow are ways to accomplish this.

The Power of Focus

We may sometimes find ourselves mired in the past or worrying about the future, but when something urgent catches our attention, we quickly snap into a state of *daas* so that we can effectively deal with it. As an example, imagine walking around your house consumed with worry over your credit-card bill, when all of a sudden, your smoke detector goes off. Suddenly, the situation that was so overwhelming evaporates from your consciousness and you focus keenly on finding the source of the smoke.

Rav Chaim Friedlander in his *sefer Sifsei Chaim* (*Menuchas HaNefesh, Vaad* 1) writes that a person can achieve *menuchas hanefesh* by focusing completely on the task at hand. Too much going on inside of our heads will rob us of peace of mind. Most importantly, we should not allow thoughts of past and future to enter our minds while doing things in the present. He quotes the Vilna Gaon, who says that **a person should think that there is only one person in the world — him — and only one hour left to live — the present one — and one task to complete — the one before him**. With this mindset, he will completely channel his power of concentration into the present moment.

The Chofetz Chaim makes a similar point in explaining the *pasuk* (*Devarim* 6:6), "And these words, which I command you today, shall be on your heart…": וְהָיוּ הַדְּבָרִים הָאֵלֶּה — **only the task before you**, אֲשֶׁר אָנֹכִי מְצַוְּךָ - which I have commanded to you — "you" in the singular form, meaning that **only to you** was it assigned, הַיּוֹם — today — **you only have today to complete it**. With this mindset, עַל לְבָבֶךָ — you will harness the power of your heart to concentrate and succeed.

This is the quality the businessman saw in my Rebbe *z"l* and it is why my Rebbe was so revered. He radiated *daas* and tranquility because he lived with focus and only in the moment. When someone stood before him, that person and his troubles were all that occupied my Rebbe's mind at that time.

The *Pele Yoeitz* (*Maamar Daagah*) teaches:

> *The past is no more, the future is not yet, why worry.... For if the matter has past, what will worrying help? Can it be undone? Was it not enough the pain of what transpired that you want to add the pain of worry onto it and live in anguish? And if the matter has not yet come to pass, if there is a solution then pursue it, and if not, then what will worrying help?*

We Have It in Us

The Piaseczna Rebbe (*Derech HaMelech, Parashas Bereishis*) writes:

> *In truth, every Jew possesses a part of G-dliness within him, except it is kept hidden by a person's thoughts, desires, and all of his other dealings with the world... If a person would simply halt the constant flow of his thoughts and desires for a moment, his G-dliness would appear to him without its usual concealments. But a person is constantly running after his thoughts: What will happen in the future? Where will his income come from? How will he achieve more honor in people's eyes? And therefore, all his thoughts continue to flood him without end...*

The words of the holy *tzaddik* are profound. There is no need to go searching; Hashem is right there inside of us. We don't need to reach up to the heavens or fast for 40 days in order to bring Hashem down into us because He's already there. All we need to do is reveal Him by emptying ourselves of all of that mental and emotional clutter. Once the noise dies down and we are in a state of *yishuv hadaas,* His light will flood us automatically.

The Rebbe continues with a remarkable yet simple solution to our tendency toward never-ending, negative, and distracting thoughts: "This person should imagine in his mind that he has, Hashem forbid, no tomorrow, and therefore he has no reason to think about his tomorrow and then he won't continue to be disturbed and distracted by such thoughts."

If there were no tomorrow, how much would there be to worry about today? If there were no tomorrow, how much of today would we spend in anger and frustration? Wouldn't we spend our last day on this world living meaningfully?

I fully realize that the thought that today may *chas v'shalom* be our last will unnerve many people, thereby causing them to dismiss this life-altering idea. They may see this mindset as depressing. It is a fact, however, that it is this mindset with which *tzaddikim* live and have always lived, and yet they remain in a state of constant *simchah*. Great people never take life for granted, which infuses their every day with vitality and a sense of urgency.

> *My father a"h was once studying Gemara with my Zaide zt"l, the Melitzer Rebbe. They were completing a sugya, and all that remained was one brief commentary. My father said that he was tired and asked that they please learn the commentary the following day. My Zaide smiled and said to my father, "Certainly, but only if you can do one small thing for me." My father said, "Anything, Tatte." My Zaide handed a paper and pen to my father and said, "Please write, I, Shmuel Ahron ben Yitzchok, hereby guarantee that both I and my father will be alive at this time tomorrow so that we can finish the commentary together."*
>
> *Needless to say, they learned it that night.*

This is how my Zaide lived and this is how your ancestors lived. They didn't take life for granted. They didn't assume there is a tomorrow, and they therefore maximized their time by only focusing their thoughts on the best use of the present moment. There can be no greater joy than living life to the fullest and there is nothing more depressing than wasting it by living life as though it is endless.

Rabbi Friedlander teaches that young people are prone to spend a meaningful portion of their day dreaming about the future and, in doing so, they never actually live in the present. Older people are always looking back; living life in the past instead of in the present. While we surely need to learn from the past and have goals and aspirations for the future, we are only meant to spend short periods of time disconnected from the present, and only when it is constructive to do so. We are meant to learn from the past and plan for tomorrow but we live in the present. We use our *daas* to do all three. The situation becomes problematic when planning for tomorrow or living in the past so consumes us that we aren't present and living in the moment.

Throughout your day as you find yourself getting dragged into the future or dragged back into the past, you can train yourself to bring your attention back into the present.

Note: Today there is another major problem we face: living while connected to our handheld devices and disconnected from the physical and spiritual world around us. In essence, we are nowhere. This poses a great challenge to our *yishuv hadaas* as people split their attention span between text, email, and internet... instead of focusing on the person and information before them.

2. Torah Study

Although we've already discussed the power of Torah study to nourish the soul (Chapter 10), here we will look at another facet of this transformative pursuit. The true and long-lasting remedy to unsettledness is to engage in self-perfection through the study of *Mussar,* because it elevates our essence and improves our perspectives and priorities.

Additionally, Hashem infused the holy Torah with the power to heal our emotional illnesses in ways that we will never understand. Just like an IV drip delivers its benefits without the patient fully realizing how, likewise, writes Rav Yisrael Salanter (*Iggeres HaMussar*), studying any area of Torah will heal a troubled and confused mind.

- **Worry — fear — depression**: We will be cured of these detrimental states of mind by internalizing Torah that builds *bitachon*. In the words of the *Chovos HaLevavos*, "It is impossible for a person to be free of worries without *bitachon*." Further, "*Bitachon* translates to *menuchas hanefesh*." I have seen many people who suffer from constant worry and anxiety helped more by working on their *bitachon* than by years of therapy. Think about it: How can anything else work? Sometimes we worry and fear situations that are real and not imaginary. We're not fabricating outlandish dangers and there is something to worry about. At the same time, there is absolutely nothing to worry about if we trust in Hashem with our minds AND hearts. With *bitachon*, all is well just as it is.
- **Anger — frustration:** This is cured by learning Torah that brings forth humility, patience, tolerance, and acceptance. The more we identify with our ego, the more injustices we perceive to be perpetuated upon us. The more we humble ourselves to Hakadosh Baruch Hu, the more accepting and tranquil we will be.
- **Materialism and honor-seeking:** The Torah teaches us why we are on this world and prevents us from getting caught up in the rat race of everyday living. Being engaged in the purposeful work that we were sent here to accomplish builds our *daas*, while drowning in worldly matters will diminish it.

Hashem, Who created the Satan, tells us that the only antidote for his poisonous tactics is Torah. The study of Torah itself, specifically *Mussar*, is guaranteed to quiet the confused mind and often does so instantaneously. The Chofetz Chaim (*Mishnah Berurah* 1:4) therefore encourages us to study works of *Mussar* each and every day.

Torah = Shabbos

Rav Dessler (Vol. 4, p. 240) teaches that inner turmoil and confusion are the result of various desires that clutter our minds. Tranquility comes from sorting them out, addressing and silencing them. This is the meaning of, "When Shabbos comes, rest comes" (*Rashi, Bereishis* 2:2). Our elevated state of mind on Shabbos allows us to let go of our yet unfinished business and adopt the mindset that, "All of my work is done." Shabbos allows us to connect to the idea that everything is from Above, and that every accomplishment ultimately flows from spirituality. In that state of mind, we can embrace the thought that, "I have done all there is to do and I can now rest." In the same way, teaches Rav Dessler, studying Torah brings a person to a state of Shabbos, because it connects us to our Creator and calms our inner battles.

Rav Dessler poses a profound question. In order to study Torah we need a settled mind, and in order to achieve a settled mind we need Torah. Don't we face the chicken-and-egg dilemma? He answers that the Gemara (*Pesachim* 54a) teaches that during creation, Hashem Himself created the first set of tongs because one cannot form a pair without anything to hold them to be forged in the fire. Similarly, Hakadosh Baruch Hu created and instilled a calming effect into Torah that takes hold when we start to learn, and builds as we study more. I can still recall the tranquility that would radiate from my grandfather's face as he placed his hand on the cover of his Gemara and began to open the volume.

Studying Torah works wonders with its ability to ground us in reality whenever we need to clear our minds of negative thoughts or make an important decision. Rav Chaim of Volozhin would advise those who had an important decision to make to spend some time learning Torah purely for the sake of learning (*lishmah*), and then rely on whatever decision came to mind as being Divinely inspired (*Keser Rosh* 61).

I encourage you to study works of Torah that speak to your mind and heart, and highlight paragraphs therein to which you most closely relate. Keep them handy and review them often. Much of the material in this book was compiled by that means.

◈ 3. We Ask Ourselves Thought-Provoking Questions

A probing question forces us to stop, focus, think, and provide an answer. Doing so will shake us into a state of *daas*. It would be great if each time we find ourselves lost in confusion or emotion, someone else could stop us in our tracks and ask us a penetrating question, but since that is not possible, we ought to learn to do it ourselves.

Rav Nachman of Breslov teaches in *Likutei Moharan* (Section 2, Torah 10):

> *The reason the world is distant from Hashem, and fails to grow closer to Him, is only because people lack yishuv hadaas, and they don't know how to settle their minds. Therefore, the main focus of a person's quest should be to try and settle himself by asking himself, what is the purpose of all the pleasures of this world, both internal ones such as physical pleasures, as well as external ones such as the desire for honor. If a person does this, then without doubt he will be able to return and reconnect with Hashem.*

When we are caught up in the web of everyday life, we tend to lose our focus on its meaning — what serves life's ultimate purpose and what does not. Rav Nachman teaches us to stop and ask ourselves, "What is the true purpose of all that I am chasing after?" One simple question can sometimes stop us in our tracks and awaken us to reality.

In order to bring ourselves to a state of *daas* we might ask ourselves:

> *How much of what is occupying my mind right now will ultimately matter?*
>
> *Will something that was done to me 20 years ago matter when I have but one day left to live?*
>
> *Do others' opinions of me mean anything in the long run? Does it even matter now?*
>
> *What exactly do I lack right now?*
>
> *How long will the pleasure I am pursuing last before I need another even bigger one?*
>
> *Do my greatest fears ever come to fruition?*
>
> *Why am I more preoccupied with the past and the future than I am with the present moment? Life is extraordinarily precious to me. Does letting go of this one worry or hurt mean anything in comparison?*

Who is losing out from this anger that I'm carrying — me or the other party?

☙ 4. Clear Your To-Do List

As we discussed, unfinished projects and matters that we push off because we dread the thought of dealing with them are *daas*-drainers. We are often amazed at how much more present and energized we feel when we finally bite the bullet and deal with the items on our "I dread thinking about it" list. People who make it their business to tend to matters immediately live with far more *yishuv hadaas* than those who procrastinate, or worse, try to sweep matters under the rug.

Make it your practice to cross items off your list immediately when possible. Make that phone call now and apologize. If you're bearing a grudge, tell the person when and how he hurt you and give him an opportunity to fix the problem. Have that difficult conversation you know is inevitable. Issues never go away when we bury them, and too much time is wasted when we postpone matters.

Sometimes we just can't check an item off our list at the moment for some specific reason. The trick then is to close the issue in our minds and only reopen it when the appropriate time comes. We file it away in a "to do at a later time" folder instead of letting it figuratively clutter up our desk. Doing so will stop the issue from eating away at our *daas*. If you are prone to ruminating over an issue that you can't resolve at the moment, here is strategy that I have found works. Write about the matter in some detail: what you would like to do about it and why you can't do so now. Now file your writing in an accessible place. Each time the issue arises in your thoughts tell yourself, "Indeed I need to deal with that but can't right now for good reasons. It's in the file and when the right time comes, I will know what to do."

☙ 5. Quieting the Mind

Another way to achieve *yishuv hadaas* is to actively do something that quiets down the inner noise of desire, confusion, worry, and anger. The Piaseczna Rebbe in *Derech HaMelech* shares a methodology which is called *"hashkatah"* — quieting the mind. Some may refer to this as meditation, but let's use Chazal's term of *hisbonenus*, contemplation. It is clear from earlier *sefarim* that people knew how to contemplate from the time that they were very young. In the coming chapter, you will find the Piaseczna Rebbe's essay on this topic, translated to English. Here are some other Torah-based methods of contemplation that quiet the mind.

"There is only Hashem"

When life proves overwhelming, you can close your eyes, take a few deep breaths and concentrate on the words אֵין עוֹד מִלְּבַדּוֹ, — "There is nothing other than Hashem." Doing this, says the *Nefesh Hachaim*, puts us into a state of connection to Hashem that protects us from all harm. This phrase, said with conviction, is a protective shield that stands between a person and all that he fears. There are many true stories of people who were saved from harm and misfortune in this manner.

In addition, if we focus on "There is nothing other than Hashem" for 30-40 seconds before starting *Shemoneh Esrei*, we will see a remarkable improvement in our *davening*. It is just what we need to clear our minds so that we can concentrate on the importance of the prayer we are about to recite: to acknowledge before Whom we are standing and His unlimited power to grant us every benefit and protection we seek. When we find ourselves worried, frustrated, or confused, contemplating the fact that there is nothing other than Him and He is our Father, will enable it all to melt away.

Breathing

When Moshe came to the enslaved Jewish people bearing Hashem's promise of redemption, the Torah tells us, the people didn't hear his voice *m'kotzer ruach* because of "shortness of breath" (*Shemos* 6:9). Rashi explains that "...they did not hear Moshe" means that they did not accept consolation, "because of 'shortness of breath' — one who is under stress is unable to breathe deeply [and is therefore unable to pay attention]."

Hyperventilation and shortness of breath are signs that a person is in a state of panic. Deep breathing is a powerful way to restore the person's equilibrium and focus. We can take this idea further by using our *daas* to become aware of ourselves breathing in and out. The Gemara tells us (*Berachos* 43b), "It is written 'Every soul praises Hashem,' and the Sages explain this to mean that "with every breath a person breathes, he must praise Hashem." However, if a person is not even aware that he is breathing, how can he ever think to thank Hashem?

In our times, the practice of deep breathing has become associated with many secular meditation and mental-health methods, but in fact, we need not stray from our own Torah wisdom to access this skill. Methods of mindful breathing are mentioned in the *sefarim* of Reb Abulafia and *Yesod Tzaddik* by Rav Shlomke of Zhvill.

Breath: How we come into existence

The *Nefesh HaChaim* (Gate 1:15) teaches that the words *neshamah* and *neshimah,* breath, are one and the same. The word "breath," however, refers to something much deeper than the air that flows in and out of our lungs; it refers to the breath of Hakadosh Baruch Hu (so to speak); as the *pasuk* (*Bereishis* 2:7) says, "and He breathed a living *neshamah* into his (Man's) nostrils."

Chazal compare the manner in which a person's life-force cascades into him to the way in which a glass vessel is formed:

> *The first stage,* ***Neshamah****, is when the breath is still in the glassblower's mouth, before it has entered the hollow blowpipe. At that stage it is breath alone. The second stage is when the breath enters the blowpipe and is extended into the pipe; it is then called* ***Ruach*** *— wind, since it is in motion. The third and lowest stage is when the wind exits the blowpipe into the glass and fills it to fashion a vessel according to the will of the glass blower. There his ruach is contained and is called* ***Nefesh****, an expression of stopping and resting.*

Based on this understanding, we can follow the *Nefesh HaChaim's* instructions for a form of *hisbonenus* in which we contemplate how the three levels of our soul, *Neshamah, Ruach,* and *Nefesh,* are blown into us with each and every breath:

Sitting calmly in a quiet room where you won't be disturbed, you can contemplate this through the following three steps:

1. Before inhaling, focus on the air outside that Hashem has supplied for you, and think *Neshamah*.
2. As you inhale think *Ruach*, and,
3. As you pause before exhaling think *Nefesh*.

By connecting our thoughts to this three-step process, we are connecting to a process by which Hashem constantly creates us, transforming us from Ayin to Yesh, nothingness to existence. We connect thereby to our essential life source. This awareness is the highest form of *dveikus* and through this lofty connection we can disconnect ourselves from all that troubles us and robs us of peace of mind.

There are several other sources of wisdom on the deeper meaning of our breathing and on methods to tap into its calming power. These are delineated in Appendix 1.

To recap: ***When we quiet our thoughts from the incessant worry over the past or future and from the noise of our daily lives, our essential self and the neshamah within us emerges. We can each develop an arsenal of techniques to free our daas from whatever shackles are restraining it. This will improve every aspect of our life and put us on the road to tremendous growth.***

17

Hashkatah: Quieting the Mind

A translation of the Piaseczna Rebbe's technique called *Hashkatah* — Quieting the Mind — with explanation.

The following essay was written by a disciple of the Piaseczna Rebbe in either 1936 or 1937. I have added some explanation in parentheses. The Hebrew version can be found in the *sefer Derech HaMelech* (page 654).

The Rebbe began with the saying of Chazal (*Berachos* 57b), "A dream is 1/60th of prophecy." As the Rebbe explains several times in his *sefarim,* the sense of self (ego) **of a person stands in the way of Divine inspiration and therefore when a person's mind and thoughts are awake, it is difficult for Divine inspiration to rest upon him. Only when the person is asleep, and his mind and thoughts are quiet, is it possible to achieve Divine inspiration since, at that time, the person lacks a mind of his own** (which would otherwise get in the way). **This is the reason why a dream is 1/60th of prophecy.**

This, the Rebbe would also say, explains why people are more inspired during *davening* than even during the study of Torah. The reason is that when a person studies Torah, he engages more of the "self," through the mindset of "I learn, I think..." whereas in prayer

the main objective is to nullify one's self to the words of the prayer. (This explains why most prayer is recited using the words of *Anshei Knesses HaGedolah* as opposed to our own words.)

However, when a person is asleep, it is impossible to accomplish anything. Therefore, the [preferable] objective would be to achieve [a state similar to] a state of sleep while being fully awake, so that one can accomplish something while in this state. This is done by quieting the thoughts and desires that constantly inundate a person, for it is the tendency of thoughts to become entangled one in the other without end. As the Rebbe once said, if a person would watch, if for even one day, his thoughts which constantly flow one into the other, then he would see that there is almost no difference between him and a person who is insane. (Ever stop and take notice of something you are thinking about and say to yourself, "How on earth did I get here?" Try tracing that thought back to an original thought and you will see how ludicrous the chain will look.) **The only difference is that the insane put their thoughts into action** (or speech) **and the sane do not, but at the level of thought there is almost no difference.**

The Rebbe then taught practical ways of how to quiet one's mind.

A person should begin to "watch his thoughts" (using his faculty of *daas*) **for a short period of time, perhaps for minutes, and to say to himself, "What am I thinking?" He will then begin to feel that his mind is slowly beginning to drain and thoughts will cease its normal flow.**

> (Author: When I first tried this, it proved to be a most frustrating exercise but I didn't give up and soon got the hang of it. You will too. The challenge is that your thoughts will keep pulling "you" in, and before you realize it, you are no longer watching your thoughts. Rather, you become part of them. The goal is to realize that you are not your thoughts and that your thoughts are being shown to you as if they were scenes in a performance. In an earlier chapter, we discussed that there is an essential YOU that can be defined as the "watcher" of your thoughts, and here the Rebbe is teaching us a technique that will help us connect to our essential selves and utilize the power of watching.

The key is not to become frustrated if you find yourself thinking instead of watching. When that happens, stop and think, OK, I was pulled in, no harm done, and then simply pull yourself back out and go back to watching.

What really helped me was to imagine myself standing behind a thick glass window, watching my thoughts from that vantage point. Imagine yourself standing in a store watching a scene playing out on the street outside. You are not in the scene; you are merely watching it. Therefore it has a different effect on you than it would if you were out in the street where the scene was taking place. Watching a scene and being part of a scene are different experiences. Try watching your thoughts from behind the store window and see if that helps.

The second thing that helped me was the understanding of why this exercise actually works in the first place. Thoughts need YOU, your attention — *daas* — to give them energy, and that's why they work so hard to pull you in. Most of our thoughts are coming from our lower self, where emotion and feeling come from, and the thoughts that we tend to get pulled into are those that are emotionally charged with fear, anxiety, fantasy, anger, and regret. These thoughts require your *daas*, your attention, to fuel them, because *daas* connects emotion to intellect, and without intellect, even emotional thinking can't take place. Beginning to watch your thoughts with your *daas* is the equivalent of pulling out the plug; the thoughts stop because they are disconnected from their power source. What I also found to be extremely helpful was to begin the exercise by focusing on breathing and only after doing that for several minutes to begin watching my thoughts.)

The Rebbe's technique has brought us to a state of *yishuv hadaas*, and he will now take us a step further — to *ha'aras hadaas*:

The Rebbe then said to begin to recite one *pasuk* or phrase such as *Hashem Elokeichem Emes* (or anything else that speaks to you such as *Tatte in Himmel, Ribono shel Olam...*) **in order to connect our minds, which are now empty of thought, to a thought of holiness. A person is now able to ask for his needs in any area in which he**

requires strengthening, such as *emunah*, love, and fear of Hashem. I then merited to hear from the Rebbe a method of using *hashkatah* to strengthen *emunah*. "I believe with a whole belief that Hakadosh Baruch Hu is the only One to be found in the world and there is nothing to be found other than Him and everything that is here on the world is a mere illumination of Him." אֲנִי מַאֲמִין בֶּאֱמוּנָה שְׁלֵמָה שֶׁהַבּוֹרֵא הוּא הַנִּמְצָא הַיְחִידִי בָּעוֹלָם וְאֵין שׁוּם מְצִיאוּת זוּלָתוֹ. וְכָל הָעוֹלָם וְכָל אֲשֶׁר הֵם רַק הָאָרַת אוֹר הַשֵּׁם, and he so repeated several times. He didn't recite these words with strength, rather very softly. I also merited to hear the Rebbe address love of Hashem and these were his holy words. "I would so want to be close to my holy Creator, I would so want to feel closeness to the great Creator."

He said that a person can use this state of quietness to fix all of his bad traits, but not to do so by addressing the negative, but rather by addressing the positive and by focusing on the opposite of the bad trait. For example, if someone is afflicted with the trait of laziness, he should never speak of distancing laziness (*atzlus*) rather of the acquisition of zeal (*zerizus*). We can see this in practice with children when they are crying; the more we tell them not to cry the more they cry. (Asking them to smile, on the other hand, works a lot better.)

A person can also quiet the mind by focusing on the minute hand of his watch or clock, which barely moves, for that will also quiet his desires and thoughts. (We also find in the Arizal (*Shaar HaKavannos, Chanukah*) that a person can contemplate the flame of a candle and the different colors it contains, orange, red, blue, clear, and the white glow that surrounds the flame.)

After this quieting exercise, a person should draw upon himself some form of inspiration from Above, and he instructed his disciples to sing the words, הוֹרֵנִי הַשֵּׁם דַּרְכֶּךָ, אֲהַלֵּךְ בַּאֲמִתֶּךָ, יַחֵד לְבָבִי לְיִרְאָה שְׁמֶךָ — "Teach me, O Hashem, Your way that I may travel in Your truth. Unite my heart to fear Your Name (*Tehillim* 86:11)," to the tune that the Rebbe composed. The Rebbe greatly stressed this idea and said that he is certain that it would bring us great benefit. He said that if a person uses this method to strengthen his *emunah* for a few weeks, then he would reach a level at which saying the words — וְאַנְוֵהוּ, This

is my G-d and I will glorify Him," will be in the sense of מַרְאִין בְּאֶצְבַּע, pointing with their finger (Hashem will be so clear a presence to him that he will feel as if he can point to Him).

◆§ Practical Applications

The Rebbe has taught us a technique that can elevate us from constricted *daas* to *yishuv hadaas* and finally to *ha'aras hadaas*. For many it will take practice, while some will be able to succeed on their first try. Ultimately, everyone can learn how to quiet their mind.

The exercise is also extremely helpful when we are trying to get to the root cause of an underlying issue or dilemma. For this purpose, a person would prepare a question or two that he would ask himself while in a state of quiet, such as, "Why do I feel anxious even though I know there is nothing to worry about?", "What is eating at me?", or "Why does my heart say NO and my brain say YES?" You will be astonished at how the answer will often appear as if out of thin air when all the noise is turned off.

This exercise can also be helpful when you are:

- trying to reach a sound decision and are being bombarded with conflicting thoughts;
- working to get to the root of an internal or external challenge so that you can effectively deal with it;
- trying to uncover the underlying fear, laziness, bias, or desire that is holding you back from reaching your potential;
- trying to come to terms with a loss, hurt, or injustice whose pain doesn't seem to go away.

You would prepare the appropriate questions beforehand, and in a state of quiet mind, ask them to yourself. Starting to think will only cause the noise to turn right back on, so the key is to just ask and watch for results.

Most of the time, the answers to life's dilemmas are within us. They are just buried under a pile of confusion.

As the Rebbe says, you can also use a state of quiet mind to rectify a *middah* that needs improvement, for with *yishuv hadaas*, you can connect what you know in your head to your heart. As an example, the *Chovos HaLevavos* in *Shaar HaBitachon* teaches the seven attributes of Hashem[14] that enable us to completely rely on Him. Contemplating those seven attributes while in a state of quiet mind will help the information penetrate the heart.

---

14. The Seven Attributes of Hakadosh Baruch Hu
Chovos HaLevavos Shaar Habitachon Chapter 3
Hakadosh Baruch Hu —
    1. **Loves you.** Just think of all of the blessing He has brought into your life. (Make a list of all of those blessings.) There is no one who loves you more. In fact, any person who loves you only does so because Hashem allows those thoughts and feelings to exist. You experienced open miracles in your life and the best way for you to show *hakaras hatov* is to have *bitachon* and trust that He will always be there for you as He has been in the past.
    2. **Thinks constantly about you** and always works on your behalf even while you are asleep. Things are happening all around you that you are unaware of and that are ultimately meant entirely for your good. Even when a situation seems bleak and hopeless you can internalize that there is so much that you don't understand and that Hashem knows better. How many times did what seemed bad at the time turn out to be pure good in the end?
    3. **Is a *Kol Yachol*, Omnipotent, and nothing and no one can stand in the way of His will.** אֵין עוֹד מִלְּבַדּוֹ אֶפֶס זוּלָתוֹ. People are fickle and weak and have no power to affect you and so you should never fear them.
    4. **Knows exactly what is good for you much more than you know yourself.** He created you from nothing and continues to sustain and infuse you with life and vitality. We know nothing at all and are fortunate that our Father in Heaven is running our lives and not us. Our tendency to worry is the direct result of our failure to internalize this fact.
    5. **Has been consistently at your side since the moment you were conceived and has taken care of your every need.** It is only because of Him that you came this far. He therefore knows you better than anyone and even far better than even you know yourself.
    6. **I am completely under His control and no one and nothing has any power over me.** I therefore shouldn't fear anyone or say anything untruthful or flattering to find favor in people's eyes.
    7. **Wants to bestow good always on both those that deserve and those that don't.** He is patient and His ability to give unconditionally is infinite.

18

The *Daas* Deposit Account

As we learned from the *Nesivos Shalom*, the Satan puts all of his efforts into bringing us into a state of *katnus*, constricted *daas*. If we use what we have already learned, these periods of confusion will likely become fewer and shorter. Nevertheless, because life is a series of ups and downs, we will inevitably find ourselves thrown into a state of confusion and irrational thinking at some point. While our goal is to spend as little time as possible in that state, we must emphasize that we are not meant to beat ourselves up when these periods set in. They are completely normal. As we will discuss in a later chapter, if we don't set our expectations correctly, the Satan will ultimately win, because despair is his most powerful method of constricting *daas*.

To avoid this outcome, let's accept right from the outset that someone may hurt us, things won't go our way, challenges that we never anticipated will materialize out of nowhere... and we will have a difficult time thinking clearly. Our objective in these circumstances is twofold: 1. To return to *yishuv hadaas* as soon as possible, and 2. To work on our skills over time so that our *daas* can withstand bigger challenges.

We can also accept the fact that sometimes, no strategy will work. You try distracting yourself, thinking positive thoughts; you even say some *Tehillim,* yet still find yourself consumed by frustration, fear, or other wretched feelings. When that happens, you are best off biding your time, sleeping it off, and trying again in the morning. The Satan would just love for us to get down on ourselves so he can use his favorite weapon — *yiush,* despair. Sometimes picking our battles, and choosing the time that's most opportune to fight them, is the very best approach.

☙ Preparing for Cold Feet and Regret

There are some decisions in life that are outright terrifying, like changing jobs, moving, making a large investment, deciding whom to marry or writing a book (I had to add that one). Our greatest fear is that we will get cold feet just as we're preparing to take the big step, or experience regret once we've acted. This fear causes untold stress and confusion and in some cases, leads to us backing out. Even if we give a situation hours of thought, speak it over with a mentor and finally reach a decision, we may still panic before or after the fact. Is there anything we can do?

Yes. It's called a pre-commitment letter.

I first used a letter like this in 2008, when the stock market was crashing. A client who was highly prone to emotional and irrational anxiety asked me to help him ride through the market, which he feared would get much worse (and it sure did). He was afraid that his irrational reaction to the temporary loss of his money would cause him to sell his stocks at the very worst time and thus incur major long-term loss. I had once heard of the concept of a pre-commitment letter, and upon further research realized that this was exactly what the doctor ordered. We drafted one.

Here is how it works: A person writes himself a pre-commitment letter during a time when he has *yishuv hadaas* and is thinking clearly. The letter provides him with the information and fortitude that he will need to grasp when he is drowning in fear, worry, and irrationality. This is like preparing a lifeline before entering a dark cave. Sometimes the letter will include a self-imposed consequence in the event that the person disobeys the provisions he's set out. He may put someone else in charge of making sure that he heeds the letter.

In my client's case, he pre-committed to refrain from selling more than 10% of his portfolio over any three-day period, and even then, only after receiving the approval of his brother, who was more rational. (We all tend to be more rational when it isn't our money that is being wiped out.)

The most important part of the letter, however, was the section in which the client wrote down all of the reasons why selling during a downturn is a terrible idea, and asked himself to please ignore the short term and focus on the long term. He gave himself a healthy dose of courage.

It worked!

I then realized this idea had many potential applications and renamed it a *Daas* Letter. Here's an idea of what a *Daas* letter might look like for someone changing jobs and/or starting a business. I helped Moshe draft this letter right before he left a cushy job to start his own business.

Moshe was in a dead-end profession and was essentially, to use an analogy, about to get off a ladder on which he had already climbed several rungs, and start at the bottom of a new, much taller ladder. His biggest fear was of himself. How would he react when he took the plunge and found himself in free fall, regretting the decision?

Here is his letter to himself:

> *Dear Moshe,*
>
> *I am writing this letter to you because I know that you are about to take a huge and scary leap into a new endeavor, and there will surely be many days when you will regret the decision and ask yourself, "Why on earth did I do this? Things weren't that bad where I was."*
>
> *The purpose of this letter is to underscore certain points and to remind you of some others.*
>
> *1. You reached the decision to make this move after many months of thought and research. You sought the advice of others and ultimately decided that this was the right way forward. You did all this in a very healthy and balanced state of mind, and right now, since you are reading this letter, you are in a*

state of tremendous fear and irrationality.

2. (Here I had Moshe list all of the reasons why he reached this decision, using real-life examples for each, such as lack of earnings growth, untapped personal potential, boredom, frustration with working for others, the difficult boss, long hours… anything that he would want to bring to mind when consumed by fear and regret.)

3. Every worthwhile endeavor entails letting go of the old and embracing the new. Every new endeavor is scary, but growth requires taking calculated risk. This is normal — par for the course. You knew that the day would come when you would be scared out of your wits and, lo and behold, the day has come.

4. There is no turning back, and even if there was, would you even want to? You would be right back on the same dead-end road from which you just fled. How would you ever live with yourself if you chickened out? Remember that the Bnei Yisrael in the desert, when facing a fearful situation, said the words, "We remember the gourds that we ate in Egypt at no cost." We all know how irrational that was, given that they had left back-breaking slavery. Their constricted daas made them believe that things weren't that bad in Egypt and they were therefore ready to turn back.

Stay strong because you will persevere, and while the light at the end of the tunnel may seem dim right now, very soon it will be shining bright. You knew it would take two years to make this adjustment and it isn't two years yet, is it?

Sincerely,

Moshe

Another situation in which a person may greatly benefit from writing a *Daas* Letter is when he is prone to mild depression. Here's one that I helped Shimon write.

Dear Shimon,

If you are reading this, it is undoubtedly because, right now, things seem dark and utterly hopeless. Life is proving difficult and you can't see a way out. You are being plagued by troubling thoughts: "I feel trapped," "Why me?" "It's not fair," "Life is so difficult," "It will always be this way."

It's all so black and your heart feels so heavy.

What's interesting is that when you wrote this letter, things looked very different. It must have been so or you wouldn't have written the following sentences:

How fortunate am I!

Look at how much I have.

I am healthy, smart, well liked. I have a great job and a loving family.

What have I done to deserve this? I surely owe Hakadosh Baruch Hu more than I can ever repay.

Why would I ever feel down when there is so much abundance in my life?

Why do the very same triggers seem to trip me up every time? Negative thoughts wash over me, cloud my vision and distort my perception. With time, they always seem to vanish, blow away, allowing the sun to shine through once again. I know that what I am feeling now is the real me and the negative thoughts arise at times when I am not being myself.

I am writing this letter to underscore that the real YOU wrote this letter, voluntarily, and with a clear mind. I am also here to assure you that the sun will shine bright for you again as it always has in the past. In the meantime, you can do something positive. Pick yourself up and distract yourself through meaningful action. Go to the hospital and cheer up someone sick. Buy your wife a dozen roses — for no reason at all — and tell her how much she means to you. Lock yourself in a room for an hour and learn a blatt Gemara, uninterrupted by your phone or computer. Sit down with a pen and paper and write down all of the blessings in your life such as the names of your children, grandchildren, close friends, and people you have helped.

Life is too short — too precious. Sure, with time, this storm will pass, but you need not wait. Seize the moment and pull yourself out. Do something to break that endless spiral of negative thought. Do it now!

Love,

Shimon

Perhaps you may think of writing a letter to yourself as odd, but is it more important to you to achieve your potential or be considered mainstream? Moshe, the man in the first letter, later told me that it kept him going for two years and he had it laminated and framed. I advised Shimon to keep a diary of all of the positive actions he took to pull himself out of depression and to keep it as an addendum to his letter. In this way, each time he finds himself in a dark place, he can read about how prior instances of depression led to a positive action that he wouldn't have accomplished otherwise.

Think about this idea. See what areas of your life could improve by documenting your thoughts when in a state of *yishuv hadaas,* to support you when you are in a state of confusion, fear, and anxiety. It works because there is nothing like hearing it from yourself. There's nothing like words on a page to bring forth rationality when there is none.

Other areas in which a letter can be used include:

- When making a choice, if you tend to second guess yourself by thinking the other choice was better. Document why you chose option A and why you didn't choose option B.
- When embarking on a project that requires motivation, perseverance, and tenacity. Write down words that will motivate you when you are feeling depleted, remind yourself of the meaning behind the purpose, and outline the steps that you need to take to re-start your engine. Trying to lose weight would be one such situation.
- If you tend to struggle with your *bitachon* during difficult periods, write down the seven attributes of *bitachon* and read them when life's challenges set in. Don't just write, "Hashem loves me." Rather, keep a diary of all of the instances in your life

when Hashem's love was undeniably apparent. You can list the attributes of your spouse, children, loved ones; your successes, possessions, health, talents, and opportunities that you were given to help others. I have this very letter on my computer and *B"H* continuously add to it.

We benefit from writing these things to ourselves because when challenges set in, they are often accompanied by thoughts such as, "Hakadosh Baruch Hu is punishing me, doesn't love me, is out to get me..." We tend to see life as pure black and thereby negate everything good in our lives, if we can even recall them at all. Pages and pages of notes, written to ourselves over a period of three or four years, are hard to dismiss, even in that constricted state of mind.

Find creative ways to put your *yishuv hadaas* into a bank account while you have it, so that you can withdraw it when you are finding yourself low or depleted.

What the Rabbi Knew

In the palace of the king the debate raged,
Each side refusing to be upstaged,
Which portends success, what's to be admired,
Talents that are given, or those that are acquired?

The king one day decided it was obviously best,
To substantiate each theory through a revealing test.
So he chose three people and gave them full command.
Each would reign over his very own land.

Samuel, David, and Joe, those fortunate three,
Were empowered to succeed in this opportunity.
They were given one solid year in which to prepare,
Whatever they'd need, the king promised to share.

Samuel was brilliant — an obvious choice.
David had charisma and a beautiful voice.
But why the third choice? Nobody did know.
He was, after all, just a "regular Joe."

The vast royal library was Samuel's desire.
Knowledge of government policies, he would acquire.
David asked to be tutored by the land's very best
Storytellers and orators. That was his request.

Joe first thought, "Why me?" and wanted to refuse.
His wife said, "Give it a try, what have you to lose?"
His request was to spend a year with the Jewish Rabbi,
And the king didn't know whether to laugh or cry.

When the year was complete, the king bade each goodbye.
Each was told, "In one year I will visit and then verify
Who made the best leader, who knew what counts most?
The one who succeeds will earn a permanent post."

Another year passed, and it was time to explore.
The king began with Samuel, feeling quite sure.
Can anything top knowledge and pure intellect?
From his subjects, surely, he had earned much respect.

The very moment the king entered his land,
He realized things were not at all as he'd planned.
The people looked miserable, sad and forlorn,
For Samuel there were only words of deep scorn.

"Rules for everything, red tape by the mile,
Since he's come here, we've had no more reasons to smile.
In all those books, from all that he had read,
Nothing relevant or practical went into his head."

Then to David the king went. Surely, he had prevailed.
The king knew well what leadership entailed.
One must lead the masses, string them along.
With his magnetic allure, what could possibly go wrong?

The once beautiful land was in bleak disarray,
Anarchy reined; the streets were in decay.
"Speeches, stories, lectures: is that all he knows?
We need systems and order to heal our woes."

It was with great dread that the king traveled on,
He knew what he'd find, the conclusion foregone.
From a leader without charisma or deep intellect,
Realistically speaking, what could one expect?

He entered the land; all seemed just right.
Wherever he looked, the faces shone bright.
"We love this man, Joe, he's the one to lead,
Oh, please let him stay; he's the one whom we need.

His laws are impartial, so balanced and fair.
We seek his advice; he has wisdom to spare.
He knows right from wrong, can tell white from black,
Since he has arrived, there is nothing we lack."

The king said to Joe, "I am truly in awe.
An outcome like this, I never foresaw.
With no special talents, who would have believed,
Where the talented failed, you clearly achieved."

"There is just one question — please tell me, dear Joe,
I can't wait any longer; I really must know.
Of all that I offered, pray tell why, oh, why,
Did you choose a year with an old Jewish Rabbi?"

Joe smiled. He'd known this question would come.
"Your majesty chose me because I seemed so humdrum,
Yet I knew that to lead, more than talent it took,
So I sought out the wise — the people of the book.

"The Jews are a wonder; in all lands they exist,
Even when all odds say they cannot persist.
I knew they know something, the formula we seek,
And so, with a Jewish Rabbi, I knew I must speak."

"Please tell me, dear Rabbi, the secret to your success.
I'm not one who's gifted, but I aspire nonetheless."
Thus, I learned what it is the Jews pass down link by link,
Not just facts and information, ***but how to think!***

So many of us wish we were created differently — more like Samuel or David perhaps. I wrote the above poem to underscore that the most powerful attribute any human being can possess is his ability to think and this ability can be improved and developed.

We give so much thought to so many things in life, but we hardly ever think about thought itself. Everything starts and ends with the way we think. As the saying goes,

- **Guard your thoughts; they become words.**
- **Guard your words; they become actions.**
- **Guard your actions; they become habits.**
- **Guard your habits; they become your character.**
- **Guard your character; it becomes your destiny.**

As we have discussed, our role in life is to make good choices, and all choice takes place in the realm of thought. Therefore, let us see if we can improve the way we think.

19

Harnessing the Ultimate Human Power

In Chapter 9, "Shedding Light on Choice," we discussed the wisdom of the mentor who has the power of discernment, and we laid the foundation for making better choices. In this chapter we will take the idea further and teach you how to improve your thinking method and optimize your benefit from this uniquely human power.

The Torah teaches that as a human being, you stand above all of creation because you possess the power of thought. The *pasuk* says (*Bereishis* 1:26), נַעֲשֶׂה אָדָם בְּצַלְמֵנוּ כִּדְמוּתֵנוּ — "Let us make Man in Our image, as Our likeness." Rashi says "as Our likeness" means, לְהָבִין וּלְהַשְׂכִּיל — to understand and gain wisdom. The word לְהָבִין, to understand, is rooted in the word *binah*. This, as we learned, refers to our ability to understand, derive information from information, make comparisons, and build new thoughts. The term *hisbonenus*, contemplation, is also rooted in *binah* because it means to remain focused on thinking until the depth of a matter is understood.

Rabbi Chaim Friedlander *zt"l*, in *Sifsei Chaim*, says that a person who effectively develops his power of thought will not only develop a higher intellect, but also, will elevate his entire essence. He goes so far as to state that a person who has advanced himself in this way exists in a realm separate from those who have not done so. This is because in principle, those in the latter group have not developed themselves much beyond their animal nature. (Please note: I didn't say that; Rav Chaim did.) Even an animal can be trained using repetition, reward, and punishment, but that isn't real thought; it is a response to various forms of stimuli.

Rav Chaim also points out that if we analyze our lives, we will notice that the vast majority of our daily routine requires almost no thought at all. Hashem created us with a nerve center in the brain that controls our organs and activates them without us realizing it. We don't need to give thought to walking, breathing, or putting food into our mouths. We can do most things that keep us alive while our thoughts are directed elsewhere. The beauty of this is that it frees our minds to think about more lofty and constructive matters. The challenge is that if we don't learn how to effectively think, our idle minds will become a hindrance to success.

Binah

Let's use an example to illustrate how *binah* elevates the human above the animal.

It is known that animals, to some degree, are capable of thought. For example, when Elsie the cow sees the farmer coming to her pen with the same blue bucket each day, she learns to think that "it's meal time" and heads over to the trough. Jack the cowhand also draws this conclusion and meets the farmer each day at the trough to see to the feeding.

One day, the farmer approaches Elsie's stall while swinging the bucket too vigorously, and Jack quickly understands that the bucket is empty; therefore, he does not head for the trough. However, Elsie heads right over to the trough because to her, a blue bucket is a blue bucket. The next day, the farmer is carrying a yellow bucket instead of the blue one, so Elsie stays put, while Jack heads over thinking, "I guess that old blue bucket finally fell apart and he splurged and bought a new one."

With time, Jack begins to notice that the farmer comes at one hour when the sun is out, and at a different hour when it is raining. Therefore, he learns to check the weather in order to know when to expect the farmer. Poor Elsie is left clueless as to when to expect him.

One day the farmer fails to appear at all. Elsie keeps waiting while Jack thinks, "Perhaps he isn't feeling well and I better go get the food myself." In all of these instances, Jack the cowhand is using the faculty of *binah* to understand, derive information, and make comparisons — something that Elsie cannot do.

Even at the basic level on which Jack the cowhand is utilizing *binah*, we can see how much it helps him understand what is going on around him, predict likely outcomes, and make informed decisions. We can therefore appreciate that the more we develop this faculty, the more success we will see in life. When we harness our *binah* to make better comparisons and derive more accurate information from what we experience/read, we can thereby develop a deeper understanding of what is transpiring inside and outside of us.

◈ We Are Compelled to Think

Fortunately, we can close our mouths, ears, and eyes when it is beneficial to do so. Stopping ourselves from thinking, on the other hand, can prove quite challenging. Our brains don't come with an off switch. Think we must, and unless we learn to harness and channel this power, our minds will be filled with nonsense, confusion, or negativity. You can visualize your thoughts as a group of wild horses that never stay still. When harnessed, this power of thought can take us to great places. When uncontrolled, it runs wild and wreaks havoc.

◈ Free Choice

Given that everything that has ever been accomplished in this world, good or otherwise, began with a thought, it is important to underscore that just as you have the power to make free-willed choices in the realm of speech and action, you also hold the power to choose how and what you think. You do not need to fall victim to random, negative or irrational thinking; you can be in complete control of what your mind generates.

The Ramchal shares the following in *Sefer HaHigayon*,

> *The uncultivated tree is a metaphor for the intellect of Man. Even with his ability to reason, the uncultivated mind will be like the tree that is not cared for. Though our mind does not stop producing many thoughts like the tree that does not stop giving fruit, untrained thinking will not compare to refined thinking, just like the fruit of a tree growing in the wild is not comparable to cultivated fruit.* ***Just as it is necessary to study every facet of reality, for without this a person can never reach his potential — so too, it is necessary to study the mental process itself so that the mind can grasp ideas in a way that is complete and perfected and not lacking and confused.***

The Ramchal is stressing that we are not helpless when it comes to thought, the most essential aspect of being human. We have the power to choose the thoughts our higher self generates; if we don't, our lower self will throw its never-ending desires and fears at us. We can think positively when matters don't go our way, allow insults to roll off our backs, and jump up with "I can" when someone asks us to undertake a task. We cultivate our minds by learning to make good thought choices, as in "I will choose not to think this, because it brings me down, and, will think something positive instead."

Not Thinking About Thinking

What happens when we fail to think about thinking? In some areas we,

- Think very little at all and act mostly on impulse, which Rav Dessler writes is the result of "laziness of thought." Instead of thoroughly thinking a matter over, we act impulsively.
- Think the same way we did as children.
- Allow our feelings to dictate the way we think.

- Adopt someone else's way of thinking instead of forming our own opinions.
- Stick to an antiquated mindset even though facts and circumstances have changed.
- Think only as the result of external or internal stimulus. Instead of choosing our thoughts, they are thrust upon us.

How often do we sit down in a room and truly think something through in a planned and structured way? What we may not realize is that thought is a skill we are quite capable of improving. Many people don't appreciate how much structure, control, and direction can be brought to the process of thought and how much positive change can be brought about by changing a mindset or perspective.

Here are several detrimental manifestations of this tendency.

- When faced with a decision, we say, "I will think it over," and then go on with our lives hoping that the answer will magically pop into our heads while we are driving our car or doing the dishes. We may as well just flip a coin right then and there and be done with it.
- When making a decision in an irrational state caused by anger, greed, or fear, we mistakenly think we thought the matter through and reached a rational decision.
- When trying to make a decision involving many variables, emotions, and biases, we find ourselves confused and paralyzed in indecision.
- When we are faced with a challenging task, we are quick to say, "I can't do that," adopting a belief that is erroneous and long overdue for a re-evaluation.
- When we try to think, we find it difficult to stay focused because we have almost no mind control.

Thinking About Thinking

Now that we have explained the detrimental results of uncontrolled thinking, we can learn how to control and improve our thinking.

The *Sifsei Chaim* points out that there are two benefits to focusing on our method of thinking:

1. To give thought to the things we do instead of performing them like "a monkey."
2. To broaden and improve the way we think by training ourselves to think more efficiently, constructively, and positively. Thinking is like a muscle which strengthens with prolonged and consistent training over time. If we don't utilize this faculty, it will atrophy and decay.

We will separate thought improvement into two categories; learning how to think more *constructively* and learning how to think more *positively*.

◆ Constructive Thinking and the Power of the Pen

In the words of the *Sifsei Chaim*, nothing facilitates constructive thinking as much as writing. Words and facts swimming inside of our heads can quickly turn into disarray, while seeing words on paper focuses the brain. Writing also gives us something with which to concretize our thought process and conclusions for future review. We will explore this later in the chapter.

Schedule Thinking Time

We schedule time for most important things, so why not thinking? When a decision needs to be made or a worry surfaces, we can say, "I will think more about this during the time that I have set aside for such things," and then go back to our day. If we don't set time aside, the worry will linger and keep resurfacing and the decision will be made haphazardly.

> *Even during the darkest days of the Holocaust, Rebbe Shaul Yedidya of Modzitz ztz"l always had a joyous disposition. People asked him how he managed this and he explained that he was just as worried as everyone else, only he kept his worries tied up and locked away. Once a day he would take them out and think about them and then immediately put them away again.*

Constructive thinking takes time and attention. To think, we need to sit down in a room, turn off our phones, and have an actual thought session. The more often we do this, the better we will become at thinking. When we say that we will "think something over" we should put a date and time on the calendar to do so. If we don't, we will end up making a decision based on snippets of uncontrolled thoughts that took place at random moments throughout our day.

Rav Wolbe teaches in *Alei Shur* that the power of thought is the highest aspect of a human and at the same time, the most fragile, in that it is easily diverted and interrupted. Any slight distraction can serve to pull us away from what we were trying to focus on. Often, even without outside distraction, we find that foreign thoughts pop into our heads as we try to stay focused on any subject matter. **Thinking requires focus and focus requires dedication of time**.

Rav Wolbe recommends that a person begin by sitting in a room and trying to focus on one thing for 4-5 minutes without any interrupting thoughts. He says that this could take up to a month of daily practice to master. Writing our thoughts during the session will make this task a lot easier, but Rav Wolbe's method is extremely helpful in training ourselves to think uninterrupted even when we are unable to write.

A Constructive Thinking Exercise

Some of our worst decisions are made in a state of high emotion and irrationality, on impulse, or before all of the facts are assembled — in essence, with little *daas*. A thinking and writing exercise forces us to step out of an emotional state, because writing requires focus and attention. It also forces us to document the facts that pertain to the decision; this creates structure and order.

At times when we are faced with a decision, we are unable to properly distinguish information from emotions. The best decisions are made only after information is properly sorted and prioritized, and facts are separated from fiction. Effective decisions are also made with the brain first and with the emotions second, as we are taught, *"Moach shalit al halev"* — the brain should rule the heart (*Tanya* Ch. 12). Yes, there are many stories of people who followed their gut and things worked out, but in most cases an informed gut is far superior to a clueless one. Let's meet our friend Moshe and use his story as a means to demonstrate how a thinking exercise might look.

Meet Moshe

Moshe shared with me that he was being offered a seemingly very lucrative fundraising role and a seemingly less lucrative commission-only salesman job. He needed to decide which position to take. He also questioned whether he had the skills for either option, and thought that perhaps neither was the correct choice. He had been playing mental ping-pong with himself for months and by the time he called me, he was tied up in knots.

When I asked him to delineate the pros of fundraising, other than the higher upfront pay, he couldn't get more than one sentence out before he jumped back with "but being a salesman has the advantage of..." The same happened when I asked him to share the advantages of a sales job. When I asked him why he thought he could/couldn't be good at either, the conversation followed the same pattern; reasons that he could and couldn't were interspersed in each sentence. In essence, everything was mashed together in his head and it was no wonder that he was thoroughly confused. He also had a difficult time separating emotions such as greed and fear from facts.

As the conversation progressed, even I was getting a headache. I gave him part one of a two-part exercise and asked him to call me upon completion. He did, and we spoke for 10 minutes about his findings. Based on the findings I gave him instructions for part two. He called a few days after that and sounded nothing like the confused man who had made the initial call. After another 10-minute conversation, he reached a decision.

Moshe was advised to sit in a quiet room and do the following.

Part One:

1. Delineate the most important attributes required for sales and fundraising, each on a separate sheet of paper.
2. List his personal attributes/weaknesses, and highlight where he was matched and unmatched for each role.

Moshe called upon completion and after reviewing his lists he quickly realized that, despite several weaknesses, he actually did have the skills to be successful at either fundraising or sales. Now it was a question of which one he **wanted** to do.

Part Two:

Moshe was instructed to think about a list of important questions and provide a yes or no response to each. Yes and no were the only two acceptable answers.

Here are some of the questions and his responses:

Would I enjoy asking people for money? No.
Would I be proud to be known as a "collector"? No.
Does the organization's cause speak to my heart? No.
Do I **want** to be a fundraiser? No.

Moshe quickly realized that it was the higher salary that was influencing him, because when faced with those questions, he understood that he would hate the job of a fundraiser.

The next set of questions:

Can I learn to handle rejection? Yes.
Can I train myself to stick to a schedule? Yes.
Can I succeed at sales? Yes.
Would I enjoy sales? Yes.
Do I want to be a salesman? Yes.

With the bias of lesser upfront pay now revealed, Moshe was better positioned to gauge whether or not he wanted to be a salesman. He realized that he did.

Most importantly, through Part One, Moshe came to understand his weaknesses, which were time management and discipline. He was encouraged when he realized that there were ways to overcome these obstacles and become successful in his career.

Before doing the first exercise, in which Moshe recognized his attributes, his thoughts of, "I can, can't, should, shouldn't," were based on conjecture and hunch. Before the second exercise, which demanded definitive yes-or-no answers, everything in Moshe's mind was a "maybe, I think so, or I am not sure." The brain can't make a decision with those wishy-washy inputs. Therefore, he was left confused and paralyzed. While I provided the roadmap, Moshe did all of the work. When the process was finished, the decision was apparent. Well, almost.

The last part of Moshe's journey was to decide whether he should become a commission-only salesman or perhaps seek a salaried job. He was still intimidated by the uncertainty of sales. Therefore, I gave him **Part Three** of our exercise, in which I asked him to detail the pros and cons of each option on a piece of paper folded down the middle. When he was done, Moshe realized that the cons of commission-based sales were far outweighed by the pros. His decision was made.

To Moshe this process seemed magical; it took mush and confusion and turned it into order and decision. All Moshe really did was **think constructively**.[15]

Enumerating pros and cons, reasons for and against, is a method used throughout the Gemara. The ruling is often won by the side that can document the largest number of factors in its favor. Learning to answer questions with a firm yes and no answer brings strength, focus and clarity into our thought processes. While "maybe" may leave more doors of possibility open, when making a decision we want the opposite; we want to close all of the wrong doors and only leave the single right one open. That's why I insisted that Moshe only answer with a firm yes or no.

When you accustom yourself to make decisions this way, you will find that with time, the pen and paper become less and less necessary. You will have trained yourself to think more methodically and rationally, and will be able to effectively do in your head everything you once did on paper.

◆§ Positive Thinking

You need not become an expert in neuroscience to know that the more we repeat any given thought or belief, the more ingrained it will become and the more readily it will appear in the future. I have come

15. And he now has the basis for a daas letter to himself.

to see the brain as the man behind the counter of a coffee shop. The first time you ask for a cappuccino with low-fat milk and one sugar, he will make the drink and serve it to you. By the third or fourth time, you shouldn't have to ask. He will be the one to ask you, "Your regular?" and you will simply nod your head. After a week or two, he will start preparing the drink as soon as he sees you enter the shop. He already knows what you want, until you tell him otherwise.

Similarly, our brains become accustomed to how we "want" to think in any given situation, and will do the work for us automatically. The brain has an inventory behind the counter; it's your subconscious. It knows what to bring to the forefront at any given time. It could be pessimism, despair, anger, and self-deprecation or it could be optimism, hope, confidence, and acceptance, depending on what is "your regular."

Once your mind becomes accustomed to thinking about something in a certain way, those thoughts will be as automatic as tying your shoes. As an example, try becoming aware of words like, "impossible, too difficult, I can't, I am afraid, wrong or bad," that may appear in your thoughts in challenging situations. These words just pop up because our cappuccino was already prepared for us as soon as events began unfolding. In these situations, our thoughts are being thrust onto us; we aren't choosing them.

So, how do we retrain our internal storekeeper so that he/she serves us something more positive and constructive?

Meet Reuvain and Shimon. Reuvain is inclined to excessive worry and Shimon lacks self-esteem.

> *Reuvain: "I worry about everything and can't seem to stop. People keep telling me that I need to have more bitachon, but that doesn't stop these thoughts from running circles in my head throughout the day, and sometimes at night as I try to fall asleep."*
>
> *Shimon: "I have low self-esteem. People say that I need to believe in myself, and I know that I should, but how do I stop constantly putting myself down? Perhaps there really is nothing to believe in. Maybe I am just a loser.*

Reuvain and Shimon are playing the same song over and over in their heads; a song that comes naturally to them and requires no effort. They know how detrimental these thoughts are, but they feel powerless to stop them. **They both need to learn how to think. The definition of thinking is chosen, constructive, empowering, and focused thought that is aimed at creating a positive mindset, deriving a solution or making a rational decision.** Worrying and putting oneself down accomplishes absolutely nothing, so it does not meet the criteria of thinking. **We may be having thoughts, but that does not mean that we are thinking.** Please keep in mind that although we are using these two examples, the same holds true for all other negative thought-patterns such as:

- Something doesn't go our way and our first thought is **despair:** "Things are always going wrong."
- Someone insults us and our first thought is **anger** and **vengeance**.
- People around us are moving forward in life and instead of spurring us to act we wallow in **self-pity**.
- We fail at something and immediately find someone/something to **blame**.

Retraining the Shopkeeper

The first step is to fill your mind with information that counters the way you currently think. Our Torah is the only "inventory" we need for this effort. There, within the Torah's vast body of wisdom, you will discover that negative thoughts — even those that seem aimed at self-improvement — are destructive. You will get a taste of a far more positive reality; you'll feel its healing and strengthening effect, and you'll want more. As we learned in the chapter on higher will, submission to Hashem's will and separation from our lower-self thinking infuses us with the *ratzon* to think differently, and the study of *mussar* motivates us to work at it until we succeed.

Even with motivation to change, we still face a challenge, because our negative thoughts have become automatic through frequent repetition. How do we shift to a different gear? The good news is that the same way we learned the negative thought-pattern, we can unlearn it. The process begins by learning to notice the negative-thoughts and replace these thoughts with more constructive ones. Our goal is to form a new habit that overrides the old one.

To accomplish this, we will need a library of **positive replacement thoughts** that we can call up, as needed, so that we can slowly train ourselves to think these new thoughts instead of the old detrimental ones. This is why studying *mussar* and reviewing what we learn is so important; it provides us with the positive thoughts that we so desperately need.

◆§ The Positive-Thinking Exercise

1. What

You begin a thinking exercise by becoming aware of and writing down the thoughts you are having in a given circumstance, as the Piaseczna Rebbe taught, by asking ourselves, **"What am I thinking?"** If you find it difficult to focus, first work on reaching a state of *yishuv hadaas* and only then explore and document your thoughts. **The goal is not to judge your thoughts, only to document them.**

Reuvain might write:

> *I am worried about the future, what it might bring.*
> *I feel like I can't let go, because if I do, everything will come crashing down.*
> *I am plagued each day with worries about:*
> *How I will make ends meet as the cost of living rises;*
> *How I will find the right spouses for my children;*
> *How I will pay for their weddings. Will people have to solicit funds for me?*
> *How will I live with the shame?*
> *How will I ever be able to afford to retire?*
> *What if I lose my job?*
> *How will my children be able to fend for themselves in this deteriorating world?*

Shimon might write:

> *I tend to feel inferior to others;*
> *As I witness people around me succeeding, I think that I can never do the same;*

Since I was young, I always knew that I would never amount to much.
Why was I born this way?
Why is life so unfair?
Why can't I be as capable as other people?
Will things ever turn upward for me?

We should write down our thoughts in detail and in an orderly fashion, as though we are documenting a business inventory. There's nothing like staring at the enemy on a piece of paper when we are all done. It may take several sessions to get it all out, but at some point, things will exhaust themselves and you'll find yourself repeating things you've already stated. Get it ALL out and then move on to step two.

2. Why?

We try to understand **why** we are having these thoughts by asking revealing questions and documenting the answers. Here are some examples.

Reuvain:

Why do I feel that I can't let go?
Do I believe that it is me that is holding my life together?
What exactly do I think will happen if I did let go? (Write it all out.)
What am I accomplishing with worry?
What do I think would happen if I stopped worrying?
Why do I think my children will have a hard time getting married?
Why do I think that I may lose my job?

Shimon:

What factors make me inferior to others?
Do I tend to focus on what I have or what I'm missing?
Why did I feel inferior as a child?
What circumstances or events cause me to feel this way?
What proofs do I have that I am inferior?
Do others agree with my self-assessment? If not, why not?
List some people you know who have fewer skills than you, and yet are successful.

Documenting the "why" serves to more fully uncover the enemy so that we can gain a deeper understanding of what is ailing us. This helps us in the most important, final part of the exercise:

3. Replacement Thoughts

The most important part of the exercise is to develop and document opposing thoughts and beliefs. These thoughts should be documented in bullet-point form and memorized for easy recall. While studying Torah or reading helpful books, it's always best to keep a highlighter handy and highlight sentences that jump out as useful positive replacement thoughts. Transfer them to a handy document.

Let's try to see how this can apply to our two friends Reuvain and Shimon.

Reuvain, as an example, can learn *Chovos HaLevavos, Shaar HaBitachon* multiple times while highlighting sentences that will serve to replace negative thoughts with positive ones.

These are ideas such as,

What is there to worry about when Hashem loves me?

- He has gotten me this far.
- He has given me all that I have (Reuvain makes a list of all that he has).
- He has provided for me always, even when I was in my mother's womb and completely unaware.
- He thinks about me constantly.
- He is my Father in every sense of the word.
- He knows what is in my best interests far better than I do. In truth, I haven't even a clue.
- The whole purpose of creation is so that I can be a recipient of His good.

Hashem is ultimately in control of everything.

- If Hashem can manage the complexities of the universe, surely He can help me with my problems.
- Why worry about other people when Hashem is ultimately in charge?
- *Parnassah* comes from Hashem and NOT from my job.

- Haven't I been worried in the past only to feel foolish afterward when Hashem demonstrated that He always works things out?
- Hashem holds the steering wheel? Unlike me, He never gets lost.
- If I really need to worry, I ought to be thinking about my next heartbeat and continued brain function. I don't because I know that Hashem has those big things under control. Why then worry about everything else which is small in comparison?

How wasteful is worry! How precious is time!

- Rarely, if ever, is there any truth to what I am worried about.
- Matters generally turn out much better than I ever envisioned.
- The issues that I should have worried about could never have been foreseen.
- Life is so precious and so short and every moment in a state of worry is a moment not lived.

Shimon could also learn *mussar* and focus on the fact that **belief** in self is a myth, while **appreciation** of self is crucial. He would also want to learn the myriad of sources that discuss the greatness of every Jew and the extraordinary powers we each possess to effectuate positive change in the world. Lastly, he would want to engage in a self-exploratory exercise and delineate all of his attributes and accomplishments and write them down.

Shimon would also remind himself that:

- While *hishtadlus*, action is in my hands, results are not.
- It is completely useless and highly detrimental to compare oneself to others.
- He was given a specific purpose in life and was provided the exact tools needed to succeed.
- People with far fewer capabilities than him have become highly successful.
- It is the Satan himself who is putting these negative thoughts into his head, with the goal of destroying him.
- Instead of accepting the poison being injected into his mind, he has the power to push back.

(Please refer to Appendix 2 called "The Power of Positive Thinking.")

☙ Be Patient

The *Sifsei Chaim* stresses that changing a mindset takes time and, as with all positive change, improvements will not be immediately apparent. Each new constructive thought, however, leaves an ever-so-slight impression in the deepest recesses of our minds. Gradually, just as a rope is woven from thin strands, these slender fibers will interweave with each other to form a cord as thick and unbreakable as the "rope that holds a horse to a wagon."

Eventually, we can look back and take notice of how far we have come. We will realize that the negative thoughts that used to occupy our minds are no longer running rampant and taking up space. Instead, positive, controlled thinking has become second nature to us. Life will still have its ups and downs, but with our improved thinking faculty, we will be better equipped to weather storms and win more battles.

Is it ever too late to embark on this transformation? Are the established habits of negative thinking ever too entrenched to overturn? No! Our mindset can change at any age; we can each choose a life free of the confusing and negative thoughts that plague us each day and rob us of *yishuv hadaas*. We can make better decisions. Successful living begins with the way we think and we should always remember that we have more control over that aspect of ourselves than we may have believed until now.

20

A Picture Is Worth More Than a Thousand Words

Rabbi Yisrael Salanter once said, "The greatest distance between any two points is the distance that separates our minds from our hearts." Intellectual knowledge is indispensable, but we gain true wisdom only when we internalize what we know so that it penetrates our hearts. Then and only then does what we know truly become who we are.

We are each working to overcome detrimental habits — fear, selfishness, inhibition, laziness, stubbornness — and we are trying to incorporate a more positive, resilient, confident, and growth-oriented attitude in life. To accomplish this, we need motivation and passion, for without the heart, integrating those attributes is impossible.

Chazal teach that the mind/brain is the place of logic while the heart is the root of feeling and emotion. The *Tanya* (Ch. 9) teaches that the נֶפֶשׁ אֱלוֹקוּת — the G-dly soul — resides partially in the right ventricle of the heart and partially in the brain. Both the brain and the heart have the ability to affect the entire human — the brain through the nervous system and the heart through the flow of blood. When they are working as a team, great things happen, because the unified *neshamah* is an unstoppable force. When they are not acting in unison, however, we are left in disarray, thinking one way and acting another or performing actions without any feeling or passion.

Once, when I experienced a difficult test in the area of *bitachon,* I went to speak to someone who I hold in high regard. I told him that I had learned *Shaar HaBitachon* in the *Chovos HaLevavos* multiple times and could quote it chapter by chapter, and yet *knowing* I should feel secure wasn't enough to make me *feel* secure. Why couldn't I teach my heart what my head already knew? He smiled and said, "When you figure out how to do that, please come back and teach me."

☙ The Challenge

In *Lashon Hakodesh,* the term for paying attention or taking note is שִׂים לֵב which literally translates to "place heart." In the language of the *Mishnah,* the term is לְכַוֵּן לִבּוֹ — to align the heart — with the mind. The reason the heart is central to this concept is that even if we try really hard to focus our minds on something, our heart will pull our thoughts elsewhere unless it is engaged in the process. We all face this issue as we try to concentrate on our *davening* and instead find ourselves thinking about everything in the world except the words on the page. When the heart wants to go one place and the mind someplace else, it is the heart that usually wins. We will soon explain why that is.

The second challenge is that the mind can't seem to educate the heart on right and wrong. Therefore, the heart continues to urge us to act as it feels. We learn new things; they make intellectual sense to us and we decide to change. We are going to go to bed early, get up on time, make more sales calls, stop smoking, lose weight, stop speaking badly about others…yet when faced with a challenge, we often find ourselves doing what we feel like doing. What is the source of this disconnect? Why doesn't our heart learn the same way that our brain does?

☙ Different Languages

The reason for this disconnect is that often, the brain and heart speak and understand different languages. The brain communicates using thoughts comprised of logic and facts. When a person learns about trusting Hashem, for example, he does so by studying ideas such as "Hashem runs the world, Hashem can do anything, Hashem's kindness is boundless, Hashem has taken care of me until now..." Logic, facts, and ideas are important because they provide the basis for the brain's sense of reality. They define right and wrong. They are the basis upon which we assess and interpret what we hear, see, and read. We need our brains to think and store memories. As it turns out, however, the brain and ideas alone aren't enough.

The heart communicates through feeling and emotion. Ideas and words only penetrate the heart when they evoke feeling and emotion, such as when someone tells you that he cares about you, or you read an inspiring story or hear an uplifting song. The heart has little use for dry facts and logic, especially when it is overwhelmed with negativity and the ideas being communicated counter powerful emotions. This is why telling yourself to "calm down" never helps and others telling you "there is nothing to worry about" usually falls on deaf ears. Your heart won't respond to such words and your brain, hearing this, has learned nothing new, because it already knew it.

So we are left with a dilemma. The brain, which is our center of learning, needs to teach the heart what it knows, but it often lacks the language to do so. The heart is essentially deaf to facts. If the brain does not learn to speak so the heart can understand, the person's feelings will run amok. His emotions will thrash around like a child throwing a tantrum in a store, and his brain will be like the parent who has no idea how to get the child to stop.

◆§ The Heart Often Wins

That the heart and mind speak different languages explains a lot, but we are still left with one more important question. Why is it that when the two are at odds, the heart often wins? The reason is that emotionally charged thoughts always overwhelm cold and dry words when they are at odds with each other. Emotion and feeling, good or bad, engulf us to the point that opposing concepts have a difficult time getting through.

The reason emotion overwhelms us is that YOU, your *daas,* is more prone to be captured by emotions, and most of what overwhelms us is driven by emotion. Therefore, emotion rules. Even if our initial negative emotions are launched by a factual situation — for instance, a financial challenge — the heart quickly takes the reins. At that point, the challenge becomes how we feel — worried, depressed, fearful, and so forth. Once the heart takes control, the brain's attempt to set things straight will rarely prove successful — that is, if the brain uses mere words.

◆§ The Heart Needs the Mind

The Gemara teaches (*Berachos* 5b), "The prisoner cannot free himself from prison," and therefore, the heart needs the mind to free it from feelings that are negative, detrimental, and destructive. The heart cannot free itself. A person who seeks to rule over his lower self must teach his mind how to govern his heart. This requires mastery of the heart's language.

If our mind learns how to speak to the heart so that the heart will understand, the benefits go far beyond alleviation of our negative emotions. We will also improve our overall power of concentration, because both aspects of our *neshamah* will be pulling in the same direction. Furthermore, we will be able to perform our actions with passion instead of going through life in a rote, ambivalent fashion. When we have *kavannah* — alignment of heart and mind — we are operating at full capacity and are able to achieve great things. We have all experienced this phenomenon when we have put both our hearts and minds into our mitzvos, jobs, or projects and given them our all. The results are outstanding.

◆§ The Power of Imagery

Given that information-based words rarely invoke emotion, one method of bridging the gap is to use a more enhanced vocabulary — imagery. If you close your eyes and focus, you will see that your heart already communicates to you using imagery, and that it is also a language that effectively captures your mind. I once asked a man who was worried about being able to make his mortgage payments what he saw when he closed his eyes. He said, "My family at first out on the street and then moving in with my in-laws." (I won't tell you which one he feared more.) People often tell me that they see visions of their greatest fears coming true several times a day or at night as they try to sleep. Whether we envision good or bad, we are often triggered by feelings of the heart.

The good news is that imagery is a language that both the heart and mind can understand. While we can write/read stories, poems, and songs that educate our hearts, imagery remains an especially effective method of bridging the mind-heart gap because the brain can easily create imagery.

Here's an example.

> *A friend calls and tells you about a family of seven children that lives in your neighborhood and unfortunately lost their father. The bank seized their home and they are now living in a dilapidated basement in abject poverty. You immediately pledge $180.00 and hang up the phone. The friend calls you back the next day and asks you for a favor; to please come with him to this family's home to deliver some much-needed food packages. Naturally you say yes. When you arrive at their basement apartment you are shaken to the core. The windows are broken, several children are crowded into one small bedroom, and mattresses are placed in every nook of the apartment for the rest to sleep on. The kitchen cupboards are bare and the sight of the children, with their beautiful, innocent faces, breaks your heart to the point that you need to hold back tears. The young mother looks so ragged, so utterly exhausted, yet her face shines with a spiritual glow bespeaking her inner peace and acceptance of her lot.*
>
> *You leave the house and immediately turn to your friend and say, "We need to help these people right now! We need to raise a lot of money, get them a decent place to live, buy the kids new clothes, food...!" Your friend responds, "I know. I told you all that the other night when I called and you pledged $180.00."*

What changed? You SAW them. Until you did you were acting from your head. You heard words such as "poor, needy, orphans..." and your head pledged $180.00. The moment you saw those words illustrated with real human beings in front of your own eyes, you were off and running full speed ahead. The power of sight and imagery is such that it awakens the emotions of the person in ways that words cannot. When we read a book, the better the author, the more he captivates us with his words. He paints a picture with his words invoking our power of imagination — which, as the word implies, is the ability to visualize images. We visualize in imagery and think in words — unless, of course, we are able to train ourselves to think in pictures.

How would that work? Let's go back to my example of the family of orphans. Suppose that your friend calls for a donation, and instead of reacting with your brain alone, you stop to imagine the situation. You imagine what the faces of these children might look like — the little boys with their big sparkling eyes and yarmulkas askew on their heads, and the little girls in ponytails, perhaps with freckles. Their clothes don't fit, their shoes are torn, and little Chedva is crying that she is hungry. Her mother can only tell her soothingly that there will be more to eat tomorrow, but today's food is finished. It's cold outside, the windows are iced over, and there's a draft coming in under the old door. Each night little Moishe'le is "in charge" of stuffing rags underneath to keep the wind out.

Now what number is going on that check of yours? Your heart is on fire and you didn't even need to leave your house. Perhaps this vision wouldn't rile you up as much as actually seeing it for real, but it would have gotten you to write a bigger check than you would have otherwise. By envisioning the scenario, you brought your heart in as a partner, and the heart writes much larger checks than the brain does.

Lest you think that the use of imagery is some new-age phenomenon, in the next chapter we will share some remarkable Torah sources that speak of this life-altering skill and also demonstrate that in prior generations, great people would commonly think in images.

21

Visualization and Imagery

In *Sefer Michtav M'Eliyahu*, in an essay titled כֹּחַ הַצִיוּר, "The Power of Imagery," Rav Dessler writes that we connect to ideas through our senses far more effectively than we connect through our intellect. As an example, for some people, *yiras Shamayim* is a sensory experience that permeates their essence, while for others, it is a purely intellectual concept; they know they should fear Hashem, but they don't feel fearful. The first person hears the *shofar* in Elul and it pierces his heart like an arrow. The second person hears the *shofar* and, while it awakens his mind that Rosh Hashanah is coming, his heartbeat doesn't quicken. His day goes on as usual. Another example: While we all know that we won't live forever, some people emotionally connect to the idea that their time is limited, and it dictates how they spend their days. They feel the urgency in their hearts. For those to whom the idea of mortality is intellectual, there's no rush to accomplish; there's always tomorrow.

Rav Dessler writes that there is only one way to take what we know and make it sensory; by using imagery of the heart. By strengthening and fully utilizing our power of imagination to bring forth sensory images, we create a powerful tool to enhance our *Avodas Hashem*.

> *Rav Simcha Zissel, the Alter of Kelm, once asked, "How were our forefathers able to reach the heights that they reached? What power did they possess that we lack? The answer: they were*

well-versed in the awesome power of visualization. The Satan knows this secret quite well, and all of his battles are fought with imagery and imagination through which he entraps our heart and catches us in his net. The only effective way to battle him is by using his own weapon — to strengthen imagery of holiness. Our forefathers would have a constant image of the World to Come before their eyes and would envision the infinite pleasure that awaits one who serves Hashem. It was with that image that they vanquished the Satan and passed their tests.

Elsewhere Rav Simcha Zissel writes, "the difference between a *tzaddik* and a *rasha* is only in the power of visualization. It is not as the world believes that the rasha lacks emunah — faith. It is rather the power of positive imagery that he lacks [which would empower him to overcome his negative tendencies]" (Chachmah U'Mussar 1:28).

When a person contemplates sinning, he can literally taste and pre-experience the pleasure he will have when he satisfies his lusts and desires. As mentioned earlier, this is how the serpent entrapped Chava, as the Torah says (*Bereishis* 3:6), "and the woman perceived that the tree was good for eating, that it was a delight for the eyes, that the tree was desirable, and she took the fruit and ate." The serpent aroused an overwhelming desire for the fruit to the point that Chava could almost taste it from a distance. This is why she succumbed to sin and ate.

Imagine if instead of tasting the short-term pleasure of sin, we had the power to pre-experience the after-effects of sin; the bitterness of regret, the feeling of emptiness and disgust that will follow? Would we still sin? Suppose we could envision the face of a holy *tzaddik* before us, a great ancestor of ours, our mother or father, standing right there and watching us. Would we still sin? This, Rashi tells us, is how Yosef rejected the entreaties of Potiphar's wife. He saw the image of Yaakov in his mind's eye.

Likewise, this is what the Alter of Kelm means when he advises using the "Satan's weapon" against him. We can counter the Satan's evil imagery with holy, positive imagery. Rav Wolbe writes (*Derashah, Parashas Chukas*) that there are three powers that influence YOU; will, thought, and imagery. In order to reach a positive decision and put it into action, you must be able to create positive imagery, because otherwise your emotions will not get behind the idea.

> *Rav Schwab zt"l was once entering a room where a large crowd of people eagerly waited for him to speak. A student asked him, "Rebbe, how does all this honor not get to you?" He responded, "As I approach the podium each time I am about to speak, I envision myself being led to my final resting place in vivid detail so that by the time I face the audience, there is no room in my heart for haughtiness.*

This is how *tzaddikim* lived. They envisioned and experienced the words of Chazal — "Remind yourself of the day of death" — and by doing so they instantly drove away all thoughts of arrogance. Arrogance resides so deep in the heart that the unadorned words, "one day you will die," would have no meaningful impact. Rav Schwab's imagery spoke directly to his feelings.

Even Moshe Rabbeinu used the power of imagery when he wanted to beseech Hashem to appoint a successor for him. Realizing that he would not be entering Eretz Yisrael, Moshe prayed, "May Hashem, G-d of the spirits of all flesh, appoint a man over the assembly who shall go out before them and come in before them, who shall take them out and who shall bring them in; and let the assembly of Hashem not be like sheep that have no shepherd" (*Bamidbar* 27: 16-17).

Why does Moshe Rabbeinu use a metaphor of wandering sheep to illustrate his point? Does Hashem need poetic speech?

I once heard a novel explanation. The *Midrash* (*Shemos Rabbah* 2:2) relates that when Moshe was tending the flock of Yisro in the Wilderness, a little lamb escaped from him. He ran after it until it reached a shady place, and there, the kid stopped to drink. When Moshe approached it, he said, "I did not know you ran away because of thirst. You must be weary." So he placed the kid on his shoulder and carried it back to the flock. Hashem then said, "Because you showed mercy in leading the flock of a mortal, you are surely worthy of tending to My flock, Klal Yisrael." **When Moshe Rabbeinu was envisioning a world without him and what that would mean for the Jewish people, he recalled**

the vision of the little sheep, thirsty and weak, wandering away in search of water. It was with this image that he stood before Hashem and beseeched that a worthy shepherd be appointed.

☙ Visualizations Prepare Us

As mentioned, Rav Shlomo Wolbe writes that a person possesses three main faculties: will, thought, and the power of imagination. While will is the deepest and most encompassing of the three, it does not have full impact on the person's thoughts and actions until he learns to create positive imagery that will pull his entire being in the direction of the will.

Rav Dessler teaches that we can also use imagery to better prepare ourselves, both intellectually and emotionally, for challenges that lie ahead. Often, when we are caught off guard by an unexpected occurrence, we make mistakes. To remedy this:

- Before a challenge sets in, we can imagine the challenge itself and how we will successfully overcome it. We can pre-experience the arguments we will use to vanquish the evil inclination and the joy we will feel when we win the battle.
- We can envision the butterflies we will feel when entering a room full of people to whom we are about to deliver a presentation, and practice what we will say to ourselves.
- We can envision how our spouse will react as we come home two hours late and how we will apologize instead of launching the counterattack.
- We can visualize all of the obstacles and pushback that we will experience when we embark on a new and worthy project, so that when they occur, we can smile and think, "Ahh, I was expecting this."

Successful business people do this all the time. They visualize how they will conduct a meeting, all of the objections that will be raised and how they will effectively address them. They visualize their success.

What's ironic is that our hearts visualize future episodes automatically all the time, but the visions usually produce fear and trepidation. We imagine our humiliation and disappointment instead of our triumph over the obstacles. Last week, as I left a successful meeting that had been potentially contentious, my colleague turned to me and said "Phew! That went a lot better than I imagined." In fact, the meeting had gone exactly as I had imagined; we were challenged, but well prepared and able to rise to the challenge. His comment, however, explained the anxiety I saw on his face throughout the meeting. He had allowed his emotions to paint the visualization. If instead, we choose to use our minds to imagine a positive outcome, then that will likely be the result.

◆§ Taming the Unruly Child in Us

Another proponent of the power of visualization is the Piaseczna Rebbe, *Hy"d*. In his *sefer Hachsharas Avreichim* he speaks often of the use of imagery and provides us with several detailed and useful visualizations.

He explains that when you use your intellect to exert influence over your lower self, you are like a father who is trying to control his unruly, destructive son. The father, as hard as he may try, cannot effectively control a son who is eager to destroy and who will turn the house upside down as soon as the father turns his back. Similarly, we cannot influence ourselves with intellect alone, because if we don't refine our feelings, we will spend most of our days fighting ourselves and often losing the battle. Furthermore, if we don't educate and train our hearts, our emotions will ultimately distort our minds to the point that evil will become good and vice versa. In other words, at some point, the father may unfortunately take an "if you can't beat 'em, join 'em" attitude and destroy his own house.

The Piaseczna Rebbe writes,

> *The hairs on my head stand on end when I hear elderly Jews complaining that they cannot withstand their temptations, not even those that they had conquered in their youth. The reason is as I stated earlier: in their youth, they served Hashem only intellectually. They didn't work to improve themselves and their feelings and to use them for holiness. Instead, they*

only restrained themselves; they only held themselves back from destructive passions. Once they grew old and weak, their ability to restrain themselves weakened.

The Piaseczna Rebbe teaches two profound lessons.

1. The mind trying to control the heart, using logic alone, is insufficient;
2. As we age, our ability to battle our negative tendencies weakens. If we've only managed to suppress those tendencies in our younger years, they will arise to harm us later in life.

Without achieving a change of heart, we are locked in a non-stop internal struggle. This exhausting battle expends an inordinate amount of our willpower which, after some time, becomes depleted. Additionally, even if we are completely on guard, circumstances will arise that will catch us off guard and our feelings will run rampant and cause destruction. A good example: A person who hasn't worked on internalizing patience tries to control his anger using logic and reasoning. It works to some extent, but when he has the inevitable "off day" in which his willpower is lagging, or when something beyond his endurance arises to "really tick him off," he'll lose his self-control.

The Piaseczna Rebbe continues:

> *We see throughout the holy sefer Noam Elimelech that when Rebbe Elimelech of Lizhensk directs a person to engage in thought, he usually doesn't use the verb "think" but words such as "imagine" and "visualize." For instance, in the first paragraph of Tzetl HaKattan he says, "Imagine and visualize that a great and awesome fire is burning before you... May our thoughts be clear, lucid, and powerful" and our thoughts cannot be powerful without imagery.*

Given that the use of visualization is an important aspect of self-refinement, we will explore two methods of using imagery.

1. Recording What We See

The *Chovos HaLevavos* (*Shaar HaPrishus* 5) encourages us to use our power of sight to record sights and images of Hashem's world and creations. We can use these images to contemplate and awaken our hearts to the greatness of the Creator. Although many of us have encountered wondrous scenery, visited holy places, and seen holy people, envisioning them in detail may prove difficult. The reason is that when we encountered them, we weren't mindfully present. Therefore, the image was not vividly captured in our mind.

The *Kuzari* (Essay 3:5) refers to the power of visualization in describing how an elevated person refines his thinking. He says that after the person clears his mind of detrimental thoughts, he dedicates his power of imagination to project images of the highest spiritual quality, which he will recall using his memory. **"He will also command his memory to retain such images and never forget them."**

How do we command ourselves to remember?

> *The year was 1999. My now married sons were young boys and I took them to the Simchas Torah hakafos of Rav Shlomo Halberstam zt"l, the Bobover Rebbe. Anyone who has ever been privileged to be there knows that watching the Rebbe dance — with his face aflame and his feet seemingly floating off the ground — can only be compared to seeing the dance of angels. There were multiple circles snaking around the shul, so that every 10 minutes or so we had the opportunity to pass by the Rebbe for just a moment and get a glimpse of his holy countenance. As we drew close to that spot, I turned to my two young sons and said, "This may be the last time in your lives that you get to see the holy Rebbe's glowing face, so when we pass by I want you to sear the memory deep into your minds so that you will never forget it." We passed, we seared, and until this day, 20 years later, we can each recall the image of the Rebbe's face, his eyes on fire and his face illuminated.*

When we know that something is important and worth remembering — when we take notice and focus completely on it — the image is seared into our memories. The *Kuzari* is teaching us that we can effectively command our faculty of memory to remember things we feel are important.

Variety, Detail, and Sensory Images

The Piaseczna Rebbe continues, explaining the importance of remembering the multiple details of each image:

> *To expand your ability to think so that you can concentrate at length and forcefully, you must fill your mind with many different visual images... a variety of images. You cannot expand your ability to think and visualize on the basis of one image alone. By nature, thought and mental images only remain in your mind when you add new images. For instance, you can only hold the thought of the evil that someone has done to you if you imagine what he was thinking, how he prepared himself, exactly how he raised his hand against you, exactly what he said to you....*

Visualizations have greater impact when they contain detail and movement. An image of a *tzaddik's* face is not as powerful as the vision of him dancing or *davening*. Rav Yisroel Salanter (*Ohr Yisrael*, Letter 9:30) teaches that tangible imagery that is sensory and brings forth emotion has the ability to awaken us to concepts and ideas. There are people who have so mastered this skill that they can conjure up sounds and smells in addition to imagery.

We can each build a library of visualizations to recall when we need them to help us through a challenge: holy people we have been privileged to meet, exalted places we have visited, uplifting events we've experienced, and visions of Hashem's miraculous world. We can infuse these visions with detail and feeling until they capture our hearts and minds. We each have our own memories and images and should review them from time to time so that they remain fresh in our minds. We should also be on the lookout for opportunities to record new visualizations.

Additionally, we benefit from adding visions of a different sort to our collection: someone who is much less fortunate than we are, someone in the hospital, *r'l*, or of an orphan or widow. The next time you thank Hashem for what you have, you can use more than mere words. You can engage your heart by *seeing* what you have and what others are lacking.

We can also build a library of pictures that are not so holy, such as the appearance of someone who loses his temper, his face red and contorted, his forehead veins popping out as he yells words he will soon regret; someone acting selfishly, turning his back on a pauper as the poor man looks on, his expression downtrodden; or someone driving like a madman with complete disregard for pedestrians and other drivers. The next time you are trying to overcome the urge to act badly, close your eyes and see that ugly vision, and ask yourself, "Is that who I want to emulate?"

A young married yeshivah student was having a difficult time keeping his eyes away from provocative sights as he walked in the streets. I suggested that the next time he passes a construction site and sees a worker ogling a passing woman, he should sear the image into his mind. Each time he feels the urge to look where he shouldn't, he can recall the image and think, "Do I want to be like him?"

Each of us needs to seek out visions and sights that we know will be helpful in fighting the personal, specific battles that keep coming up for us. In doing so, we will slowly train our hearts to feel the beauty of goodness and be repulsed by the ugliness of evil.

2. Create Your Own

Try closing your eyes and envisioning a pink elephant. Now try envisioning the pink elephant climbing up a ladder.

Were you able to do that? Most likely you were, and yet I will assume that you have never seen a pink elephant climbing a ladder. That's your power of imagination at work. Children can spend hours in a world of their own making, and we were once no different. Somewhere along the way, we discarded this skill; perhaps we didn't believe we had any use for it. Now is the time to open up that tool box, retrieve what you've stowed away and put it to good use.

The power of imagery to influence our hearts emerges powerfully in the Torah itself, especially in its descriptions of the seminal events that forged us into a nation — crossing the *Yam Suf* and receiving the Torah. Although none of us physically stood at Har Sinai when the Torah was given, or crossed the *Yam Suf* when Hashem split it, we have enough information to imagine what it was like. I have met people who are able to experience the splitting of the *Yam Suf* in vivid detail, all based on the images provided by the *Midrash* and other sources. The Alter of Kelm writes:

> *The Torah, Gemara, and Midrash are full of lively and sensory images and if people learn them well and preserve them in their memory, they will be able to recall them in their imaginations and, without question, they [the images] will effect a positive change in their hearts.*

Reading the Torah's descriptions, we notice that it goes to great lengths to vividly depict the wind that blew, the wall of water, the sound of the *shofar*, the lightening… all so that we can envision these momentous events in a way that will capture our hearts. The Torah paints powerful images with words to assist the essential task of ensuring our faith in Hashem and His *Hashgachah Pratis.*

The Alter of Kelm (*Chachmah U'Mussar* Essay 132) says something even more profound. A person is accustomed to envisioning only that which he has already seen with his eyes. We all know what a lion, whale, and mountain look like. When we envision them, we aren't using imagination, but rather, the power of recall. Furthermore, seeing a single bird, for example, doesn't make us think, "Wow, how wondrous is Your world, Hashem," because we have grown accustomed to them.

Suppose, however, that we were able to see 1.5 billion red-billed quelea as they swarm across Africa's savannah, or 10 million fruit bats in Zambia or millions of wildebeest stretching for miles and miles across the Serengeti. Imagine all of the oxen, lions, zebras, and every other animal on Planet Earth gathered in one area spanning hundreds of miles. How many people would flock to see a spectacle like that?

The Alter of Kelm encourages us to use the power of imagination to multiply many times over the individual visions that we have stored in our memories so that the next time you say, "How wondrous are Your creations, Hashem," you can close your eyes and allow your heart to flood you with feelings of awe. You can close your eyes and take a trip around the world and envision the spectacular sights that are out there: millions of animals, insects, birds, mountains, trees, canyons, ice caps, rivers, and deep oceans. Envision getting into a rocket; travel into orbit, and view the world from that vantage point. (For readers who want to expand their knowledge of Hashem's creation, I recommend *Visions of a Compassionate World*, by Rav Menachem Epstein, *Hy"d.)*

Sometimes we get so wrapped up in our own myopic lives and our daily issues that we forget that there is a big and wondrous world out there. Life brings constriction of *daas*, perspective; we achieve a connection to Hashem in a state of expansion. You can spend $250,000 to book a ticket for a trip into outer space, or you can study photos of planet earth from outer space and launch yourself into orbit whenever you feel like opening up your heart and mind to Hashem's greatness.

The next time you are groping for *bitachon* and are using thoughts of "Hashem runs the world" to calm down, try envisioning all of the animals out there that somehow have what they need to eat, and the perfect harmony and inter-dependence of all of creation. Don't just think the words, "Hashem is good to me." Try instead to envision everything that you have in your life: your faculties, relationships, possessions...... When saying the words *"Ad heinah azarunu"* — until now, You have helped us — envision as the *Chovos HaLevavos* says (*Shaar HaBechinah* Chapter 5), the moment that you were conceived and were protected in your mother's womb, a perfect environment, where you were formed cell by cell, limb by limb, growing with absolutely no effort; your miraculous birth; the nourishment Hashem provided you through your mother and your early childhood with all of your needs being fulfilled.

The next time you are struggling to gain control over your lower-self instincts, take the advice of Rav Yisroel Salanter (Letter 9): A person should use the power of imagery to arouse his heart and limbs to fear Hashem by picturing calamities that befall people. He can thereby internalize what punishment could look like *R"l. There is one caveat, however*: Take care that you don't visualize calamities when you're grasping for *bitachon*, or conversely, visualize Hashem's unconditional love and care when you're about to sin.

You can use the power of imagination before performing an action that arouses fear of failure. Imagining a successful outcome breeds courage and confidence. Imagine walking into the room and making a fabulous presentation. In your mind's eye, see that as objections are raised, you effectively address them and finally, visualize the handshake when the deal is closed. Don't be among the people who envision the opposite; failure and humiliation. As we said in an earlier chapter, davening along with positive thinking, the product of *bitachon*, leads to positive outcomes.

To recap:

- We need to engage our hearts to be successful at anything we wish to accomplish, because we need passion and fervor to overcome challenges.
- We need to involve our hearts because otherwise, emotion will pull us to places we don't want to go.
- We need to educate our hearts to desire that which is good and positive and to have an aversion to negative feelings/emotions.
- The heart has no use for the words that speak to our intellect, but that is the only language our brains are accustomed to speaking.

The solution is that the brain can learn to use the language of imagery and visualization when communicating with the heart. To do so, it will store and create a library of images that can be used along with, or instead of, mere words.

Exercises:

Close your eyes and —

- Spend a few quiet moments visualizing the faces of holy people, one by one. Let them appear and depart at random and then try to have them appear as a group.
- The Reishis Chachmah writes (*Shaar HaKedushah* 4:23) that when we pray we should imagine ourselves standing in Gan Eden before the holy *Shechinah* in a place of purity. Rav Elimelech of Lizhensk writes (*Lech Lecha*) that we should imagine ourselves praying in the Holy Temple.
- If you find Gan Eden hard to imagine, picture yourself in a holy place that you are familiar with and that warms your heart. What are you doing? How are you feeling?

Try to visualize yourself soaring like a bird; looking down at mountains, valleys, jungles, and oceans while thinking, "How wondrous are Your creations, Hashem." If you can, launch yourself into outer space and see the planet and universe from that vantage point.

Rav Chaim Vital writes (*Shaarei Kedushah* 3:5) that a person should turn his attention away from all physicality and conjure up an image of himself ascending into the upper worlds in order to receive light from the source of his soul. This is extremely powerful when we find ourselves overwhelmed with fear and trepidation. By unshackling our power of thought from this world, we free ourselves of the potential for negativity to harm us.

- In your mind's eye, play images of all of the blessings you have in your life. Your family, each member one by one, your close friends, mentors, possessions… while thinking of Who gave it all to you.
- Replay the happiest and most fulfilling experiences you have ever had since you were a child: An important milestone that left you feeling uplifted. The moment you experienced the successful culmination of your hard work.

Each of these exercises will bring you to a state of *yishuv hadaas* and cause your heart to swell with *emunah* and *bitachon*. Some people may think this is weird, but please don't let that stop you. Better to be a bit unconventional and highly successful than mainstream and just getting by.

22

Confidence

I once played a thought-provoking game with my children at the Shabbos table. I posed the following question: Imagine you walked out of our front door and, to your utter surprise, a space ship was parked on the lawn. A door opens, a ramp is lowered, and out comes a creature from another planet. He informs you that on his planet, many galaxies away, live tens of thousands of Jews who know absolutely nothing about Judaism. They're looking for someone to come and teach them what they need to live a well-balanced observant life. There is only one issue; space on the ship is limited, so you can only bring five written works along. You, as the master teacher, are charged with heading back into your house and choosing what those five written works are going to be. What would you choose as your five?

The question was designed to be tricky in that the first four are obvious and indeed within minutes all of my kids agreed on a *Tanach, Siddur, Shulchan Aruch,* and *Shas*. It was at number five that the real debate began. *Rambam, Zohar, Chinuch*... There were so many to choose from and the debate raged on for a while until I said the words "*Chovos HaLevavos*" and they all became quiet. After giving it some more thought, we all agreed, for us at least, it had to be the *Chovos HaLevavos*, the *sefer* that teaches a Jew how to think and feel — the *sefer* regarding which my great-grandfather the Noam Elimelech, and others such as the Chasam Sofer, designated as an integral part of a person's daily Torah study; the *sefer* to which so many turn for answers to all of life's challenges. It is the roadmap for a thinking and feeling Jew.

The *sefer* that almost wasn't written at all.

Rabbeinu Bachya devotes the introduction of his *sefer* (*Chovos HaLevavos)* to describing the extensive process that led him to the decision to write the *sefer*. He explains the research he undertook to establish the need for a *sefer* that teaches the obligations of the heart. Based on this, he concludes that nothing of the sort had ever been written. He also concludes that despite the overpowering need, he is not the right person for the job. It is at this juncture that he teaches us some profound and life-altering lessons, which, in the coming chapters, we will explore and internalize using the Hebrew translation of the *Lev Tov*. You'll be amazed at the transformative power of these lessons, as have been the many people around the world with whom I've shared them. Let's begin with Rabbeinu Bachya's disclaimer:

> *However, as I set out to bring into action my decision to author this sefer, I realized that a person like me is not worthy of writing this work. I evaluated myself and determined that I do not have the skills that it would take to break down the wisdom of conscience into roots, branches, and categories in a way that this compilation would be as orderly and organized at it would need to be.*

Contrary to this self-evaluation, any student of *Chovos HaLevavos* will attest that it is almost unsurpassed in the orderly fashion in which the information is transmitted. Everything is separated into gates, steps, and categories, and numbered in ways that make recalling the information easier for the student. For example, many who have learned *Shaar HaBitachon* will recall that it is neatly organized into groups of seven, the seven attributes of Hakadosh Baruch Hu which provide the foundation for us to completely rely on Him; the seven differences between the life of a person who has *bitachon* and one who does not; and the seven fallacies of a person who demands collateral from Hashem. Rabbeinu Bachya also provides an exquisitely ordered explication of the factors that strengthen or weaken each gate. Although the *sefer* was written nearly 1,000 years ago, someone learning it today feels as though Rabbeinu Bachya is speaking directly to him, addressing the very issues we face in this generation. He knew exactly what needed to be done and proceeded to do it in the most brilliant way possible, yet at this juncture he truly didn't believe that he could.

☙ Self-Evaluation

The words Rabbeinu Bachya uses to describe the process by which he determined his fitness for the endeavor was, "I evaluated myself."

Anyone seeking success in life needs to become aware that we each perform countless self-evaluations over the course of any given day, and that we are often not conscious of doing so. Even worse is that most of our self-evaluations are done in milliseconds, because we have already long ago convinced ourselves of our so-called "limitations" in any given area and therefore, we rarely revisit that initial evaluation. Instead, we strengthen that initial belief each time a situation comes our way by quickly thinking, "I can't do that." Perhaps we once tried and failed, or perhaps we don't believe that we have the necessary skills, and that negative evaluation sticks with us, sometimes for life.

As we discussed in an earlier chapter, the belief that we have the capabilities to successfully complete an undertaking is what gives birth to the will to undertake it. Lack of confidence in our capabilities stifles the potential for growth.

What would you have advised?

Here is Rabbeinu Bachya's assessment in his own words:

> *In my eyes the task was too difficult for me,*
> *My mind was too weak to grasp the subject,*
> *I do not have the skills that it would take to break down the information in an orderly and organized fashion.*
> *I don't have sufficient proficiency in the Arabic language, (the sefer was originally written in Arabic, the language spoken in Spain at the time).*

Rabbeinu Bachya offers four compelling reasons why he's not up to the task. Think about them and try to imagine that you were alive in that generation and Rabbeinu Bachya came to ask you what he ought to do. Remember you don't yet know the end of the story. How would you have advised him? He was at a crossroads, deciding whether or not to dedicate a major portion of his life to a task that he felt inadequate to complete. If he went forward and failed it would have come at the expense of other worthy endeavors. Would you have advised him to proceed? Would you have proceeded were you in his situation? In our minds, Rabbeinu Bachya would have been completely justified in abandoning this task, but we would be left without this critical roadmap for life.

And now let's stop and ask, Was he correct in his self-assessment, incorrect, or were those perhaps words of humility?

We can safely eliminate humility as being the source because of what he will go on to say in the following paragraph. Also, the *Chovos HaLevavos* itself clearly states in *Shaar Hachniyah* that a person can only attain humility once he has fully understood his own self-worth, inherent talents, and attributes.

Let's therefore explore the first two options. While we don't know what was truly going through Rabbeinu Bachya's mind, examining each option will teach us important lessons.

1. His self-evaluation was correct

Rabbeinu Bachya was not up to the task. Well, if that's true then how did he successfully write the *sefer* and do such a splendid job? The answer is that there has never been a human being in history who has been up to any great task, and that certainly holds true for writing a *sefer* that has impacted generations upon generations. Anything great that we accomplish is beyond our physical capabilities; we ultimately rely on *siyata d'Shmaya* to succeed. Ask someone successful in any given area how he succeeded. If the person is in touch with reality and not subject to an inflated ego, he will answer that it was a miracle, beyond what was naturally possible. He himself would have never believed it possible; many of these individuals walk around in a state of utter amazement years later.

We are never allowed to forget the Source from which our abilities and successes derive. The Torah teaches in *Parashas Eikev* "And you may say in your heart 'My strength and the might of my hand made me all this wealth.' Then you shall remember Hashem, your G-d, that it was He Who gave you the strength to create wealth..." The *Targum Onkelos* translates this to mean that in business, even thoughts to buy or sell are placed into our minds by Hashem. This teaches us that when we think, "I can" or "I did," we are denying Hashem's hand in everything. The term "self-made" is therefore a form of heresy.

There is another side to this mindset that addresses failure rather than success. When we think, "The lack of might in my hands is why I didn't achieve wealth, success...," or "I can't do this," we are also denying Hashem's hand in everything. If your efforts weren't the cause of your success, they couldn't be the cause of your failure, either. To be clear, we aren't speaking about a person who was negligent, lazy, or reckless; we are discussing someone who did his proper *hishtadlus* yet feels that he fell short because "he" fell short.

If it's ultimately all Hashem, then in reality, what difference does it make if we think we can or can't do it, if we don't know the language well enough, or our mind is not strong enough to grasp the subject? As the Yiddish saying goes, "When Hashem wants it to be so, a broom can shoot bullets." I once shared this point at an event hosted by the Belzer Chassidus and a participant came to me and said that he once heard in the name of the late Belzer Rebbe *zt"l* that *"Ich ken yah, ich ken nisht, zennen beider kefirah."* (I can, I can't, they are both heresy.) That's why Rebbes are great. It took me an entire paragraph to say what the Belzer Rebbe said in nine words.

He was able — just not able enough on his own

If you look at the reasons that the *Chovos HaLevavos* gives for thinking, "I can't," the underlying message is that he felt he wasn't gifted enough in the required areas. This is important to note, because clearly if someone is completely lacking a given talent, he is likely meant to focus his efforts elsewhere. Those who aren't artistic won't be artists and those who find numbers frightening best not try to master finance. As we will discuss later, the more common issue is that we often think that we know what constitutes being "good enough" at something, and also believe we have a realistic assessment of our own inherent capabilities. Often we do not.

☙ Why Moshe Had a Speech Impediment

The Ran (*Derashos* 3) shares a powerful explanation to when Hashem instructs Moshe to go to Pharaoh. Moshe Rabbeinu reminds Hashem several times that he is speech impaired, in the hopes that Hashem will either heal him or choose to send a more capable emissary to Pharaoh. As a child, I would always think, "Please, Hashem, heal him. He deserves it. He's Moshe Rabbeinu!!"

Indeed, the Ran asks why Hashem didn't simply heal Moshe Rabbeinu. His answer is profound and should give great strength to anyone who thinks he isn't up to a task and therefore won't succeed. The Ran explains that if Moshe would have stood before Pharaoh and delivered a beautifully enunciated speech, then the Jews would have said, "Wow, Moshe can really get things done! Two hundred and ten years of slavery and it turns out that all we ever really needed was an eloquent orator." Moshe was given a speech impediment so that it would be obvious that liberation was undeniably brought about through the Will of Hashem and not the eloquence of Moshe. The message, says the Ran, is **"that the Jewish people should know that natural obstacles/ shortcomings are not obstacles to Hakadosh Baruch Hu."**

The Sfas Emes adds that not only are there no natural obstacles to Hashem, but in fact, everything He does is miraculous. The Sfas Emes writes that the birth of any child is an open miracle, and that life begins in this way to remind us that our entire lives will be experienced in the same manner. We are each capable of accomplishments that are above nature.

We all know people that have excelled despite the world's predictions to the contrary. With Hashem's help a person can overcome their perceived limitations. An important aspect of *bitachon* is that we learn to put our self-estimation calculators away — the ones we use to calculate odds of success — and throw away the measuring tape we use to gauge ourselves when approaching a task.

History books are replete with people who succeeded against all odds and people who had everything going for them yet didn't succeed. Calculating the odds of success, while sometimes an appropriate part of normal *hishtadlus*, can limit our potential when the assessment becomes the stop sign preventing us from stepping up to a challenge.

The definition of confidence, according to the Torah, is not our trust in the might of our hands, intelligence, or creativity. It is living with the mindset that **"My Father in heaven can do anything. I am His child and therefore anything is possible."** While we are each endowed with unique capabilities and talents, confidence that is built on the self can always be shaken whereas confidence built on the omnipotent Creator is unshakable. It's the difference between anchoring oneself to the finite versus the infinite.

Confidence can alter reality

I once lectured to a group in Israel on this topic and several months later received the following email, translated from Hebrew.

> *Dear Reb Naftali,*
>
> *I attended your lecture in Belz several months ago and wanted to thank you for the impact your words had on my life. I am a sofer by profession, 41 years old, and years ago I believed that my safrus was as good as it would ever get. After hearing you speak and internalizing your words, something almost miraculous occurred — my skills improved significantly. So much so, that today, I am able to charge 35% more for the tefillin and mezuzos I write, and can now support my family with greater dignity.*

I was astounded by his words at the time. Can a person's handwriting actually improve based on his perspective? In retrospect, I shouldn't have been surprised at all. Our perspective often creates our reality. From the human perspective, improving one's script writing at the age of 41 may seem like an insurmountable task, but Hashem can do anything. Our challenge is to believe in Hashem's assistance, and in doing so, we are able to transcend our own perceived limitations.

What does *hishtadlus* mean?

If Hashem is the cause of everything, we may wonder how our *hishtadlus*, our input, factors in. I once heard a wonderfully insightful *shiur* from Rav Shlomo Brevda *zt"l* on the *pasuk* in *Mishlei (3:5)*, "Trust in Hashem with all of your heart, and upon your intelligence do not rely." The Vilna Gaon expounds, "Do not rely on it even as a walking stick." A person who walks with a cane primarily relies on his feet and uses the cane as a backup. We are meant to rely completely on Hashem and not at all on our intellect, not even as a backup. Does that mean that we don't prepare for that big interview or learn all of the facts before delivering a presentation? Of course not; we are obligated to do our part. What, then, is the correct approach and mindset?

Rav Brevda provides an illustration through the story in *Tanach* when David HaMelech was captured by the Philistines, who quickly realized that they had captured the man responsible for the deaths of tens of thousands of their soldiers. Accordingly, they fully intended to kill him. As David sat in prison, he thought of a brilliant idea. He realized that the king had an insane wife and child and would therefore take pity on someone who had gone mad. Therefore, he feigned insanity. He spoke complete nonsense and drooled as he stood before Avimelech, the king. Avimelech then turned to his advisors and proclaimed, "Do I lack lunatics in my kingdom?" and instructed that David be expelled from his country. The ploy worked and David's life was spared.

Brilliant! What an *einfal* (idea)! It actually worked!

Lest you think that David spent even a moment patting himself on the back, he quickly took his quill and wrote the magnificent chapter (*Tehillim* 34) that we recite every Shabbos morning: "*L'Dovid beshanoso es t'amo lifnei Avimelech vayigarsheihu vayeilech* — To David, when he pretended to be insane before Avimelech, who drove him away. It is a chapter replete with *emunah* and *bitachon,* because while David may have conceived of and carried out the plan, he knew where great ideas originate, and that success is 100 percent from Hakadosh Baruch Hu. The plan could have just as easily backfired, or Avimelech could have seen through the ruse, or the idea might never have entered Dovid's mind. This is what the Vilna Gaon means when he adjures us not to rely on our intellect even as a cane. We must use our intellect to its fullest capacity, but we may not ascribe any credit or results to it. On the flip side, had the plan failed, David would never have blamed himself either. He knew that Hashem runs the world, not him.

In summation, for those who think that they can and for those who think they can't, the truth remains the same — "you" can't, but Hashem can, and for that reason alone, you can. *Hishtadlus* means doing what we are meant to do without relying on a positive or negative self-evaluation to calculate the odds of success. We should always feel empowered knowing that we are being guided and assisted by the Master of the Universe, and our limitations are therefore of zero consequence.

Rabbeinu Bachya therefore wasn't wrong; no one was up to the task of penning *Chovos HaLevavos,* and his limitations were not imagined. However, given the importance of and the need for the *sefer*, Hashem provided Heavenly assistance to Rabbeinu Bachya once he shook off his thoughts of inadequacy, stepped up to the task, and attemped to write it. In fact, this is how Rashi was able to write his commentary using *Ruach Hakodesh*. Do you think that Rashi thought to himself, "Wow, seems this task requires nothing less than *Ruach Hakodesh* and what a coincidence, I just happen to have it." Of course not! Rashi knew that the task called for skills that were beyond human, yet he also realized that Hashem would give them to him if he undertook the task in earnest and did his very best.

We will close with a lesson taught by the Ran (Derashos 10) who explains the aforementioned *possuk,* "Then you shall remember Hashem, your G-d, that it was He Who gave you the strength to create wealth..."

> *You will note that the Torah does not state "remember Hashem Who gave you wealth" for if it did it would negate the potential that is entrusted with the person which is meant to serve as a conduit to the creation of wealth. This would be incorrect.*

The Ran is stressing that while Hashem gives us the strength to succeed, and we must always recognize that without Heavenly assistance success would never be possible, we must take the initiative and act. *Hishtadlus* reflects our partnership in creation. It is our responsibility to put in effort to maximize the many gifts we are blessed to receive.

Stepping into greatness

I was recently asked to address a community abroad that had lost most of their *Parnessei Hador* — supporters of their community — because these wealthy individuals had relocated to other countries. Needless to say, there was a huge degree of despair in the room, and many were contemplating moving themselves. I explained to those present that the *Chovos HaLevavos* says that Hakadosh Baruch Hu constructed the world so that there are always givers and receivers: *Olam chesed yibaneh*. This holds true in every community and therefore, I posited, it must hold true for this one. The proof was in the way in which the community had functioned throughout the generations until the present time. Because the community was now lacking givers, many of those sitting in the audience would now need to shed their fears of failure, inhibitions, and outright laziness and step up to become the pipeline of abundance for the rest of the community.

Hakadosh Baruch Hu wants to bring a flow of goodness into the world and wants to do it in a way that His hand in it will be apparent. Therefore, He seeks volunteers who believe in Him. It's as if a huge waterfall is hovering just above, and the ones who step into the role and become vessels will serve to channel that abundance to the rest of the community. I urged the people in that room, "If you think you aren't up to the job, good! Just go ahead and do it and always keep in mind why Moshe had a speech impediment. You can be the next person about whom people proclaim, 'If he can succeed then Hashem MUST be running the world because who would have ever thought THAT GUY would ever be THAT successful.'"

We will now consider the second option…

2. He was underestimating himself

Rabbeinu Bachya was indeed up to the task and his self-evaluation was biased at that moment in time, causing him to underestimate his own capabilities. Relating back to the toothpaste incident, there was a lot more in him than he knew existed.

When I once presented this possibility at a conference for educators, someone came to me after my lecture, quite upset, and said, "Are you implying that Rabbeinu Bachya lacked self-esteem? We are not allowed to even think that." To this I responded, "I didn't say anything of the sort. I am merely presenting the possibility that Rabbeinu Bachya himself is telling us that he underestimated himself, and if that is so, he did it to give *chizuk* and direction to all future generations of Jews who will face the identical issue in their own lives, namely a lack of confidence in a given area. They will now be able to point to this *sefer* and say, "Wow, this great *tzaddik* was human just like me. He expressed doubts regarding his own capabilities and look at what he went on to achieve. I am NORMAL! B"H!"

This is precisely why Rabeinu Bachya wrote the introduction to the *sefer*: to teach a person how to research and analyze a subject before any great undertaking is decided upon and then to prepare himself to battle the voice of "I can't" that will surely surface and dissuade him from the decision. In a later chapter we will explain where this voice of "I can't" comes from and how to battle it.

In summation, whether the cause for Rabbeinu Bachya's hesitation was the first or second reason, or both, he concludes by stating that he ultimately decided that his job was to do the very best he could and then rely upon Hakadosh Baruch Hu to help and guide him to perform the task. Before he reaches that conclusion, however, he goes on to teach us many more profound lessons that we will now explore.

23

Cold Feet

Rabbeinu Bachya continues…

And when I decided to remove this heavy burden from myself and refrain from writing this sefer, I questioned myself and suspected that I was choosing the path of tranquility and certainty. I was afraid that abandoning my original intention was due to a will rooted in self-gratification and it was this will that swayed me toward the path of rest and tranquility and provided the push for me to abandon my plan and to sit among the lazy instead.

Rabbeinu Bachya, in revealing his inner struggle, teaches us several profound lessons.

At the age of 19, as a descendant of Chassidic lineage who was learning in a Litvish yeshivah, I faced a dilemma. Litvish boys tend to marry at a later age. If I followed the path taken by my yeshivah friends, I would be heading, at the age of 20, to learn in Eretz Yisrael for two years that upcoming Elul zman. Subsequently, I would return to the US at the age of 22 ½, or 23 to begin shidduchim. I decided to ask my father a"h, for permission to finish the year and then head to Eretz Yisrael. He responded, "You may go to Eretz Yisrael whenever you think best, but your birthday is on Pesach, and I want you home by the Pesach when you turn 22 to begin shidduchim.

Here was my dilemma: If I waited until Elul to leave for Eretz Yisrael, then I would only be able to learn in Brisk for a year and a half. If I left five months sooner, right after Pesach, I could be there the full two years, but I would be going all alone. My friends wouldn't arrive until Elul. I gave the matter much thought and decided that leaving after Pesach was the right thing to do.

I went to speak to my Rosh HaYeshivah, Harav Shlomo Feivel Schustal, shlit'a, and explained my reasoning to him. He wholeheartedly gave me permission to leave early and assured me that he would help me get into Brisk. As Pesach approached, I began to second-guess my decision. I worried that if I went all alone, I would have a hard time finding chavrusos, and an apartment, and besides, I was learning so well where I was. Why rock the boat?

And so, back to my Rosh HaYeshivah I went to inform him of my change of plans. After I had delivered what I thought was a pretty convincing argument to stay, even throwing in the point of how much I was gaining from his shiur, he flashed his warm and radiant smile and shared with me these amazingly insightful words. "Naftali, when you came to me a few months ago, I was speaking to your head and I liked what it had to say. Now, I am speaking to your feet and I don't like what they have to say."

Before I could even ask, "Rebbe, my feet?" he continued. "You have a case of cold feet. I don't know about you, but I always make it my business to listen to my head and never to my feet." Needless to say, my plane tickets were booked that very same day and the decision turned out to be the right one.

Rabbeinu Bachya realized that his thought to abandon his plan to write the *sefer* was rooted in cold feet and potential laziness. Therefore, as we will learn, he quickly ignored it.

What separates the successful from the unsuccessful is the ability to identify the motivation behind every thought to act or not to act. Like detectives, we need to learn to pick up and identify clues, because the truth is always right there if we know where to look.

The question is, How did Rabbeinu Bachya know that his decision was rooted in fear and laziness and not the result of an honest self-assessment? How did my Rosh HaYeshivah know that my second decision was the result of cold feet while my first decision was rooted in sound judgment? How can we each know which ideas are coming from the head and which from the feet? Think about how much better and more productive life would be if there was a way to know.

1. Your first reaction

Put yourself in the shoes of Rabbeinu Bachya. You have spent several months seeking a *sefer* on your desired topic in the hopes that it had already been written. When you realized that it didn't exist, you performed extensive research to ascertain the need for the *sefer*. You finally came to the realization that there was a clear and present need for the *sefer*, that it hadn't yet been written by anyone, and that it was therefore imperative that you undertake to write it. Just as you are about to begin the crucial task at hand, the thought that, "I am not the right person for the job," enters your mind. Before you undertake this monumental task, you decide to quit lest you engage in an exercise in futility.

What would you expect your very first feeling to be upon reaching the decision to quit? Let's try multiple choice:

1. Utter disappointment
2. Sheer physical relief (as in PHEW! someone just untied all those knots that were in my stomach!)
3. A deep feeling of sadness
4. A feeling of emotional release (*B'H*, I am free to stay in my comfort zone)

Would it be 1 and 3, or 2 and 4?

If the answer is 2 and 4 then you can be 100% certain that you just had a conversation with your feet. The reason is that when a person has a higher will that cannot be brought to completion, he feels a sense of deep disappointment. The relief that a person feels upon abandoning a worthy endeavor is the result of choosing the self-serving will over the higher-purpose will. The lower will provides that feeling of relief and contentment because it fears hard work and potential failure above all else.

In my story, without question, the first decision was one that thrust me into a self-imposed challenge for the sake of personal growth. The second decision was an attempt to alleviate that challenge because as I got closer to it, I wanted to "chicken out." My Rosh HaYeshivah saw that I wasn't distressed enough by the fact that I would not realize my aspiration to spend two full years in Brisk, because at that moment, my need for safety and comfort overshadowed the higher goal.

2. It's rarely all or nothing

Abandoning anything completely is usually a sign of laziness or fear. No one should completely negate a decision that was reached after much thought and research without applying an equal amount of thought and contemplation to the possibility that there really might be a way forward, or at least a compromise. As you contemplate walking away from something worthwhile that you either decided upon or have already embarked upon, ask yourself,

- Was I in my right mind when I first made the decision to proceed? If so, then what has fundamentally changed?
- Must the plan be completely abandoned? Is there perhaps a solution? A compromise?

At times, the right answer is to discuss the matter with a wise person who isn't biased as you may be at that moment. If a person is sufficiently invested and motivated to see something come to fruition, he drops his ego and seeks answers wherever they can be found. Let's think about what ideas a wise person might have shared with Rabbeinu Bachya. What ideas would have addressed his concerns regarding his inability to write the *sefer*?

- Write the *sefer* in Hebrew and allow someone else to translate it to Arabic.
- Work with a partner who will edit the information and organize it in a way that you feel you are incapable of achieving.

- Since there was nothing of the kind written at that time, even something less perfect would have a tremendous impact on Klal Yisrael, so go ahead and do the best that you can. This is what he ultimately decided to do.

It is fascinating that he proceeds to author a revolutionary *sefer* without needing any of the solutions or compromises listed above. When he realized the source of his negative thoughts, he completely dismissed them and proceeded as though these limitations never existed.

Rabbeinu Bachya may have quickly realized that he wasn't crushed enough by his decision to abandon his plan to author the *sefer*. Perhaps he felt a bit too relieved by the prospect of following the comfortable route. He may have realized that at the very moment he reached the decision to quit, he no longer felt motivated to seek a solution or a compromise of any sort. And so, he goes on to teach us the crucial lesson: "NEVER LISTEN TO YOUR FEET!"

You will need a high degree of self-awareness and integrity if you are going to identify the true motivation behind your decision to quit anything worthwhile. We have a strong tendency to convince ourselves that our choice to quit something is a rational one. The place to identify our true motives is in our emotions, because emotions are often the source.

Are you thinking of abandoning or saying no to a worthwhile undertaking?

Was that relief you just felt? If so, why?

Why are you no longer putting any thought into finding a solution?

Where did your original motivation and excitement for the project go?

If you remember to ask yourself these questions and answer them honestly, you can cut through the clouds of confusion that surround your decision-making and see the right path clearly laid out before you.

24
Laziness

Rabbeinu Bachya admitted that he almost chose to "sit among the lazy" and determined that it was laziness that drove his thought to abandon his plan to write his *sefer*.

Laziness is an extremely detrimental *middah* which can cause untold hardship to people entrapped by it and to those who depend on them. Bills can pile up unpaid, laundry can sit undone, and a person's life can literally fall apart when he fails to exert himself and take responsibility for his life.

To someone who isn't afflicted with this tendency, it can seem utterly absurd and, of course, irresponsible: "The man's world is literally falling apart, his house is heading toward foreclosure and he fails to do what it takes to find a job. How can he be so lazy and negligent?" Often the subject of this indictment is asking himself those very same questions. He would argue that if he only knew of a solution, he'd gladly change his ways. I have met many people, good people, who struggle with this issue. Sadly, the people who care about them most are often the ones who must drag them to seek advice, because the lazy person is unmotivated to do even that.

The *Tanya* explains human laziness as a product of one of the four elements of which we are made — earth, wind, fire, and water. Earth has no power to move on its own, unlike the other three elements which move, rise, and flow with vitality. In the words of the *Mesillas Yesharim*, Chapter 6:

> *Now realize that the natural tendency of man is to be extremely sluggish for the earthiness of physicality is dense and this is why man does not desire exertion or work. One who wishes to merit to properly serve the Creator, blessed is He, must overcome his nature, strengthen himself, and be diligent. For if he leaves himself to his sluggishness it is certain that he will not succeed.*

Before you completely despair, or run out and sign up for earth removal surgery, remember that you are comprised of the other three elements as well, and that a lot of good comes from earth. Almost nothing would grow without earth. Furthermore, if you had it removed you would have nothing to keep you grounded. The *Sifsei Chaim* points out that Adam is named for the element of earth within him, even though "*Midaber*" — one who speaks — might have seemed a more fitting name. He quotes Rav Shamshon Raphael Hirsch who explains that Adam also means *adameh l'Elyon*, "likened to the Above," because when we elevate the earthiness in ourselves, we merit to rise above all of creation.

While the outward expression of laziness includes sluggishness, procrastination, or decision abandonment, the underlying causes are not necessarily the same for all people. The cause could be self-indulgence, fear, uncertainty, or confusion. It's important that we identify which of these ails us, because the remedy is somewhat different depending on the root cause. We will now examine each.

Laziness Rooted in Self-Indulgence

Let's face it, work is just plain demanding. Exertion takes energy and doing nothing at all is much more comfortable. While some people are blessed with boundless energy, many find relaxation to be a more natural and enjoyable state of being. The Maharal (*Nesivos HaZerizus*, Ch. 2) states that laziness is the result of a person's physical body and nature overruling his soul and thereby nullifying the soul's purpose. The soul came into the world to accomplish; it knows how precious time is and being of a spiritual make-up is not subject to the heaviness of the body. Chazal teach that the more physical something is, the denser it is. The heavy body wants to relax; because the body erroneously calculates that doing nothing is in its best interests, it blocks the will of the lighter soul.

As we explained in an earlier chapter, a higher will needs to pass through the lower seven *Sefiros* — also known as *middos* — on its path to *Malchus* and completion. When *Ratzon* — will — passes through all seven *middos* without hesitation and blockage — and is even energized and enhanced by the lower *Sefiros* — then the person is in a state of *zerizus*, alacrity. We have all experienced this at times in our lives when we've gone from initial will to action in the blink of an eye. When Avraham Avinu saw the angels before him, he was off and running without the slightest hesitation, despite that fact that it was three days after his *bris milah*. Sometimes, however, events don't flow as they should and higher will, even when it begins with great promise and energy, hits a roadblock along the way.

◈ *Chesed*

The first of the lower seven *middos* is called *chesed*. This is a word that usually brings to mind an extremely positive connotation, because *chesed*, in its healthy state, means expansion of self — the ability to project outside of oneself, giving, sharing, and doing for others. When higher will passes into a healthy *middah* of *chesed*, it is energized with enthusiasm and excitement. *Chesed* creates an emotional connection to an idea and generates the euphoric feelings that we associate with doing things for others.

However, *chesed* can turn the wrong way. Chazal discuss a negative force that is present in creation, which is called a *klippah* — a husk — that can adhere to a *middah* and conceal the spark of spirituality in it to various degrees, depending on the density of the *klippah*. In the *Sefer Tanya*, a *klippah* is defined as a spiritual shell that conceals G-dliness. [16]

16 In every *middah* there lies the potential for both a positive and a negative expression. As an example, Avraham represents the epitome of the *middah* of

One manifestation of a *klippah* is that it can cause a given *middah* to be directed completely in the wrong direction; for example, *chesed* can be directed inward instead of outward. Here the *klippah* literally traps the *middah* and causes it to be directed back toward the person himself. We can visualize a *klippah* as a thick black sock covering an illuminated light bulb. Not only will the light not shine outward but the heat of the bulb will build up, perhaps causing the bulb to burst. In the case of a *klippah* of *chesed,* the person is expansive and kind, but in an egotistical way: selfish, narcissistic, self-pitying, and lazy. He does a great deal of *chesed,* but his primary beneficiary is himself. This, as we know, isn't kindness to anyone at all, because such a person is ultimately leading himself down a road of self-destruction.

The other implication of a *klippah* is that it blocks out rational thoughts that would otherwise serve to rectify the *middah.* The higher will needs *chesed* to energize and expand its ideas. *Chachmah* and *binah,* the *middos* that are the root of rational thoughts, are like the wise and discerning parents who must channel *chesed's* impulses outwardly toward others, and warn it against the destructive nature of laziness and self-pity. However, the *klippah* makes *chesed* impervious to these messages. As a result, the person operating within this *klippah* can't grasp the truth, and is instead content leaving matters as is, within his comfort zone. *Chachmah* and *binah* have no more chance of getting through to *chesed* than a parent trying to get through to a child who has put in a pair of earplugs and locked himself in the closet.

Laziness, rooted in self-gratification or indulgence, is often a manifestation of the *klippah* of *chesed,* and knowing this will help us find the cure. The positive side of this condition is that if there is a closed shell, there is a seed inside. Likewise, a person who finds a strong *klippah* of *chesed* within himself can be certain that there is a

---

chesed while the *sefarim* tell us that the *klippah* of *chesed* gave birth to Yishmael, who epitomized promiscuity. It is for this reason that the Torah states, when discussing an immoral relationship between a man and his sister, *"chesed hu (Vayikra 20:17)."* The *middah* of *chesed* can result in both positive and perverted expansion. Yitzchak represents the *middah* of *gevurah,* restraint — strength, through his vigilance and fear of Hashem, while Eisav was born from the *klippah* of *gevurah* which is the root of anger and murder.

seed of lofty *chesed* hidden inside, waiting to be revealed. Cracking open the shell of laziness will unleash a torrent of positive expansion, and it's all right there beneath the surface, buried in the earth of which we are comprised.

⁂ Laziness Rooted in Fear of Failure

There's an expression, "If you don't try then you can't fail." Many people don't even realize that the reason that they are "so lazy" is they are afraid of failure, because fear is often buried very deep inside of us.

Here are the next words of Rabbeinu Bachya:

> *And I knew that many intellectual undertakings, which were within the person's reach to achieve, were lost due to fear that prevented them from attempting them lest they fail to actualize them. And that many deficiencies in the actualization of a person and their character traits are the result of this fear.*

Fear of failure: Rabbeinu Bachya spells it out for us, in black and white. He lets us know that there is nothing more debilitating than this self-destructive tendency. People controlled by their fears bring all sorts of failure upon themselves rather than risking the failure that trying might engender. They underearn, underachieve, dare not try new things and settle for mediocrity or less in many areas of their lives in order to play it safe. All of us are sometimes inclined to stay in our warm and cozy comfort zones, where there are no risks and therefore there is no growth, rather than expose ourselves to the taste of disappointment.

The fear of failure extinguishes any will that passes through it. Unlike indulgence, which stems from the *klippah* of *chesed,* this manifestation of laziness stems from the *klippah* of *gevurah.*

Our forefather Yitzchak epitomized the *middah* of *gevurah,* which is a healthy fear, awe, restraint, vigilance, and caution that engulfs and permeates a person who internalizes the fact that he is in the presence of the Master of the Universe. The fear of losing that relationship motivates him to restrain his natural tendencies and to act with caution and precision. He is protecting an extremely valuable asset at all costs. The *Chovos HaLevavos* teaches (*Shaar Ahavas Hashem*) that the outcome of this fear is that Hashem infuses us with a deep sense of love, so that what begins as restraint leads to us drawing closer to Him. This is the picture of healthy fear.

Just as with *chesed*, a *klippah* over *gevurah* turns this *middah* inward, and instead of fearing Hashem, we fear loss of self or ego. We choose to abandon a plan not out of self-indulgence, but rather because we don't want to risk a blow to our egos by trying and possibly failing. We fear what others will think of us and what we will think of ourselves when it becomes clear that we couldn't succeed even though we tried. We fear the shame that is associated with that failure. Ironically, through our inaction, we are actually assuring that a greater loss of self will take place eventually, when we experience the ultimate failure — the failure to achieve and live up to our potential, responsibilities, and life's mission.

Interestingly, since in this case the person's will is allowed to pass through *chesed* without blockage, the person is sometimes quite excited by an idea before he eventually abandons it out of fear. The self-indulgent person never allows himself to become enthusiastic because he knows all too well that this idea will translate into too much work, whereas for the fearful, work isn't what is frightening him; failure is.

From this perspective we can understand why words like, "Stop being so lazy!" and "What are you so afraid of?" often have no effect at all. This is because the person already knows that he ought to get up and do something, and that his fears are unfounded, but that information doesn't penetrate his lower self where the impasse is taking place.

◆§ Uncertainty and Confusion That Lead to Hesitation and Procrastination

We sometimes procrastinate because we honestly don't know which way to proceed. This is called "decision-paralysis." It may occur when we lack information or when we have gathered too much information, and now find ourselves overwhelmed and utterly confused. If there is no laziness present and uncertainty is the true underlying cause, then the remedy is to have extra *kavannah* during the blessing of *Atah chonen l'Adam daas* and/or to find someone who can help you process the information and make a proper decision.

True uncertainty, however, is sometimes not the underlying reason. Rather, laziness is. We hardly ever admit to ourselves, and certainly never to others, that we are doing nothing because we are self-indulgent or petrified of failure. We rarely admit that we are stalling and procrastinating because we are lazy and instead, we use a very noble term to describe our tendency to postpone matters. We say, "I am merely being '**cautious**' or 'waiting for the right time.'" Caution — *zehirus* — is such a noble trait; what can possibly be wrong with that?

Well, Rabbeinu Bachya tells us...

> *And I remembered the saying that "part of being cautious is not being too cautious." I told myself, that if everyone who intended to perform some good act, or to provide guidance to others regarding the path of righteousness and correctness, would stand by and wait until perfect conditions were present and he reached the depths of understanding and found the purest language, then not a word would have been spoken by man since the prophets, whom Hashem had chosen as His messengers.*

Sometimes laziness manifests itself as overthinking, overanalyzing, doing too much research or waiting for perfect conditions to present themselves before stepping out of our front door. We procrastinate by spending too much time gathering data, thinking, analyzing, speaking to a million people... because we are afraid to make a decision or don't want to begin the work at hand.

Here are some examples.

- Those who spend their entire lives coming up with great ideas and executing none of them because they never reach a final decision on how best to proceed.
- Those who will not begin a project until every variable that lessens the likelihood of failure is perfectly lined up.
- Those who paralyze themselves with confusion by asking too many people what they think about any given idea.

- An older man or woman who is still looking for a perfect mate lest he or she marry the wrong person.

These are examples of people who believe that they are embracing caution and circumspection, because it is the prudent and responsible thing to do. They do not realize that their "caution" is simply an expression of laziness, rooted in fear of failure, self-indulgence, or both.

> *I once worked with an older salesman who would often come into the office and do absolutely nothing for much or all of the day. He would just sit there immobile, staring at the phone as if in a trance. I would sometimes ask him, "Phil, is everything OK? No sales calls today?"*
>
> *He would respond, "I have been in sales a very long time and I have learned many tricks that increase the probability of my success (choose one):*

- *NEVER EVER make calls on Monday, people don't like being bothered on Monday.*
- *Friday is definitely out — their minds are already on the weekend.*
- *Don't even think about calling if it's raining outside. That puts people in a bad mood. (Never mind that many of his prospects were in California!)*
- *Never call people first thing in the morning; before lunch; right after lunch; at the end of the day; when there is bad news; when the stock market is down."*

> *After writing down all of Phil's "wisdom," I soon realized that this left me only a few hours a week to make sales calls and that, even then, I had to first check the weather, news channels, and stock market before dialing! I also realized why, after so many years in the business, my co-worker really hadn't found much success in sales.*
>
> *I decided that since no time was a good time to make sales calls, any time was as good as any other. You wouldn't be surprised to learn that some of my best sales calls were made when I got the guy on the phone on a rainy Monday while he was chewing on a pastrami sandwich or on a Friday when he*

had his golf clubs already in hand, with one foot out the door for the weekend.

The lesson is that there is no good time to make sales calls if excuses are what you are seeking, and there is no bad time if you are truly looking to succeed.

☙ Confirmation Bias

Laziness can sometimes manifest itself in what is known in behavioral psychology as confirmation bias. This means that when we are contemplating a decision, we only allow information that supports our true beliefs and desires to penetrate our minds; meanwhile, we render ourselves impervious to information that counters our bias. With this mindset, the person who prefers not to act will be pulled toward voices of pessimism and negativity and will judge words of optimism as unrealistic. He only hears what his lower self wants to hear. "After all, if so-and-so says that I am sure to fail, then it would be utterly silly to go forward. Right?"

Take an idea, any idea, and you will find someone who will say that it will work and someone that it will not work. If you are blinded by the desire to follow through on that idea no matter what the drawbacks, you will only listen to those with a rosy, even if unrealistic, outlook. Conversely, if you want to stay on the couch and avoid the challenge, you'll adapt any excuse you can find to support your inaction. Someone who seeks the truth weighs both opinions carefully; he isn't stopped in his tracks by a lack of unanimity. The ability to discern excuses from legitimate reasons to abandon an idea is a skill-set that distinguishes the highly motivated and successful from those who underachieve.

Another aspect of confirmation bias is resistance to rethinking a plan when new information becomes available. Because switching tracks means expending more thought and effort, the lazy person sticks with the path already chosen. He therefore only accepts input that supports that path.

In summary: We discussed several underlying causes for laziness, a highly detrimental trait. Whatever the cause, the expressions are similar — sluggishness, decision paralyses, or the abandonment of a decision. Different underlying causes produce different nuances. One person may get excited about an idea and one may not. One may gather lots of data to analyze and one may not even allow an idea to "go into one ear." Uncovering the underlying cause of laziness is not all that difficult because the clues are usually hiding in plain sight. What to do about it will take a bit more work and we will discuss that in the next chapter.

25

Embracing Alacrity

Now that we have a deeper understanding of laziness and its detriments, we are motivated to combat it. Winning this battle turns a person's life around in positive ways and brings unimaginable fulfillment and joy. If laziness is a trait you have to contend with, as many of us do in different areas, overcoming it may very well be key to achieving the purpose for which you were put on this world.

In this chapter, I will share nine strategies to bring more *zerizus*, alacrity, into your life.

☙ 1. Awareness

The first step to self-improvement is to become aware of the underlying cause of your laziness, procrastination, or sluggishness. We want to see our enemy for what it is and then greatly reduce our tolerance toward this trait that lays the groundwork for a lifetime of failed endeavors. We can utilize a thinking and writing exercise to uncover what is holding us back and then to develop a plan to improve. If after this exercise you are still unable to uncover the cause, you would surely benefit from speaking matters over with someone wise.

As I wrote this chapter, I received a call from a young man who shared with me that two years ago, he was jobless and $100,000 in debt. Today, he has paid back every penny and expects to earn $250,000 selling real estate. What changed? After hearing a lecture, he spent quality time in deep introspection and realized that fear of failure was keeping him on the sidelines in a state of mental paralysis. He picked himself up and began relentlessly knocking on doors. Once he saw his fear for what it was, he was utterly repulsed by it. Today he is passionate regarding activity.

Oftentimes awareness is all we need.

⧼§ 2. Redirecting Our *Middos*

Keeping in mind what we learned in the previous chapters, we can each develop a plan to remedy the underlying cause of our laziness. We can do this by directing the *middah* toward its intended purpose, slowly peeling away the *klippah* that encases it. For someone who tends to be self-indulgent, embarking on a regimen of acts of kindness and volunteer work can be an effective way to get off the couch and experience the joys and fulfillment that outwardly expressed *chesed* brings.

For a person mired in fear of failure, the remedy is to redirect that fear toward Hakadosh Baruch Hu by working to develop greater *yiras Shamayim* and *bitachon*. When we are all alone in a room, we may fear spiders, but when we are standing in the King's inner chamber facing His Majesty himself, we will not even notice a daddy long-legs crawling up our arm. We are designed to fear the Almighty and feel awe in His presence. If we don't utilize the *middah* of *gevurah* that way, we will fear spiders, loss of ego, failure, and all sorts of other circumstances that are ultimately of no eternal value. We are also meant to use *gevurah* to restrain our impulses and perfect our adherence to *mitzvos*. The more we fear slipping in our *ruchnius,* the less we will fear failing in our *gashmius*.

How do we know that a *klippah* is obstructing our progress in life? The sign is that we've thought, analyzed, pinpointed the cause and the symptoms of our laziness, but still cannot rally the strength to change. Once we are able to put the *middah* of *gevurah* to good use, the results prove astounding.

◆ 3. No More Excuses

The *Mesillas Yesharim* (Ch. 6) writes that many times we are fully aware of our obligations and yet do nothing, due to a powerful laziness that overcomes us. What makes laziness so insidious is that a person often comes up with all kinds of logical arguments to justify it: "... and he does not see that these arguments do not come from his logical thought; rather they stem from his laziness, which overcomes his rational thinking."

Let's stop and think about some of our own excuses that may be masking laziness:

- Other aren't doing it.
- What's the point? It won't change anything.
- I am overworked as it is.
- I am satisfied with the status quo.
- I can't do more.
- I am not good at that.
- It's too late for me.

The fact is that as long as we are making excuses for ourselves, life won't improve. If you seek growth, it is imperative that you step away from your fabricated reality and see yourself through the lens of pure *emes* — truth — and ask yourself, "Why am I not moving forward as much as I can? Am I lazy? Afraid to fail?" When we shed the light of *Daas* onto the issue we will have taken a giant leap forward.

◆ 4. Living With a Sense of Urgency

"Why do today what you can put off until tomorrow?"

That saying may sound silly, but deep inside, most of us adhere to this motto in regard to some area of life. We know we are procrastinating, but we tell ourselves that some day we will have time to make things right.

The Piaseczna Rebbe starkly reminds us that we are not guaranteed a tomorrow and urges us to take full advantage of today. While no one wants to think about their last day on this world, as we discussed in the chapter on *yishuv hadaas*, there can be great benefits to living each day of life to the fullest and not taking time for granted. When laziness and procrastination are causing us to postpone important matters, we can ask ourselves, "What if I knew that I won't...

...have as much time as I would like to make something of myself?
...be given another opportunity to finish what I started?
...make things right in the future?
...be able to apologize to the person ever again?
... get another chance to tell them how much they mean to me?
...have another opportunity to perform this mitzvah?"

What would I do differently today?

Rav Nachman of Breslov speaks of the power of the Satan to keep a person in darkness by encouraging him to believe "there will be time later." Only when it's too late does he reveal the truth that, "there wasn't enough time." In the chapter on visualizations, we mentioned that the Piaseczna Rebbe *HY"D* in *Hachsharas Avreichim* provides detailed visualizations that can help a person internalize important concepts. In chapter seven of that *sefer* he shares a visualization of a man who contracts a dreaded illness *R'L*, and follows his thoughts until the moment he closes his eyes for the very last time. Each time I learn this chapter, I am left shaken to the core. It arouses a sense of urgency and appreciation for life that remains with me for quite some time.

The holy Piaseczna Rebbe *HY"D* was known to have lived in a state of elevated *simchah* even during the darkest days of the Holocaust, during which he lifted the spirits of the downtrodden Jews in the Warsaw ghetto. He teaches that living with the awareness that life is short and time is precious spurs stupendous growth and inspires the happiness that comes with living with a sense of mission.

While the Rebbe wrote his visualization for a broad audience, I fully appreciate that readers may be sensitive to the topic of death and therefore only included excerpts in a footnote. I urge you to skip it if it may disturb you.[17]

---

17 "But I have not come to depress you. I do not want to depress you, and you must take care not to get depressed, because depression is very far from the service of Hashem... Only in order to subjugate the spirit of the evil inclination and to arouse the good inclination does the Talmud state, "a person should visualize the day of his death."
A man has grown ill a number of times, but after a day or two, thank G-d, he recovered. But now he doesn't know what is happening, because this time he cannot shake it off... For the past two nights he has been in great pain and was unable to sleep... His heart knows the bitterness of his soul and senses that his end is coming

We can apply this concept to the person who constantly finds himself mired in information-gathering and then indecision. A large part of the

---

and he is completely shocked by the realization. He always knew that he wouldn't live forever, but now that his heart is telling him that his end is near, his whole body shakes. How great is the distance between the knowledge of death and death itself. His sons, daughters, and wife calm him down. "It's nothing, it's nothing. You will get well. You will get out of bed..." His friends come to visit him and they soothe him, bless him, and encourage him. At first, perhaps their words do reassure him, but when his suffering grows worse, his thoughts again return to oppress him. "How pleasant it would be for me to be with you, my children, and my friends, and how bitter it is for me to leave you and go far from you to a dark pit, all alone... Who knows who knows? I only hope that at least you will remember me just as I wish to remember you..."

And in his mind he begins a personal reckoning: Who knows what will be done with his soul? While his body was strong and his drives enticed him, even when he examined his deeds his evil inclination blinded him so that he didn't see his flaws. And if he did see anything wrong, he smoothed it over so that it wouldn't appear so low and evil in his eyes. But now he is close to death *R'L*, and he has no drives and no desires. Now he sees everything as it is: sins, flaws, and in general his days and years spent on foolish, meaningless things.

And even if he occasionally learned Torah, prayed, and performed *mitzvos*, others who saw him then thought that it was all genuine and honest, but he himself knows his thoughts and intentions — whether he was acting for the sake of Heaven or to be thought of well. It is possible that only a small handful of all of his Torah learning and service to Hashem in his entire life was for the sake of Heaven.

What did he do with himself and with his life? Of all his pleasures and joys that he enjoyed in his many days and hours, nothing remains except for a feeling of revulsion and disgust... Oh, how bitter are the pangs of death, and how difficult it is to bear them while he is immersed in feelings of shame and disgust for himself and his entire life. He wishes to curse the day that he was born into such a polluted life and into such bitter sufferings. What did he do with the years of his life? What could he have done with them? How happy he would be if he had done everything in the way of the Torah, of purity and piety. He would have at least worked to improve his character... Who knows what will happen to him? Who knows if Hashem will not, Heaven forbid, cast him away. What can he do? He wishes to tear his flesh, but now nothing can help...

I ended his words early because the remainder is quite frightening and I apologize if reading this sent shivers up and down your spine. Some people make a *cheshbon hanefesh*, an accounting of their life, every day, some wait until Yom Kippur, while others put it off until the very end. Some don't even get the chance to do that. The sooner a person accepts his mortality, the sooner a sense of urgency will set in. Laziness stifles urgency, excuses stifle growth, and a zero-tolerance stance toward laziness and excuses is best embraced starting today. Life is short.

issue is that he feels little urgency to reach a decision because there is no time limit. Limits are sometimes imposed upon us by bosses or circumstances, and that is often a good thing. When none are present, we can each learn to self-impose them. I once advised someone who had the tendency to shop for information without end. The plan we created required that before he embarked on his next project, he must make a list of no more than three people from whom he would seek information, and then choose only one person to whom he would bring all the information he had gathered. He also had a maximum of 30 days to reach his final decision. He himself was surprised by the results. He reached a decision in far fewer than 30 days and did so with an uncluttered and rational mind.

◆§ 5. Become Innately Suspicious of ...Easy Routes and Shortcuts

The *Mesillas Yesharim* cautions us that whenever we have two choices, we should be extremely wary of choosing the easier option, because the underlying motive is often laziness. He encourages us to "examine, probe, and question" before ever choosing the path that is easier.

> *Every leniency requires examination, for although it may be correct and proper, it is more likely that it is the counsel of the evil inclination and his deceptions. Therefore, one must examine the leniency with probing and thorough questions and, if after all this the leniency is warranted, then it is surely good.*

As we learned, our body, the source of laziness, wants something that is easier and more instantly gratifying, while the soul seeks self-sacrifice and delayed gratification. Naturally, we are inclined toward the body's will; the status quo is easier than work. Coming to a state of *daas* will awaken us from the trance into which the lower self can put YOU.

A person may ask himself:

Is this the easier route? If so, can I justify that it is the best way forward?

Do I generally tend to seek shortcuts in life?

If difficulty were a non-factor, would I still choose this route?

If I could be certain that the more difficult path forward would lead to success, would I still choose this route?

Is there something about this undertaking that I am afraid of right now?

... Your First Inclinations

Rav Dessler writes in the name of the Alter of Kelm that when a **person who is prone to laziness** is deliberating about whether and how to proceed in a given matter, **he should try to recall what his first inclination was and do the opposite**, because our initial inclination likely stems from the evil inclination that is buried deep inside of us. Effective decision-making takes time; we weigh options, costs, and benefits and don't act in haste. Because the Satan wants us to act rashly, he speaks up before we have any time to think.

In those areas of our lives where we know that laziness exists, we should learn to question and challenge our initial beliefs and inclinations.

☙ 6. Don't Hesitate

The *Mesillas Yesharim* (Ch. 7) provides two remedies for laziness, one which applies before initiating a deed has begun and one that applies afterward.

> *When an opportunity presents itself or a good idea enters your mind, you should quickly seize the opportunity and perform the deed. With each passing moment the danger grows that an obstacle will arise that will prevent you from performing it. Secondly, once you have begun the deed you should hasten to complete it. This haste should not be like someone who desires to cast a burden off himself; rather it should stem from the concern that you may not merit to complete it.*

As we discussed, urgency is a remedy for laziness. No one is lazy when his house is on fire or a big black pit bull has just run out of an alleyway headed in his direction. We have to learn to create a sense of urgency and act quickly once the decision to act is reached, because hesitation will open the door for distraction, excuses, and rationalization to set in. When we jump into swift action, we are engaging the elements of *ruach* and *eish* — wind and fire — which are within us. These are the sources of zest, enthusiasm, and agility. We must act before our earthiness subdues them.

Closing Our Ears to "His" Arguments

The *Midrash* says that when Yaakov Avinu was about to be buried, Eisav showed up and claimed that the last plot in *Me'aras Hamachpeilah* — the family burial site — belonged to him. A debate ensued. Yaakov's descendants argued that Eisav had sold the rights of the firstborn, and Eisav demanded to see the contract that proved this. Since the contract had been left in Egypt, they sent a member of the tribe of Naftali to run as swiftly as a deer to fetch it. Chushim, the deaf son of Dan, watched the events that were unfolding, understanding only that which he could see. He asked, "What's going on?" When he was told of the issue, he said, "And until the contract is brought my grandfather's body should lie here in utter disgrace?" He then lifted a sword and killed Eisav.

Rav Chaim Shmulevitz asks, What did Chushim see that all of the others missed? Did no one else notice that Yaakov's body was lying in a disgraceful state? The answer is that because Chushim was deaf, he was not privy to the back-and-forth of the debate with Eisav; therefore his resolve was not weakened by the rationalizations that arose in that interaction. Participating in the conversation and "trying to understand" Eisav's point of view, while normally an integral part of effective communication, in this instance served to cloud the brothers' sense of right and wrong. All Chushim saw was Yaakov's remains lying in disgrace, and so he did what needed to be done.

In the *Parashah* of *Bereishis* (3:15), Hakadosh Baruch Hu, the Creator of all, provides us with the secret formula for destroying the Satan's evil plots. It comes in the form of six words: *"Hu yeshufcha rosh v'atah tishufenu akeiv"* — He (Man) will pound your head, and you (snake) will bite his heel. A snake doesn't need to bite a person on the head in order to kill him. A bite on the heel is enough because the venom only needs to enter the body and, with time, it travels to the vital organs and does its damage. The Satan knows better than to come to us with an argument aimed at our head — words that directly counter our beliefs and best interests. He didn't come to Chava and say outright, "Eat from that tree now!" because her response would have been a flat-out "No way!" Furthermore, she would have then been on guard against him, making her suspicious of all of his future arguments. Instead of taking that futile approach, the Satan started out by posing a seeming innocuous question which brought her into a "discussion." He "bit her on the foot" and the poison did the rest.

The remedy, says the Torah, is to step on the Satan's head; nip him in the bud. Don't get into a debate and discussion. Rather, get right to the work at hand and tune him out completely. There is no danger as great as the danger of hesitation and procrastination, says the *Mesillas Yesharim*, because it opens the door for "him" to enter.

You may be wondering at this point whether this recommendation encourages people to respond impulsively. How can acting without thought and planning be rooted in Torah wisdom? It isn't! We should rarely go into anything worthwhile blindly. We are aiming always to achieve a healthy balance between deliberation and alacrity. The *Mesillas Yesharim* is referring to the point in time that comes after we have already thought, planned, and concluded that an idea has merit. At this point, we are only deciding when to proceed. It's that time — between conclusion and action — that is fraught with danger.

☙ 7. Engage Your Heart

We have already discussed the power of visualization. Now we will demonstrate how it can prove a highly effective tool in combating laziness.

The *pasuk* says (*Mishlei* 24:30-32),

עַל־שְׂדֵה אִישׁ־עָצֵל עָבַרְתִּי וְעַל־כֶּרֶם אָדָם חֲסַר־לֵב: וְהִנֵּה עָלָה כֻלּוֹ קִמְּשֹׂנִים כָּסּוּ פָנָיו חֲרֻלִּים וְגֶדֶר אֲבָנָיו נֶהֱרָסָה: וָאֶחֱזֶה אָנֹכִי אָשִׁית לִבִּי רָאִיתִי לָקַחְתִּי מוּסָר

"I passed by the field of a lazy man and by the vineyard of a man lacking [an understanding] heart. And behold, it was all overgrown with thorns; nettles had covered its surface, and its stone fence lay in ruins. I observed and took it to heart. I saw it and learned a lesson."

Rav Chaim Shmulevitz, in *Sichos Mussar* (Essay 67), says that Shlomo HaMelech is teaching us that the root of laziness is that the heart is disengaged; the person fails to internalize what he knows. The remedy for laziness is to ***teach the heart what the mind already knows.*** Shlomo HaMelech was able to see and learn because, unlike the lazy man, he applied his heart to the matter.

What was it that Shlomo HaMelech saw?

Shlomo HaMelech (who had mastered the faculty of *mo'ach shalit al halev* — intellect over emotions), even while looking at sheer desolation, was able to envision a beautiful field with luscious fruit trees, a new fence, and greenery all about. He had the power of vision and his heart was awakened. He also envisioned the work that it would take to succeed, the obstacles he would encounter and the nagging doubts about the worthiness of the entire endeavor, which he knew would surface in his mind. He could see himself sweating profusely while trying to swat annoying fruit flies away from his face as he began to regret his decision to undertake the project. Shlomo HaMelech was able to hear the voice saying, "Give up already," loud and clear even before he started a project, and he prepared his responses ahead of time. When those thoughts would surface, he would never be caught off guard. As Rav Dessler teaches, if a person can learn to envision a test beforehand, he is far more likely to prevail.

In contrast, the lazy man saw only thorns, mud and a whole lot of work. Therefore, he went right back to his recliner thinking, "It's just not worth it."

Want to get off the couch? Then get yourself excited! Taste the success now. Imagine the meeting, the challenges that will come up, and the successful outcome. Imagine the smile on the person's face when you shlep out on a cold winter night to visit him at his bedside. Hear his words as he says, "I cannot tell you how much this visit means to me and how much you have lifted my spirits." See yourself as a successful person in the area of your life where growth is needed. Envision all of the moments of fulfillment that you will merit to experience. Success in the areas of *ruchnius* and *gashmius* come with so many wonderful benefits, but all the Satan wants you to see is how much work it will take. He presents us with visualizations of stress, failure and rejection to scare us into procrastination. Grab his weapon out of his hands and turn it right back at him.

◆§ 8. Break Tasks Into Pieces

The Satan wants our heart to feel that our undertaking is insurmountable, because this leads to despair and laziness. We can counter him by taking a large task and dividing it into smaller, achievable goals. Remember my friend Andy Burian who taught us the lesson of the steeple? This step-by-step approach was the brilliance of Rav Meir Shapiro *zt"l* in creating *Daf Yomi*. Finishing *Shas* can seem like an impossible task to many people, but learning a *daf* a day is doable. In this manner, tens of thousands of Jews have achieved their dream of completing *Shas*. The same method can be applied to our careers and other areas in which we seek achievement and growth.

Rav Nachman of Breslov (272) explains the *pasuk* (*Tehillim* 95:7) הַיּוֹם אִם בְּקֹלוֹ תִשְׁמָעוּ — "Today, if you hear His [Hashem's] voice" — to mean that we should only focus on the day and hour before us. Otherwise, life will seem too large a burden. One hour, one day, isn't so tall a mountain to climb. This mindset will also prevent us from thinking, "I can do it tomorrow," because *ha'yom* teaches that the only thing Hashem expects from us is what we can do *today*.

A successful life is the cumulative outcome of many successful minutes, hours, and days. Building a tall brick wall can seem overwhelming, but placing a single brick is not. Nevertheless, we benefit by envisioning the tall, sturdy brick wall before we begin the task. Perhaps we would also want to think about it once in a while when we need a dose of motivation, but most of the time we ought to be focusing on the brick right there in our hand.

◆§ 9. Burn Your Bridges

When our nation left Egypt, Hashem took us via a longer route so that we would be unable to return to Egypt when we encountered battles. The *Sifsei Chaim* (*Zerizus, Vaad* 13) quotes Rav Dessler, who explains that the reason for this is what military strategists call "burning all bridges." When a battalion would enter enemy territory, they would torch the bridge they crossed over because when soldiers know that there is no option to retreat, they fight for their lives and find the courage to advance and win. Rav Dessler advises, "Don't just accept it upon yourself to improve; change your situation in a way that compels you to improve."

Sluggishness that is rooted in fear of failure leads to hesitant and highly hedged action; we develop lots of fall-back plans before we step outside the front door. Therefore, we need to burn all bridges that lead back to safety and cut all safety nets.

> *Years ago, a new neighbor moved into the office next to mine at the bank. I introduced myself and we began to chat. He told me that he had left the real-estate field to enter Wall Street and intended to work very hard to be successful at it. He then added, "And if things don't work out, I can always go back to real estate." I told him that this may prove to be to his greatest detriment.*
>
> *Years earlier, when I went to my former boss to resign my position and let him know that I was entering Wall Street, he graciously said, "If things don't work out, your office will be waiting for you." I said, "That is very kind of you but I will definitely not be coming back." I intuitively knew that what I was about to do was going to scare the wits out of me and I had to burn that bridge to the ground.*
>
> *My new neighbor lasted six months before he returned back over his safe and secure bridge.*

I have seen many people make this same mistake — they go out on a tightrope with great trepidation, make sure there are lots of nets under them, and then under exert themselves because they have removed the greatest motivation to succeed — the fear of not succeeding. Fear of failure is like a jet engine; if it's placed in front of you it will push you backward and if it's placed behind you it will propel you forward. Fear of failure can cripple or motivate depending on how we use it. The more safety nets we construct for ourselves, the less courage we will need to muster. Conversely, burning all bridges brings forth a fear of failure that proves motivating.

Rav Dessler taught us to change our situation in a way that forces us to improve. The following story illustrates how he did just that in his own life.

> *Rav Dessler once decided to quit smoking. He came to yeshivah that morning and called in a student and said, "I have come to realize that smoking is unhealthy so as of today I have stopped." He then called in the next student, and the next. By the fourth or fifth, word had gotten out: The Mashgiach had quit smoking. One student finally said, "Rebbe, we all know you quit smoking. There is no need to call in any more students." Rav Dessler smiled and said, "I'm not calling each of you to inform you. I'm doing it to make it impossible for me to ever start again. The next time I have an urge to break my resolution I will think, 'I called every single student of mine and told them that I would quit smoking. How humiliating will it be if I start again!'"*

It's absolutely brilliant! You might tell people whom you respect, as many as you can, that you are starting *Daf Yomi*, and ask them to please check up on you once in a while to see where you stand. Several people recently asked me how to stick with the *Daf Yomi* program as we approached *mesechtas Eiruvin*. I suggested that on the first day of the *mesechta*, they should call several people they respect and invite them to a *Siyum* in 104 days and ask them to put it on their calendars. Tell your closest friends that you are going to work diligently on your *Shemiras halashon*. Before you begin an initiative for which you fear you will lose your resolve, announce it to as many people as you can. Set yourself up for mass-scale embarrassment and leverage your aversion to humiliation to achieve your goal.

To recap: ***We've outlined nine strategies to combat laziness:***

1. **Become aware of the underlying cause of your laziness;**
2. **Break through the *klippos* that keep your *middos* from being constructive.**
3. **Don't accept excuses from yourself.**
4. **Live with urgency, making each day count.**

5. **Be suspicious of taking shortcuts and following your first impulses, both of which are often the suggestions of the *yetzer hara.***
6. **Overcome hesitation and procrastination before new obstacles set in.**
7. **Get excited — engage your heart in your goals.**
8. **Focus on taking your next step rather than climbing the entire mountain.**
9. **Burn your bridges; don't leave yourself an easy path for retreat.**

MOST IMPORTANTLY, *DAVEN* FOR *SIYATA D'SHMAYA* TO HELP OVERCOME THE OBSTACLES OF LIFE.

Now you are ready to draw up battle plans and go to war against the highly detrimental tendency toward laziness. No matter which of your goals you ultimately achieve and which prove beyond your reach, you will have accomplished the one, critical overarching goal of your life. You will have grasped each opportunity Hashem put before you and taken it as far as He willed it to go. You will have not let your mission in life slip through your fingers, but rather, you will have embraced it and given it your best.

26
Taking Control

Let's assume you've absorbed everything we've discussed so far. Now you know why you procrastinate and are no longer making excuses for yourself. Your stomach turns when you hear words like "There must be an easy way," because you know that there are no shortcuts to success. You can close your eyes and envision yourself as the successful person that you want to be. You are prepared to torch the bridges leading back to your old way of life, and you are firmly committed to live life with urgency. Excellent, but we aren't quite done yet.

The Rambam says that the only way to fix a *middah* is to go to the other extreme for some time, and then slowly come back to the middle. Therefore, your next step will be to actively seek out toil and difficulty. No, I am not kidding.

Laziness is cured by actively seeking difficult undertakings: things that go against your inherent nature. Walk up three flights of stairs even though the elevator is working. Leave your car in the driveway when possible and take a brisk walk. Several times a day as you feel yourself drawn to inaction, take action. This strategy will prove life-changing in many areas of life beyond laziness.

A man came to talk to me recently after I had spoken at a conference on the topic of confidence. He asked me to meet with his son. The issue the young man was facing was that he was extremely shy and withdrawn. This had already led to social issues in yeshivah, and the father was concerned that, if left uncorrected, it could have repercussions for shidduchim as well.

Father and son came to my home and I spent close to two hours with the most delightful young man a person can ever hope to meet. However, his handshake, lack of eye contact, and low tone of voice, all yelled, "I don't believe in myself!"

I taught him something that I had learned, and he listened to every word carefully. He also agreed to check in with me every thirty days for the following three months. Today, less than a year later, in his own words, he is "a completely changed person." I saved a beautiful voicemail that he left me before the Yamim Noraim, which had me in tears, in which he expressed his gratitude for the positive change in his life. Tonight he called to tell me that he is engaged to be married.

What was it that I taught him?

In his *sefer, Pirkei Kinyan Daas,* Rav Shlomo Wolbe quotes a profound idea from his Rebbe, Rav Yerucham Levovitz *zt"l.* In a diary of resolutions that he took upon himself before Yom Kippur, Rav Yerucham writes in reference to himself that, "He stopped and realized that in actuality he was not in control of himself at all, because, in truth, he was being ruled by his physicality and desires, which were corrupting his intellect with their disruptive ideas."

To remedy this, he accepted upon himself to do five things each day that were directly counter to his bodily desires, and imposed a penalty of 10 *kopeks* per day (I can't even tell you if that's a lot or a little) if he failed to follow through.

Rav Yerucham realized that he could take back control of his life by training himself to do more than just say "no" to his weaknesses; rather, he would do the opposite of what his urges demanded! This is a simple yet profound idea. You train yourself to do more than suppress your detrimental habits and whims; you actively and conscientiously do things that are diametrically opposed to them.

The Alter of Kelm had a daughter who, as a child, displayed selfish tendencies. Each day he would take a few kopeks and sit her down with a pushka. He would have her lift each kopek and place it in the pushka while repeating the word "tzedakah." This is how he cured her of this reprehensible trait.

Here is what I taught the young man to do, and all of the credit goes to him because he followed the directions to the letter. Each morning, he was to prepare a short and interesting topic of conversation. It could be a *dvar Torah*, something in the news, or a short story; it really didn't matter. Throughout the day, he had to seek out three people and initiate a conversation with them by saying, "I saw something really interesting this morning..." He was to address three new people each day, and he couldn't approach the same person more than once every two weeks. I also wanted him to up the ante each week by choosing people in whose presence he felt a bit more intimidated.

He used Rav Yerucham's formula, and after 30 days he called to report on progress. Just from his tone of voice I knew that it was working. He spoke with a poise and confidence that was nowhere to be found when we had first met. A few months later he was cured; he has become a popular and confident young man. The voicemail he sent me came from his new yeshivah in Eretz Yisrael. It was a joy to hear.

Rav Yerucham's formula helps a person break free of nearly any detrimental tendency or *middah* that is plaguing him. With *siyata d'Shmaya* it will work. What we are training ourselves to do is take back control of our lives in the areas where desire and weakness are controlling us. Each time we say, "No, and as a matter of fact I will do quite the opposite," we prove to ourselves that we really don't need to be pushed around and we are able to take control of our lives. We have free-choice, as Rav Dessler taught us.

Here are some examples of how this technique can be used.

- Those who are afraid to *daven* for the *Amud* (lead the *davening*), can stare their fear in the face and ask themselves, "What is the downside of getting up there? Am I so childish that I will allow an immature fear to prevent me from serving Hashem in this beautiful way?" They should then immediately approach the *gabbai* and volunteer before the voice of fear starts speaking again.

- Those who are petrified of public speaking should volunteer to speak at the next family *simchah* or speaking engagement. To my knowledge, no death certificate has ever had "speaking at a *Sheva Berachos*" listed as the cause of death, and yet the National Social Anxiety Center states that the fear of public speaking is the most common phobia, ahead of death, spiders, and heights. The National Institute of Mental Health reports that public speaking anxiety, or glossophobia, (they even have a name for it) affects about 73% of the population. Imagine that, 73% of people would rather be dangled over Niagara Falls with a tarantula crawling up their leg than stand at that podium and speak about the *chassan* and *kallah*!!
- Finicky people can try eating foods each day that they don't particularly like. For example, if you like the dark meat of the chicken, you would eat the white meat. If you like lots of sugar in your coffee, use less, or none at all.
- Those who carry grudges should find someone in their shul with whom they have an issue, and buy him an *aliyah* this Shabbos. Send someone for whom you have hard feelings a bottle of wine or fruit basket for Shabbos with a note saying, "Time to put the issue behind us." Break every grudge you have one by one. Start taking in your next-door neighbor's garbage cans on collection day, AFTER the Sanitation Department takes the garbage.
- Learn to greet everyone you meet with a "Good morning" or "Good Shabbos," even if you tend to keep to yourself.

☙ Climb Rung by Rung

The Piaseczna Rebbe (*Hachsharas Avreichim* 9:4) teaches that you should embark slowly on a path of growth by choosing issues that are merely annoying to you. Then you can work your way up to those that you abhor. As you grow, you will learn something quite remarkable about yourself; you really do have the power to control your desires and your lower-self instincts. In the Rebbe's words:

> If you do not want to be one of those people who are at the mercy of their hearts, but one of the righteous people who control their hearts, who are not subject to whims and crushed by the force of every desire — if you wish to control yourself and be the master of your soul, then you must begin with minor feelings.
>
> For instance, if you are brought two slices of meat, and your glance falls on one of them because you like it more, then eat the other one. Do not say, "What is the point? Both are permissible."
>
> Have compassion on yourself and your soul and begin your battle with the smallest buds of your desires. Then you will turn yourself into a warrior who rules himself, whose heart is in his hand.
>
> But if, Heaven forbid, your evil inclination has taken hold of you and you have been brought a dessert that you find most appealing and more difficult to resist, you may find an excuse to dismiss this entire exercise and say, "What difference does it make whether or not I eat this? Everyone else is eating it."
>
> Therefore, do as I have urged you above. Gaze dispassionately at your desire. Tell yourself: "Is it true that my desire to eat this dessert is so strong? Perhaps doing so would not be a sin, but I have learned that I am controlled by my desire, completely subjugated to it, so that I find it difficult to refrain from this dessert. If I skip it, I won't be lacking anything, yet how strongly I am driven to have it!"
>
> Mentally gaze at yourself and your desire, contemplate it, and say, "I know that I am not a *tzaddik* but I hadn't realized that I am such a wretched, lowly glutton, completely taken over by my desire for dessert!"
>
> Meditate on this. Review it with a dispassionate gaze — once, twice, three times or more. Then you will be amazed how, with Hashem's help, your desire will weaken and even melt away entirely.

This is not by any means an exercise in self-loathing; it is just the opposite — an exercise in self-respect. The Rebbe is teaching us a profound idea. That when we realize that we are being pushed around by our desires and whims, we can say to ourselves, "Seriously, don't I have the inner strength to resist a chocolate-chip cookie?" The realization that in certain areas of our lives we are not in control, and that a force far weaker than us is, will motivate us to wrestle back that control.

Improving a trait or breaking a habit is difficult, but within your reach. If a stick is bent, you need to bend it carefully but completely in the opposite direction in order to straighten it out. Bend yourself in the same manner and don't worry, you won't snap. On the contrary, once you are upright, you will realize that you are far taller than you ever imagined.

27

"Don't Let Perfect Be the Enemy of Good"

Are you a perfectionist?

Do you tend to set your expectations too high?

Do you:

Insist that things must be done a certain way or not be done at all?

Immediately take notice of what's not right and hardly notice what is?

Find yourself unable to turn your attention away from something that, to your mind, "needs fixing"?

If you answered "yes" to any of these questions, then I deeply empathize with you.

I confess; I am a recovering perfectionist. I was once really proud of the title "perfectionist," but that's no longer the case. I have come to learn, the hard way I might add, that while aiming for a degree of perfection in life is healthy, when the three letters "ist" are added to the end of the word, it can become problematic.

Addressing this issue, the *Chovos HaLevavos* continues.

> *And if everyone who wanted to perfect themselves in the areas of their character traits were to abandon that pursuit upon realizing that perfection was beyond their reach, then we would be left empty of good deeds, lacking in beautiful middos,*

and instead, chasing after expectations that will only lead to disappointment. The trail of goodness would remain desolate and the path of kindness abandoned, for it isn't within the power of anyone to reach the epitome of perfection.

We have already discussed the idea that waiting for perfect conditions before embarking on a project is often a symptom of laziness. Rabbeinu Bachya is now teaching that, in general, trying to achieve perfection in life is a ploy of the Satan that stands between us and accomplishment.

The often-repeated mantra of perfectionists is, "If it's worth doing, then it's worth doing right." While there is nothing wrong with working toward the goal of doing something right, it is important that we keep several things in mind.

1. Our own definition of "right" may not be the true definition. Our egos often lead us to believe that things must be done a certain way, when in actuality something that seems "less than perfect" will do just fine. We must fight this tendency by focusing on the fact that an undertaking may not necessarily be best served by something that makes us feel good about ourselves. We often go into an undertaking with a hidden agenda; revealing this agenda frees us to be more flexible, which leads to superior outcomes.
2. People who live by their own definitions of "right" tend not to work well with others and rarely delegate tasks because in their mind, "No one will do it like I will." Unless a person plans on doing most things himself, learning to compromise is an essential element of long-term success. Furthermore, after working with others, we often learn that we actually don't know everything (shocking, I know), and that our definition of perfect was actually imperfect.
3. At times, at the outset of an undertaking it can be difficult to envision how it will be possible to succeed, given the variables at hand. Nevertheless, along the way we usually manage to figure things out. If that dearth of confidence and vision prevents us from taking those first steps, then it becomes detrimental to our ability to achieve. The *Chovos HaLevavos* teaches this lesson from

experience. Rabbeinu Bachya admits that he began his *sefer* with far-from-perfect conditions, but that didn't stop him from making an earnest attempt. The results were nothing short of miraculous.

4. Some things cannot, under any circumstances, be done to perfection. That is when the Satan will throw the "If you can't do it right, then best not to do it at all" slogan at us. Do you notice how inspiring and lofty that slogan sounds? People are often proud of being perfectionists and they chant the Satan's motto with great conviction. With this mindset, says the *Chovos HaLevavos*, many worthwhile endeavors never get off the ground.

This, the *sefer* teaches us, is a HUGE mistake. Perfection should not be our goal and is not in our control at all. Only Hakadosh Baruch Hu is perfect. Our mission is to do the best we can. Our role in life is to make progress in areas that require effort and growth, and not to set our sights on reaching ultimate perfection. We will never be a perfect father, mother, spouse, advisor, lawyer, teacher, daughter, or Rabbi. Therefore, it's time to stop making perfection our goal. Life is a journey of self-rectification and NOT of self-perfection.

The perfectionist, ironically, settles for a far lower level of achievement than his non-perfectionist counterpart. The non-perfectionist may eagerly undertake an effort to reduce his anger, thinking, "Even if I still lose my temper once in a while, every time I manage to overcome it will be an achievement and will prevent me from doing or saying something I will regret." He is willing to try his best and keep moving forward with whatever results he can manage to achieve. The perfectionist, in contrast, never moves off home base. "What does it help to hold my anger back 10 times if I still get angry 20 times?" he thinks. Similarly, the *lashon hara* speaker keeps speaking *lashon hara,* because he believes that he'll inevitably slip up. The overwhelmed homemaker leaves the mess on the floor because her house will never be what she would call "neat."

In truth, a person who struggles with anger may never reach a point at which he completely rids himself of that trait, but he undoubtedly can vastly improve his relationships. The person who works on *bitachon* may never be able to sail through life without a worry, but perhaps he'll worry less about the small stuff. The homemaker may never achieve the immaculately clean home she envisions, but she can at least enjoy those times when she looks around and sees that things are in order for the time being. The *Chovos HaLevavos* is teaching that perfectionism is not a reason to abandon a path of improvement, because success in NOT defined by perfection.

◆§ The Goal of Perfection Derails Us

The founder of an organization that helps challenged boys recently came to seek my advice. Despite his heart of pure gold and the very best of intentions, things were not going as planned. His organization was a mess and facing shutdown. It was easy to see why. He was trying to accomplish too much for too many because in his mind this was "the only way to do this. No one can be turned away."

I asked him, "Can you imagine if the founder of every worthwhile organization began with a perfectionist mindset? 'We help everyone or no one at all.' Would any of them survive? 'We help every patient, childless couple, and provide every poor family all of their needs.' While those are great aspirations, they are unrealistic and somewhat detrimental to the underlying goals. If you don't narrow your focus and realize that solving the totality of the problem is beyond your reach, you will soon become another story that ends, 'We achieved nothing in our quest to achieve everything.'"

◆§ Essential vs. perfect

Great people are never those who do everything perfectly. Rather, they are people that do more things proficiently than other people, and also do the essential really well. The key is to focus our efforts on those tasks that are most important and essential.

Here's an example. Were we to list the attributes of really great teachers we might say, "They care about children, are inspiring, tell good stories, listen well, know the subject matter, speak with clarity, are empathetic, responsible, kind, have a sense of humor, and an upbeat disposition." If they are good in all of those areas, then they are great teachers and highly sought after. If they are exceptional at even one or two of those things, then they are truly a catch, as long as the other elements are also present. They need not, however, be the very best at anything. Someone, on the other hand, who can enthrall an audience for hours with their stories, tells side-splitting jokes, and yet is disorganized and irresponsible would make a terrible teacher.

Teachers who are looking to excel need not seek perfection at anything. What they need to do is understand how much more outstanding they would be if they had some level of proficiency in an area that is essential, yet is currently lacking in them.

◆§ Core vs. Ancillary

Successful people learn to differentiate between the core objective of a project and the elements that enhance it but are not essential. They strive to achieve the core objective as best as possible, and are ready to compromise on the ancillary aspects when doing so is for the benefit of the overall objective or facilitates working with others. In other words, they can let someone else's idea prevail when it doesn't affect the essence of the project. The timing and location of an event may be essential, but the font of the invitation is probably not. Being able to discern upfront what is essential and what is not is a key to successful outcomes. Compromise requires humility and it demonstrates that we are at all times cognizant that Hakadosh Baruch Hu runs the world and that success can only be achieved with His guidance and blessing.

◆§ Learning to Say "No"

While on this topic, it is worth mentioning that some of us may yearn for a perfect image or reputation in one or more areas of our lives: to be the perfect friend, mother, neighbor, *baalas chesed*. However, in our quest for perfection we may burn ourselves out, for we are trying to achieve the impossible.

"Sarah is ALWAYS there to help. 24/7."

"Shimon has a heart of gold and gives the shirt off his back to ANYONE."

"Leah will NEVER let you down."

Wow! Who wouldn't want his name associated with accolades like that? On the surface all may seem rosy, but behind the scenes things are often different. Many "perfect people" have confided to me that behind the façade of a perfect reputation lies weakness and low self-esteem. They feel like spineless doormats and wish they believed in themselves enough to speak, act, or refrain from acting as they feel is right. They don't do so because they don't believe that the world will love and appreciate an imperfect version of them.

For many, one of the most important yet difficult words that we can teach ourselves to say is "NO."

Yes, "no." This observation doesn't refer to those for whom the word "no" is their default response. Those people have another issue to tackle. This refers to those who:

- Are afraid to say "no" when they know they should.
- Won't say "no" to someone who is taking advantage of them.
- Consistently come to the rescue of someone who should be helping himself.
- Won't say "no" when their instinct tells them they are tapped out and need a break.
- Say "yes" even when helping someone will come at the expense of their loved ones.

Why do some of us often say "yes" when we shouldn't? Why can't we say "no" even when we know we should? Might we be seeking a perfect image; that we are always available, ready to give, bend over backward? Does our lack of self-esteem perhaps tell us that if we are less than perfect, we are unworthy?

Here are two things I learned the hard way:

1. Always saying "yes" is rarely a sign of goodness and strength. It is often a sign of weakness.

2. **Over the long term, you won't be able to say "yes" at all if you don't learn how to say "no."**

The drive for a perfect image takes its toll, and one day we start hating ourselves for being a pushover. Then we completely burn out. We go from all yes to all no. If you learn to utilize the word "no" responsibly, you will merit to say "yes" many more times over the longer term and do so with far more satisfaction and fulfillment. You will also feel a whole lot better about yourself. A healthy perspective starts by abandoning the idea that others will ever regard you as perfect and that worthiness and perfection are one and the same.

"He" thrives on disappointment

Rabbeinu Bachya teaches us that when we seek perfection in any area of our lives, we set ourselves up for disappointment, which ultimately leads to complete abandonment of a goal. That's exactly what the Satan wants, and he knows how to get us to throw in the towel. He can't easily stop us from aspiring to accomplish, because we are doers by nature. Therefore, he puts the noble pursuit of perfection in our minds, knowing that it can't be achieved. When we realize that perfection is unreachable, we either quit before we start or burn out from our futile efforts. Either way, he wins and we lose. When a whole group of people takes this approach, great causes and ideas can be abandoned and forgotten.

What we perceive as very little is quite a lot

As humans we like to see results, discernable results, and when they are not forthcoming, we may find ourselves thinking, "What is the point of toiling if things don't seem to be much different than when I first started?" This mindset is highly detrimental and is another one of the Satan's essential tools. Unless it is overcome, it prevents otherwise capable and growing people from reaching their fullest potential.

The *Chovos HaLevavos* (*Cheshbon HaNefesh* Ch. 5) teaches that no advancement should ever be small in our eyes; even one proper word spoken or one forbidden sight refrained from has inestimable value. An analogy for this would be the movement of the sun. When measured from earth, the movement of the sun in one hour appears to be a few feet. However, in reality, the earth has shifted relative to the sun a distance of 67,000 miles during that same period. What, on the surface, appears to be a little movement was actually quite a lot.

Rav Nachman of Breslov, who was known for his deeply mystical stories, illustrates this concept with one of his most insightful stories,

"The *Tzaddik* who Fell into a Depression."

A great tzaddik once fell into a deep state of depression to the point where he literally could not move from his bed. In his attempts to cheer himself up, he reminded himself of things that he had accomplished in his life, but each time he did so, there was an insidious voice inside of him that pointed out an imperfection in that accomplishment. This only served to give him more reason for depression. And so he slipped deeper and deeper into despair.

Then he found something to be happy about; he remembered that each morning we thank Hashem for creating us a Jew with a special mission in life.

Thoughts like this can never be mingled with depression. When a person tries to cheer himself up with thoughts of his own accomplishments, the Satan will always be able to bring up the inevitable imperfections of any of man's deeds. However, the fact that we were born Jews is purely the result of the mercy of Hakadosh Baruch Hu, and therefore, it must be perfect.

Having grasped this bit of happiness, the tzaddik began to cheer himself up. Fueled by ever-increasing happiness, he ascended higher and higher into the upper worlds — light years away. When the tzaddik began to descend, because joy comes and goes, ebbs and flows, he was astonished to find that he actually landed back in the place from which he had originally started his journey. If he moved from there at all, it was perhaps by a hair's breadth, כְּחוּט הַשַּׂעֲרָה*, an infinitesimally small distance that the human mind cannot even comprehend.*

The tzaddik simply could not get over the fact that in the upper worlds he had flown so far, yet in the lower worlds he seemed to not have advanced at all. It proved to him how precious in Hashem's eyes is even the smallest forward movement that a person makes in this world — even if it is no greater than a single hair's breadth.

To understand why this is so, we must understand that this world is a mere dot in the realm of the universe and that the universe is a mere dot in the realm of the upper worlds.

We all know what a wheel looks like. There is a hub and a rim and spokes that attach the two. The difference in distance between the spokes where they meet the hub is mere millimeters, but this translates to a difference of inches at the level of the rim. Now imagine that you removed the rim and extended the spokes up into the solar system and you didn't even stop there but just kept on going and going. Imagine the difference in distance between one spoke and the other in the upper worlds. They would be many light-years away from each other.

As Rav Chaim of Volozhin teaches in *Nefesh HaChaim*, Jews span all of the universes in that we have our feet firmly planted on this world while our soul is planted in the highest realms. What we do with our feet down here makes an impact all the way up there. A hair's breadth of progress in this world translates to a leap of light-years in the worlds above. We need not run miles from where we are to accomplish great achievements.

The perfectionist must learn to appreciate the vast impact of each and every accomplishment and advancement, and understand that the objective in life is to move a hair's breadth. Often, advancement will be indiscernible, especially in the early stages of growth. We must also remember that we are not here for results; we are here to toil. The need for perfection is nothing more than ego, which is not only unflattering, but highly detrimental to our most important goals in life.

28

What Do You Expect?

Perfectionism, the focus of our previous chapter, is the root of a particularly destructive off-shoot that warrants its own discussion. That is the tendency toward unrealistic expectations. Like perfectionism, this is a mind-set that causes us to burn out and abandon worthwhile projects that might well have succeeded.

Whenever we embark on an undertaking, we have expectations: How long should this take? How much work will it entail? How will we define success? How likely are we to succeed on the first try? Those who aspire to accomplish their goals need to master the skill of setting realistic expectations. This is a function of *binah.* If a person jumps into action before clarifying these issues, the undertaking quite possibly will lead to tremendous heartache and disappointment, not to mention a whole lot of wasted time, energy, and money.

Successfully taking a task from start to finish requires tenacity, motivation, and, most of all, resilience — the strength that allows us to experience setbacks, get back up, and keep going. One of the most prevalent causes of loss of resilience is the great, deep abyss that seems to open up between our initial expectation and the reality that unfolds. If we embark on a project without having set realistic expectations, each obstacle we face makes us think, "Is this normal? Am I doing something wrong?" As more obstacles arise, we think, "This can't be normal. I must be doing something wrong," and ultimately, "I am not going to succeed at this. I should give up."

Each obstacle and setback chips away at our resilience and drains us of our motivation. Sometimes a project takes longer than we thought it would, which spurs us to think we are on the wrong track when we are actually right on track.

For example, a young man who had just begun working in the commercial mortgage industry came to ask my advice. He was ready to quit and try something else. "It just isn't working for me," he said. I listened to what he had to say and then sentenced him to six more months of hard labor. I asked him to come back to me after that period if he still hadn't started to see success. It is now several years later, and *B'H*, our conversations are now only about the many clients he has acquired and how well he is doing. So many people quit perfectly good projects and careers too early, not due to laziness or fear, but rather, due to having set the wrong expectations up front.

☙ The Barking Dog

Setting the right expectations also minimizes unpleasant surprises that cause us to lose our focus. Imagine Freddy is beginning his paper delivery route for the first time. The boss tells him that when he rides his bicycle down Elm Road and reaches the third house, there will be a huge black pit bull that will bark loudly at him, but he need not worry because it is chained to a fence. As Freddy reaches the house, he fully anticipates what is about to happen and isn't all that startled. Without that conversation, the poor kid would have jumped off his bike and run for his dear life.

Now let's imagine Shimmy is beginning his first day in a sales job. His boss hands him a call list and a phone. Shimmy makes his first 40 calls and is hung up on 40 times. We call that 0 for 40. Shimmy heads straight into his boss's office and quits. The boss realizes that he goofed by not having "the conversation" up front, so before he hands the list and phone to Dov, his next hire, he takes him out to the parking lot and shows him a brand-new Lexus. He says, "Do you see this shiny new car? It belongs to David, the salesman who sits right near you. He makes 60 calls a day, gets hung up on 55 times, and yet he had enough cash to buy that car outright." Now, each time a prospect hangs up on Dov, he will think, "Well, David seems to have the same issue, yet somehow he drives a new Lexus." Can you see how a change of perspective and expectation can mean all the difference between success and failure at anything?

I will share a personal story that taught me the great importance of setting the right expectation and definition of success upfront. The lesson proved to be the difference between pushing onward and turning back.

☙ Building Pisom and Ramses

The year was 2008, and with the great market crash I watched in horror as many years of growth in my client accounts evaporated in less than two weeks. For the first time in my life, I could imagine what our forefathers felt like in Egypt as they toiled to build Pisom and Ramses, only to see their work sink into the ground. I was ready to throw in the towel on my profession (opening a bookstore sounded like a nice safe idea). I felt awful, somehow responsible, and went to seek advice from the Skwere Rebbe shlit'a. After I poured out my heart and shared my reasoning for seeking another profession, the Rebbe asked me two questions.

"Did you in any way lead your clients to believe that you were a prophet and could predict the future of the markets?"

"No, to the contrary I always stress that I don't have a crystal ball and that markets are impossible to predict."

"Will your clients be better or worse off if you decided to leave Wall Street?"

"They would likely be worse off because the next person they work with may not be using the Torah to dictate his morals and ethics."

The Rebbe smiled and said, "Then I don't understand the issue. You are doing exactly what your clients hired you to do and they need you to keep doing that. Quitting is not an option."

What was my colossal mistake? My expectation and definition of success were both wrong. I expected to earn money for my clients at all times and defined success that way. I believed that I was responsible to make sure that happened. ***I was wrong.*** *I have no control over those things — all I can do is deliver a better client experience in the areas where I do have control. Care, diligence, unconflicted advice, transparency, and honesty — beyond that, I must do my best to navigate the markets knowing full well that a great storm can appear at any time and cause great setbacks. (Indeed, as I finish writing this book the world finds itself in another such period of turmoil.)*

This is true in every endeavor. We are only in control of the effort, not the results. I once met a woman who devoted herself to working with special needs children. She had burned out and lost her enthusiasm. The work, which was once so rewarding to her, seemed to have lost its meaning because, in her words, "I'm not seeing any progress." Of course she wasn't seeing progress. She had set herself up for failure by setting up the wrong criteria for success, which was that her clients would get better. However, her job was not to remediate her clients, but rather, to allow then to live with more dignity and less discomfort. Each time she accomplished either of those worthy goals, she has succeeded. Healing others is never in our hands; we can only aim to improve the factors over which we have control. In this woman's case, that meant easing her clients' burdens and restoring their sense of self.

This is so important that it cannot be stressed enough. Our ability to act with consistency and eventually prevail is greatly influenced by how well we think we are performing, and that depends on the upfront expectation that we set for ourselves. It's highly possible to set ourselves up for failure right from the get-go by setting unrealistic expectations.

If a person expects to turn a profit in a business after one year, he will fail even before he starts. If we expect to have perfect *bitachon* after learning a *sefer* one time, we will be very disappointed, and will likely not review what we learned. If we set unrealistic expectations for an important undertaking, we will inevitably quit when we begin to realize that our expectations are impossible to meet, or alternatively, we will put unwarranted pressure on ourselves and increase our pace until we burn ourselves out. I have met many people in their early thirties who were burnt out, not from life, but from self-inflicted emotional wounds that resulted from seeing themselves as failures for not having "made it" yet.

◆§ Toil Is Par for the Course

Chazal set another important expectation for life using three words, אָדָם לְעָמָל יוּלָּד (*Iyov* 5:7) — Man was born to toil. The *Mesillas Yesharim* (Ch. 9) further explains, "A person must internalize that he is not in this world for relaxation, but rather for toil and effort."

We should expect to work, and work hard, even in retirement. We live in a society where comfort, leisure, and enjoying ourselves have become an unalienable right. When people don't have it easy they think, "This is unfair and not what I signed up for," or "What am I doing wrong?" However, Chazal inform us that we were put here to toil and that should be our expectation. If life doesn't thrust toil upon us, then we should seek ways to exert ourselves on our own, or life will be lackluster as best. With the proper expectation in mind, exertion will be like a breath of fresh air — the breath of life itself!

◆§ Getting It Right

Setting realistic expectations can be tricky and we sometimes tend to be too conservative or too aggressive. We should aim for a balance between optimism and realism. We find this balance by investigating and learning how much time and how much work it took others to accomplish what we've set out to accomplish; this is our guide.

We can spare ourselves much aggravation, both before and during an undertaking, by seeking someone who has already accomplished what we are setting out to achieve. He may tell you, "What you are experiencing is completely normal. I experienced the same thing. It took me even more time to see any progress at all." With those few words, all of your self-doubt just melts away. Or he may offer some valuable pointers as to what you can be doing better — mistakes he made that you need not repeat.

We shouldn't wait until our motivation is depleted, or worse yet, we have already thrown in the towel, before we figure out that we have set our initial expectations too high. Before we undertake a project, whether the goal is self-improvement, mastering a talent, growing in Torah, changing our career, embarking on a business venture, or any other goal, it is imperative that we seek the advice of a *chacham* — a wise person. As Chazal say, there is no one wiser than someone who lived through the test.

When I entered finance, I sought such a person and he set my expectations for the first 2-to-3 years of my career. We had an eye-opening conversation during which he advised me to "expect nothing at all to happen for at least two years and be pleasantly surprised if something does happen." Those words were extremely helpful to me as I watched so many of my colleagues burn themselves out when progress took longer than they expected. The wise person knows where the black pit bull lives and how many people will hang up on you, and he can let you in on this crucial information. It takes humility to seek the advice of others, but it surely pays off.

Writing down our expectations is also beneficial. As we explained, when we veer from a state of *daas*, one crucial tool for bringing ourselves back to that state is to have the information prepared in advance. This jogs our memory of what we thought when we were thinking logically.

However, the Satan knows this and will surely not leave you alone simply because you set proper expectations up front. He will figure out how to introduce self-doubt and confusion nonetheless. I recall thinking to myself that perhaps the person who had helped me set my expectations was wrong as I witnessed some of my colleagues experiencing success earlier than I did. I feared that I would learn after two years that I was doing something fundamentally wrong and that the time and effort would be wasted. Looking back after two years, I realized that my mentor had been 100 percent on target.

To recap: ***Unrealistically high expectations are almost always disappointed, which leads to a sense of doubt and failure. Avoid this pitfall by seeking advice of those who have "been there." This will enable you to bounce back and persist when the inevitable delays and complications arise.***

29

Removing Your Blinders

On Wall Street, it is often the smartest people who make the costliest mistakes. Trained professionals completely miss or misinterpret information that in hindsight should have been blatantly obvious to them. As an example, in 2008, trillions of dollars were lost because what the geniuses said "could never happen"... happened. The housing market collapsed. Banks were wiped out, economies cratered, and millions were left unemployed.

During the 2008 debacle, I realized that there was something deeply wrong; otherwise intelligent and educated people had maintained the strongest of convictions upon the weakest of arguments.

I have seen this story repeat itself over and over, and not only on Wall Street but just as often on Main Street. People often ignore, miss, or misinterpret information that is staring them right in the face.

They-

- Close their ears to the warnings of those who care about them and forge ahead to marry the wrong person.
- Don't seek, or ignore, advice and jump into business ventures and investments that are clearly doomed from the start.
- Rigorously defend a position that is blatantly false.
- Maintain positive or negative beliefs about themselves or others that are completely unsubstantiated and bordering on the ridiculous.

- Believe that if something has not yet happened, it never will.

There is one word that explains this — **bias**. Following the 2008 meltdown, I began to study biases in earnest, and while they come in many colors and flavors, the common denominator is that when we are biased, we are, for all intents and purposes, deaf and blind to information that is staring us in the face.

In 2008 the world wanted to believe that selling homes to millions of over-leveraged homeowners with little income would not lead to financial meltdown. With the mantra, "Housing prices have never gone down," people lulled themselves to sleep at night. They had to convince themselves, because if they were wrong, the implications were too enormous to consider. With 20/20 hindsight it was all blatantly obvious; a house of cards MUST collapse to the ground.

We each have an instinctive inclination toward information that makes us feel good about ourselves and supports our ego. This is one reason we often gravitate toward data that aligns with our own viewpoints. In addition, as we've discussed, human beings favor the course of least resistance. We'd rather take it easy. Because rethinking a viewpoint often demands more research and a new approach — which translates to "work" — we resist it. Lastly, it's hard to admit we've been wrong.

All this leads us to reject valuable information that opposes our current desires and beliefs. If the counterargument to our position is too stark to ignore, we respond by inventing creative rationalizations that enable us to stick with our position. In essence, we only see what we want to see, and hear what we want to hear.

Rabbeinu Bachya spells this out for us:

> ***And I understood that the desire of people to experience the pleasures of this world is great... When faced with the opportunity to indulge in something that they desire, they fabricate for themselves words of falsehood [justifications] in order to partake of these pleasures... And when others try to enlighten them in the hopes of setting them straight, they concoct nonsensical reasons, find false proofs, ask all sorts of "questions," find fault***

in their words... to justify their unwillingness to heed the rebuke.

Rabbeinu Bachya realized that his inclination to avoid a struggle was the catalyst for his belief that he couldn't write his *sefer*. He warns us that if we fail to recognize our bias toward lower-self desires, it will warp our sense of right and wrong and lead to the creation of a library of justifications for our lack of progress. We must also be aware of the bias toward always being right and our aversion to ever feeling guilty — other causes of self- justification.

If you recall, in my introduction I told a story about a class that I delivered to Jews and non-Jews at a university, which spurred many in the room to clamor for more. We will now discuss the concept I introduced to them.

◆§ What Aristotle Couldn't See

Rav Elchonon Wasserman (*Kovetz Maamarim,* Essay 1) asks two profound questions on the *mitzvah* of *emunah*:

1. We say in *Krias Shema* each day, "Do not stray after your hearts," which the Sifri (*Bamidbar* 15:36) teaches is a prohibition against heresy. Isn't heresy a function of warped knowledge and reasoning and, as such, shouldn't it be attributed to the brain instead of the heart?
2. How can we expect a young child in yeshivah to embrace complete *emunah* — faith in a Creator — when some of the greatest human minds such as Aristotle and other philosophers denied it?

Rav Elchonon answers that the belief that Hashem created the world is actually quite obvious and logical. A person has to be an utter fool not to see it. In the words of the *Chovos HaLevavos* (*Shaar HaYichud*) there must be a Creator because "nothing creates itself."

It's actually quite simple once we strip away all of the nonsense that we have absorbed over a lifetime of exposure to Western society's ideals. "כִּי הַדָּבָר אֵינוֹ עוֹשֶׂה אֶת עַצְמוֹ" — Because a thing cannot create itself. This wondrous world didn't just happen.

This point, says Rav Elchonon, actually flips the second question on its head. How was Aristotle so blind to the obvious truth?

There can only be one answer: bias. The Torah (*Shemos* 23:8) teaches the power of bias when it prohibits a judge who has accepted a bribe from issuing a ruling. "Bribery blinds the eyes of the wise," the verse attests. Even if the bribe is worth as little as a *perutah* (approximately 3 cents), this pittance renders the person unfit to judge. This prohibition pertains to everyone and anyone. Were you to walk into a *beis din* and Moshe Rabbeinu himself was one of the three judges, and you slipped a $5.00 bill into his pocket, he would need to immediately recuse himself from the case because he is now biased. This assumes that even Moshe Rabbeinu, who was Hashem's emissary when He split the sea, who stood at Sinai, and spent 40 days in Heaven studying Torah, can't see past what amounts to a cup of coffee and a Danish (at least as of the writing of this book, it still does) and is therefore unfit to issue an untainted ruling. The Torah bears witness to this fact. Why is this the case?

Heed carefully the words of Rav Elchonon, words that will change how we think about every decision we ever make from today and onward:

שֶׁהוּא חוּק הַטֶּבַע בְּכוֹחוֹת נֶפֶשׁ הָאָדָם כִּי הָרָצוֹן יַשְׁפִּיעַ עַל הַשֵּׂכֶל — **There is a law of nature that our desire will influence our intellect.**

Once a person takes a bribe, he is biased, because he has developed an inclination toward the giver. No matter how small that inclination may be, it renders him incapable of making an unbiased decision. The Torah is teaching us that as a rule, **a decision made in a state of bias is by definition faulty.**

Bribes and biases come in many forms. For example, if someone has always dreamed of finding a spouse who is endowed with certain physical features, and he/she meets someone who fits that description, he/she will have a bias that may cause him/her to overlook any negative character traits. Sadly, we have all heard stories of people who "fell" for someone because of physical appearance or financial status, only to wake up years later and realize they made a terrible mistake. The people around them saw the flaws, even pointed them out, but their input was dismissed. Later, when the disappointed spouse is asked, "Didn't you see any of this when you were dating?" the answer will be "no." This answer is the truth; the person was blinded by the qualities he or she desired. When we like someone, we may justify his every wrong, and when we dislike someone, we may minimize or negate entirely his every attribute.

If someone wants to strike it rich or believes himself more capable than he truly is, he will see gold where others see dirt. If he has held a position for a long time, the last thing he wants is to admit that he has been wrong all those years.

Another form of bias arises when we are deeply invested in something. The more time, energy, and money we have invested, the more we are biased toward it. Aristotle lived within, and was supported by, a Greek culture focused on physical beauty, material pleasure and their pursuit. He justified his worldview through his belief that the world had no creator, because in a happenstance world, there is no right and wrong, purpose and accountability (remember the Israeli CEO from chapter 4). The thought that he was wrong would upend everything that he stood for and pursued all of his life; it would make him accountable. To him that was a very scary proposition. Because he desired to continue living as he did, he could not allow other possibilities any place in his worldview. When a person is so biased, his brain can never be big enough to see through the bias and recognize the truth. Therefore, Aristotle denied Hashem's existence until the end.

This is why the Torah says that heresy is rooted in the heart, the organ of desire. It's our heart that leads us astray, not our brain.

Baruch Hashem, young Jewish children are not afflicted with these terrible horrific biases. They can therefore sing, "Hashem is here, Hashem is there, Hashem is truly everywhere," on top of their lungs with great feeling. Without bias, they are blessed with 20/20 vision.

◈ Cognitive Dissonance

Justifications are a natural derivative of what is called cognitive dissonance. Cognitive dissonance is the mental discomfort we experience when we simultaneously face two or more contradictory beliefs, ideas, or values.

As an example, most of us want to believe that we are inherently good and righteous people. What happens when we do something that is not so good and not so righteous? We experience mental pain, partially associated with guilt and partially associated with what is now a contradiction: "How could I have done 'that' if I am good? Am I perhaps not good?"

Some people will admit that they made a mistake and quickly rectify it so as to restore their sense of self-worth. Others choose an easier route; they justify their act. "I am not bad because what I did wasn't bad." "Even if it was bad, it was the other person's fault. He had it coming. He provoked me." People have gone as far as writing books based upon total falsehood in their quest to convince themselves and the world that they are right about something obviously false.

◈ False Questions

There is a story told of Rav Chaim of Volozhin in which one of his most promising pupils had strayed and ultimately left the path of Judaism. Rav Chaim met him years later and asked him, "My dear student, what happened to you?" The pupil answered, "Rebbe, I am tormented by many questions. If you would only answer them all I would surely return."

Rav Chaim replied, "Before I answer your questions, please tell me exactly when and how these questions began plaguing you."

The man told the following story: "As a means of reviewing each day's lessons, I used to walk in the forest alone while deep in thought. One day, I passed a young non-Jewish woman, who to my utter surprise, greeted me by saying, 'Good day, sir.' I was unsure of what to do and hastily responded, "Good day to you," so as not to be rude.

"It was the first time something like this had ever happened to me and I genuinely hoped that it would be the last. The next day, I thought about taking a different path but decided against it and it happened again. It was as though she was waiting for me to pass by so she could greet me. Again, I responded, only this time she also asked me my name and I told her.

"On the third day, she asked me why I often wandered in the forest. I explained to her that I was studying Torah and needed solitude to contemplate my studies. She seemed curious as to what Torah was and began asking all sorts of questions. This continued and each day we would converse about Judaism until in truth, I began to even look forward to these conversations, which served to open my eyes to questions that I had never thought of — questions that led me to doubt the very foundations on which my religion was based. I ultimately decided to leave.

"Now Rebbe, please allow me to share these questions with you."

Rav Chaim replied, "You don't have questions at all. You have *tirutzim* (answers/excuses/justifications). You were attracted to a non-Jewish woman and were seeking justifications in order to assuage your guilt. **To questions there are answers. To *tirutzim* there are no answers, because one cannot answer an answer!"**

A fellow who used to attend my *kiruv* classes would always pipe up with "questions" about all sorts of scientific findings that, in his mind, conflicted with the Torah I was teaching. I would never answer him. One day he approached me and asked, "Naftali, why do you answer other people's questions, sometimes even the very same questions as I ask, and yet you never answer mine?" I told him the story about Rav Chaim of Volozhin and he smiled because he realized that I was correct in my assessment.

This student, despite having attended many classes, having been to Israel, having spent many Shabbosim with my family and with the families of other rabbis, had not made a single commitment to *Yiddishkeit*. He had an antipathy to rules and restrictions no matter how meaningful and logical they were. He remained blind and deaf to the truth. Naturally he would have questions, because each class served to shake his tenuous perception of reality and leave him in a state of cognitive dissonance. No one likes to feel guilty and insecure in his beliefs, so people justify their guilt with questions.

Then this student asked me a great question: "How do we know where our questions are coming from?"

I explained to him that a true question motivates us to seek answers

— to research, study, and speak to wise people in the hope of uncovering the truth. It is asked with humility and a thirst for knowledge. It pushes you forward and allows you no rest.

An excuse is asked with a feigned curiosity and brazenness; there is no drive to find an answer because we sincerely hope there isn't one. Its sole purpose is to justify inaction or actions of the wrong kind. "I don't understand the data you are sharing so I will just keep on smoking until I do" or "How do I know the man collecting charity at my door is legitimately in need? I won't give a dollar until I find out for sure." We then proceed to do nothing toward finding the truth. We don't allow the solutions posed by others to penetrate our minds before we dismiss them outright.

Our goal is to discern questions from justifications, to seek answers to questions, and to COMPLETELY IGNORE excuses.

How do we overcome our biases? This is truly a topic for an entire book but I will share some fundamental ideas that should help you get started.

☙ Identify the Bias

Awareness — I'll bet you guessed I was going to write that. There's a popular book of challenges called "Where's Waldo?" We know he's hiding somewhere in a mass of faces, and it's the player's challenge to zoom in on him. We must learn to play, "Where is my bias?" and find it hiding among our many thoughts.

The Torah tells the story of Eliezer, the servant of Avraham, who goes to seek a wife for Yitzchak. When he reaches Aram Naharaim, he asks Hakadosh Baruch Hu to arrange a situation in which a woman will approach him and offer to provide water for him and his camels. This would serve as his sign that she is the one chosen to be Yitzchak's wife. As he later recounts the story to Besuel, Rivkah's father, he begins the narrative by relating the initial discussion that he had with Abraham. When Avraham asks him to undertake the mission, Eliezer asks, "*Ulai lo soveh ha'ishah laleches acharai*" (*Bereishis* 24:5) — "Perhaps the woman should not wish to follow after me (to where Yitzchok lives)?

When these words are initially spoken to Avraham the word אוּלַי, *ulai*, is written correctly with the letter *vav* after the *aleph*, while the second time, when the conversation is repeated to Besuel, it is written without the *vav* as אֻלַי. Rashi says this word actually means "to me." Eliezer had a daughter, and he was letting Besuel know that he had always hoped that she would marry Yitzchak.

Rashi's explanation raises a question: Why isn't the word spelled without the *vav* when Eliezer first speaks to Abraham? Furthermore, what is the Torah's purpose in implying this meaning when nothing comes of Eliezer's hopes and his coded message? I believe the answer is as follows:

There are two words used in the Torah when someone is expressing uncertainty about a future event: פֶּן or אוּלַי, *pen* or *ulai*. פֶּן is used when someone is afraid of something happening (lest) and אוּלַי is used when the person is hoping that it will happen (perhaps).

Eliezer used the wrong word when he initially spoke to Avraham. Since he was talking about the possibility of failing at his mission, which would happen if the woman would refuse to follow him back to the home of Yitzchak, *pen*, rather than *ulai*, would have been the correct word. Eliezer recognized the message of this mistake; somewhere inside him, failing in this mission was not a negative. He wondered why this was the case and he recognized the answer. He was biased by his hopes that Yitzchak would marry his own daughter.

At the time that he was speaking to Avraham, he was not yet aware of his bias and so the word *ulai* is written with a *vav* and by the time he spoke to Besuel he was aware so it is written without, meaning 'to me." What did he do when he realized he was biased? He recused himself entirely from the process and asked Hashem to show him a clear and undeniable sign so that his bias wouldn't be able to get in the way of his mission.

In this story lies the answer to our question. How did Eliezer first become aware of his bias? He checked his motives after he sensed that he felt, thought, and said the wrong thing at the time. Our words, thoughts, and actions will always tell us what is really going on inside if we only pay close enough attention. We should question our motives if we feel relief when disappointment is called for. If we hear bad news about someone and our first reaction is a degree of satisfaction, even if it is quickly replaced with "How can you even think such a thing?" we have learned that we have internal work to do. If we are generally threatened by being wrong, we should question the veracity of our positions. Once we become aware of our bias, we can be sure that we need to investigate our motives in that area.

☙ Counteract Your Bias

If your decision is based on your pre-existing viewpoints, ensure that you gather information from varied sources, consider different perspectives, and discuss your findings with people who think differently. Listen carefully to what they have to say. Before making decisions, always play devil's advocate and challenge your conclusion in as many ways possible.

It sometimes makes sense to only seek information that goes against your beliefs for some time before going back to evaluate what you initially believed to be true. A client was once bent on making what I determined to be a bad and biased investment. I asked him to seek out five reasons why the investment could go sour and then come back to me. He did just that and reversed course.

Remove yourself

Eliezer countered his bias by taking himself out of the picture, as every judge must do. If someone calls for information regarding someone toward whom we have negative feelings, we must be extremely vigilant about what we share because whatever we do say will likely be tainted. If a person seeks our advice and we have a personal conflict that inclines us toward or against a position, we should reveal the bias to the individual and ask that he consult someone else.

Ask an unbiased third party

If you know that a desire, bias, or conflict of interest will warp your decision-making skills — for example, when you really want or don't want something at any cost — then it is best to seek the counsel of someone who can help you with that decision. It is imperative that you reveal your bias to the individual so that he can be cognizant of where and how your views have been formed.

When we want something badly enough, everything about it looks rosy and when we don't want it, it's all black. If we aren't completely transparent with the people from whom we are seeking counsel, then their advice is worthless. In finance we use an acronym GIGO — garbage in, garbage out — to underscore that flawed inputs lead to flawed outputs. Advice is only as good as the information you provide the advisor, unless you are speaking to a prophet.

To recap: ***The ability to overcome biases and conflicts of interest is a hallmark of highly successful people. They tend to make better decisions and rarely fall into common traps and pitfalls. They are keenly aware of where their conflicts lie, and employ safeguards to protect themselves from their influence. They are highly mindful of their faulty tendencies and aware of the personal biases that can lead them astray.***

30

The Enemy Within

As I'm sure you've noticed by now, throughout this book I have referred to the Satan as our enemy — a tangible force against whom we are here to do battle. In this chapter, we will confirm the truth of this concept and learn why an accurate perspective on "him" is crucial in our efforts to achieve success.

The *Chovos HaLevavos* teaches us…

> *Every person's enemy resides between his ribs — the Yetzer Hara that is inside the person, who is his greatest enemy, greater than all of his other enemies.*

Years ago, when the opportunity arose for me to enter the finance profession, I was unsure whether I should take the giant leap forward. In truth, I was petrified. It was an entirely new field, an extremely challenging and competitive one, and I thought of many reasons why I wouldn't be successful.

While I was deliberating my decision, I mentioned my considerations to someone I know and he proceeded to tell me that he doubted that I would be successful in this field, and enumerated his reasons. Naturally, I found this insulting and left his house agitated. My mind was ringing with unspoken outrage: "Does he think me incapable? A failure? I will prove him wrong!"

Then I stopped and asked myself the following question. What was the difference between what he had just said to me and what I had been telling myself over the course of the past few weeks? In reality, there was no difference at all. I myself doubted that I could succeed and had rehearsed the reasons in my own mind over and over. Why was I furious at him for saying these things when I wasn't at all angry at myself?

When was the last time you got angry at yourself for putting yourself down? When have you ever treated yourself the same way you might treat anyone else who told you the kind of things that you often tell yourself? When did you ever respond with outrage when your own brain produced thoughts such as, "I can't; I'm not good enough; I will fail; I lack confidence, charisma, talent, brains, *mazal*..." When was the last time you stopped being nice to yourself as a result of a self-inflicted insult?

Considering how often we put ourselves down, we should be angrier at ourselves than we are at anyone else who may have ever slighted us. We should stop looking in the mirror, brushing our teeth, eating dessert, wearing nice clothes... as a punishment. Ask yourself, why don't you?

One obvious answer is that it's difficult to get, and certainly to stay, angry at yourself. Therefore, you cut yourself a lot of slack and allow the voice inside of your head to play "put-down songs" incessantly and without consequence. After a while, you even begin to believe the lyrics to be true.

This is a huge mistake, and contributes to the lack of success found in many people. The mistake is that we treat this insidious voice as if it is ours, when in truth, says the *Chovos HaLevavos*, it isn't our voice — it's the Satan's. If you are the type of person who does get angry at yourself, then I am here to inform you that you are taking your anger out on the wrong party.

Rabbeinu Bachya teaches us that our worst enemy is the one that speaks to us from within our rib cage. The challenge, as he says later in *Shaar Yichud HaMaaseh*, (Ch. 5, see also *Nefesh HaChaim Shaar* 1, Ch. 6, note 7) is that this enemy has so efficiently intertwined, buried and camouflaged himself inside of our consciousness, emotions, and thoughts that we don't see him for who he is. We think he is us and that it is we who desire and are drawn after harmful behaviors. We therefore treat him as we treat ourselves, with love, compassion, and endless patience. Instead of banishing him, we make a warm and cozy place for him inside our heart, soul, and mind and allow him to neutralize his nemesis, the *yetzer tov*, our best friend in the world.

❧ Redemption

In the Torah's account of our redemption from Egypt, we find four expressions of redemption: the first one is וְהוֹצֵאתִי אֶתְכֶם מִתַּחַת סִבְלֹות מִצְרַיִם — and I shall take you out from under the burdens of Egypt. The Chiddushei HaRim of Ger expounds that another meaning for סִבְלֹות is to tolerate and be patient with, as in the word סַבְלָנוּת. Through their years of slavery, the Jewish nation became accustomed to suffering, and the first step of redemption was to open their minds to that fact. Likewise, our personal redemption can only begin when we realize, and become unwilling to tolerate, the evil Pharaoh who oppresses us from within.

The Sfas Emes (*Parashas Ki Seitzei*) offers a similar idea, quoting the Chiddushei HaRim's explanation of the *pasuk* "when you go out to wage war on your enemy." The meaning, he says, is that only when a person frees himself and stops identifying with the Satan can the war begin. The first battle is the one within us.

The tendency to tolerate the voice of the enemy is the root of laziness, self-pity, low self-esteem, depression, and many other detrimental behaviors. Think about the idea of self-pity for a moment. Are YOU actually pitying and feeling sorry for yourself? Is it YOU who wants what the voice of fear and complacency are communicating to you? Are we perhaps pitying our worst enemy? When we don't recognize that we are fighting a war, and don't recognize the face of the enemy, we display patience and tolerance toward the most destructive force in our lives.

One of the Satan's greatest weapons is to distort our own self-assessment and not allow us to recognize our true qualities and potential. We suggested in an earlier chapter that Rabbeinu Bachya was underestimating himself when he concluded that he was incapable of authoring the *sefer.* He later realized that he was seeing things from a biased point of view — that of the enemy within him.

In my story above, I ultimately recognized that the person from whom I had sought advice about a Wall Street career perhaps did not want to see me succeed financially, but he was far from my greatest nemesis. There was no hate in this person's heart; at worst, he felt threatened by the success of others. On the other hand, the Satan, who had been speaking to me and through me for all those prior weeks, had far more malicious goals. He wants to see me depressed, poor, sinful, feeling like a piece of garbage, and ultimately dead.

Because the Satan will stop at nothing to get what he wants, we need to learn all of his tactics as they are described by Rabbeinu Bachya in *Shaar Yichud HaMaaseh,* and then go to battle. In this ongoing war, "Know thine enemy" is rule number one.

We need to employ our faculty of *Daas* to start recognizing the destructive voice inside us and labeling it for what it really is. It's "his" voice and NOT yours. Each time it speaks up you should be thinking, "Oh, it's him again... Doesn't he ever give up?... There he goes again... I know exactly what he wants and I am not going to give it to him."

◆§ Get Angry!

A verse (*Tehillim* 4:5) says, רִגְזוּ וְאַל תֶּחֱטָאוּ — "Infuriate yourself and do not sin." The Gemara (*Berachos* 5a) expounds that a person should constantly infuriate his good inclination and unleash it against his bad inclination.

The Piaseczna Rebbe writes (*Tzav V'Ziruz* 41):

> *You cannot distance your evil inclination unless you learn to hate him; meaning to awaken in the heart a hatred toward him for his desire to annihilate you from both worlds and to confuse your mind and heart. Through the awakening of hatred in your heart it will be easy for you to conquer him.*

◆§ The Power of *Netzach*

The Ribono shel Olam gave each of us phenomenal strength that derives through the *sefirah* of *Netzach* — the power to compete, conquer, and emerge victorious. How do we activate and reveal this powerful, yet latent, force? We start by realizing that we are in a fierce competition. When a person realizes that he is in a competition, that the other party is his worst enemy who wants nothing less than to destroy his life in this world and the next, he will become extremely angry and fight with all he has. If we fight, we win, because Hakadosh Baruch Hu steps in and helps us; Rabbeinu Bachya assures us of that. Our job in life is to go to battle.

We can get our children to do anything if we turn it into a contest. People overpay for items at auctions because money becomes secondary to their desire to best the other bidder. People spend $5.00 for the 10% chance of winning a $2.00 teddy bear because the thrill of winning a game is worth it. We need to learn to activate that will to win and channel it toward meaningful undertakings, because *Netzach*, brings forth monumental fulfillment and growth. There is no greater pleasure or thrill in the world, because each win brings us closer to our mission.

Here are the words of the holy Piaseczna Rebbe:

> *Then you will feel a type of pleasure within yourself. You may not understand the meaning of this pleasure. You may feel that it comes simply in response to your having been delivered from your desire — that it is the pleasure of your victory against your desire, of having been a warrior in the army of Hashem. Your understanding of this pleasure is correct, but incomplete. There is another cause behind this pleasure, a cause unknown to you. This pleasure that you are aware of, this pleasure of your victory, comes from a cause unknown to you.*
>
> *A part of your soul was clothed in a polluted garment of an evil feeling. You removed that evil garment, and so this part of your soul was revealed to you without it. And that is the unfathomable reason for your pleasure. You feel that with*

your victory you have come closer to holiness. Primarily, it has brought you closer to the holiness within yourself, to your soul.

Netzach, teaches the Piaseczna Rebbe, reveals latent powers within us. It squeezes brand-new toothpaste out of the tube that you never dreamed contained one more iota. An aspect of self is set free from the grip of the Satan, from the shackles of limitation. I can't stress enough how much adopting this mindset and way of life will likely turn things around for the better.

The father of a kallah once came to see me several weeks before his daughter's wedding; he was completely hysterical. His daughter adamantly wanted to call off the wedding and refused to change her mind even though everyone absolutely adored the young man to whom she was engaged. He asked if I would please speak to her. While I am neither a therapist nor a marriage coach, I agreed to a call.

The kallah informed me that "Hashem is so good to me and opened my eyes so I could realize how wrong I was about my chassan. How wonderful is Hashem that He allowed me to see this before I made the huge mistake of marrying him!"

I asked her to give me some examples of what she was seeing and she provided several.

"When we were first becoming acquainted, he made me laugh and I liked that, but now I realize that he doesn't take life seriously enough. He would be so considerate, always asking me about my day, my job... and I therefore thought he had sterling middos. Now I realize that an interest in these trivialities are unbefitting a Ben Torah and he will surely spend his days in idle chatter. What I saw as him being accommodating, I now realize is him being a pushover. He is very thought-out and goal oriented and I really liked that, but I now see him as someone who will surely control me." (A controlling pushover — can you see the contradiction in that?)

I had just witnessed the holy words of the Rambam in real life. As he writes in the second chapter of *Hilchos Dei'os*.

כַּךְ בְּנֵי אָדָם שֶׁנַּפְשׁוֹתֵיהֶם חוֹלוֹת... הֲרֵי אוֹמְרִים לְרַע טוֹב וְלַטּוֹב רַע, שָׂמִים חֹשֶׁךְ לָאוֹר וְאוֹר לַחֹשֶׁךְ שָׂמִים מַר לְמָתוֹק וּמָתוֹק לְמַר.

To paraphrase: when one is afflicted with a disease of the soul, it causes bad to seem good and good to seem bad, darkness is light and light is seen as darkness, bitter to taste sweet and sweet to taste bitter.

Situations that literally seemed good and sweet one day can seem evil and bitter the very next.

Of course this *kallah* had zero proof of any of this and I knew with absolutely certainty that I was talking to "her feet" and not her head, yet I faced the challenge of getting HER to see. How would I succeed where better people than me had failed? She had heard the words, "You are just scared to get married," many times during the past week and it clearly wasn't changing anything. I realized that I had to activate her *Netzach*.

I asked her to close her eyes and picture herself 50 years from now, sitting at the *mitzvah tantz* of her grandchild. There she is, the matriarch of a beautiful family, having reached the pinnacle of a Jewish life. Her sons and sons-in-law are now dancing with the *kallah*, her granddaughter, while she and her husband look on beaming with *nachas*. Her feelings of gratitude to Hakadosh Baruch Hu are welling up inside of her, causing tears to run down her face as she looks around the room and sees the "fortune" that she has amassed over her lifetime. She is surrounded by dozens of *Yiddishe neshamos* — children, grandchildren, and soon, there will be great-grandchildren. This moment represents the climax of her life and *b'ezras Hashem* she will have many more experiences like this awaiting her in the years to come.

I explained to her that there is a holy voice inside of her, one of a dear and close friend, who wants this vision to one day be a reality and he wants it more than anything in the world.

"He is dressed in white, his face glows, and he was there beside you, holding your hand, during the *shidduch* and engagement process. Sweet tastes sweet and light illuminates when he is in the driver's seat.

"And then, there's is an enemy inside of you who wants to rob you of all that you just envisioned. He sees your wedding day approaching and he is frightened by what will be. His hatred for you is worse than the worst hatred ever shown by one human being to another. He is dressed in black, has yellowed crooked teeth, horrible breath, and smells awful. He turns light to dark and sweet to bitter and here is a vision of what he wants:

"You are at the very same *mitzvah tantz,* only it isn't your grandchild's wedding, it's your grandniece's. You know what they are all thinking as they look your way. You've seen that look of pity a million times before. If only she would have followed through on the engagement to that wonderful, caring boy with a great sense of humor but she broke it off. He's a grandfather by now. We all tried to reason with her but she just refused to listen."

"So," I asked the *kallah,* "who are you going to allow to win this battle? I agree with all of the wonderful things that you said about Hashem, only He isn't the one that you are listening to right now. If a woman never meets her *bashert* she can live a happy and fulfilling life nonetheless. You, however, will look back with regret at having met your *bashert* and turned him away."

The *kallah* awoke, as though from under a spell, and she became very angry that night. She fought her enemy all the way to the *chuppah* and the couple is *Baruch Hashem* happily married with several children.

We need to learn to unleash the power of *Netzach* inside of us. We need to become infuriated at the voice that is preventing us from reaching our potential and dragging us down into the gutter. We never sell ourselves short — "he" does. The ugly, bad, filthy Satan that will knock us down because he doesn't want us to finish *Shas,* succeed in business, feed our families with respect, help others, treat ourselves with dignity. He wants us unemployed, not going to *minyan,* not treating our spouses as we should. He wants us to underestimate ourselves all day long.

So long as we are alive, he will keep trying, hour after hour, day after day, through voices playing inside of our heads: "You are no good, look at how much wrong you have done, how little you have done right, others are so much better than you, look at what they have and you don't have, so many wasted opportunities, it's pointless at this juncture to even try because it's all hopeless, so much has been lost never to be regained." If that doesn't work, he will try another tactic, he will lure us with fake promises of happiness and fulfillment, and lead us down a path of emptiness and desolation.

Let's review once more the words of Rav Nachman of Breslov (*Sichos Haran*, 6) that describe the Satan as someone who runs around a marketplace with his hands closed. He asks each person, "What do you think I have in my hands?" Each thinks, "Surely he has what I want," and so they run after him. In the end he opens up his hands and shows them all that he has absolutely nothing. Likewise, the Satan lures us with his hands closed and we chase after him thinking he has what we want — wealth, happiness, fame, fulfillment, honor — and in the end, when it is too late to turn our lives around, he opens his hands and shows us that he has absolutely nothing at all. He has fooled us and thereby caused us to waste our lives.

Is all this making you really angry? GOOD! This is precisely what the *middah* of anger was given to us for — to unleash it against HIM. The Piaseczna Rebbe writes (*Tzav V'Zeruz*) that a person cannot successfully vanquish the Satan until he learns to utterly despise him.

If ever one was meant to activate his power of visualization, it's in the battle against the Satan. Create an image of him and see him talking to you when that insidious voice starts up. Mine has yellowed teeth, blisters on his face, and smells like a sewer. What does yours look and smell like?

Yell at "him"

My great-grandfather, the holy Rav Naftali of Ropshitz *zt"l* was known to display great self-sacrifice in order to immerse himself in the *mikvah* each day. Once, during the bitter cold Polish winter, he went down to the river to immerse himself only to find it frozen solid. As he stood there in the bitter cold, hacking away at the ice, the voice inside of him was saying, "Naftali, Naftali, what are you doing? Don't you think Hashem would understand if you skipped a day? Look at how cold it is outside. You are obligated to protect your health! Go back home where it's warm. No one will ever know."

My Zaide just kept on hacking away while the voice kept on protesting. When he finally broke through the ice, he jumped into the freezing water and immediately the voice changed its tune to "Naftali, Naftali, how righteous you are. What a *tzaddik*! Look at your level of self-sacrifice. Who can compare to you? You risked your life to serve Hashem. How great is your reward!"

When he came out of the water, he said to the voice, "Thank you for clarifying something that has always troubled me. Chazal call you "an old fool" and while I understood that you are old — it was you after all who spoke to Chava in Gan Eden so long ago — I always wondered, Why do they call you a fool? Today, I learned the reason. Did you have to jump into the ice-cold water with me? Couldn't you have waited for me outside, where it wasn't as cold, and started your *gaavah* speech about my righteousness after I came out? You really are a fool."

Tzaddikim would often speak this way to the Satan. They would often yell at the voice inside of them and they would pay close attention to his tactics. One need not be a great *tzaddik* to want to win. Each of us can get better at lowering our tolerance for the enemy inside of us, and the more we recognize who is speaking to us, the more battles we will win.

Set realistic goals and wear him down

Remember my friend Andy Burian and the steeples that saved his life? Let's analyze that story a bit more deeply and try to understand what was going on inside of his mind on that march.

> *The enemy speaks: "Your feet are so cold and bloody. You are so weak and will never make it to the end of the march. What point is there in suffering any further? Lay down on the snow and the misery will come to an end."*
>
> *Andy: "You are right — there is no point."*
>
> *The older man speaks: "Look, young boy. Do you see that steeple over there? That's as far as you need to walk."*
>
> *Andy: "I can walk that far. That's not far at all."*
>
> *The enemy speaks again: "It's not true! He's deceiving you. It's not to the next steeple or the one after that you must go.*

You need to walk many, many more miles and will never make it. Give up now!"

Andy: "I will choose not to focus on that. Rather, I will focus on each steeple. Whether I make it to the end or not, do you think I am so weak that I cannot march to the next steeple? I obviously can."

We already mentioned the brilliance of *Daf Yomi*, the ultimate steeple-to-steeple program. I recall when I started my first cycle, the enemy would badger me each day with put-downs like, "You will never finish. It's too difficult." The challenge went away when I started retorting, "Who's trying to finish? I am merely going to learn tonight's *daf*. Are you suggesting that I am incapable of even doing that?" So it went until learning the *daf* became as habitual as my morning coffee and my enemy finally left me alone.

If we set realistic and achievable goals, we arm ourselves with ammunition that will vanquish the enemy. We are in a battle; a battle for purpose, mission, and success. "His" job is to derail us and our job is to build strategies to neutralize him. We will prevail.

31

Ups and Downs

You are 17 years old. Your brothers don't understand you. Tension between you builds. Differences proliferate and you are treated more and more like an outcast. They ultimately turn against you and throw you into a pit with snakes and scorpions. As you lie at the bottom in utter darkness, you can hear them deliberating your fate — to kill you or spare your life. Suddenly you are pulled out of the pit only to realize that you're being sold as a slave. You are forcibly stripped of your precious coat, the one your loving father gave you as a gift, which will soon be soaked in sheep's blood and used to feign your death. Your new masters sell you to others who then sell you yet again.

You end up in Egypt, the most spiritually corrupt land on the planet. Not a soul knows who you are and not a single family member will be searching for you. You lie awake at night worried sick about the pain this is surely causing your father. "Does he even know I am alive?" you wonder.

Just as you seem to be settling into your new role, your master's wife fabricates a slanderous lie about you and you find yourself locked in a cold dungeon. Can we envision anyone reaching a lower point in their lives than this?

As we try to place ourselves into Yosef's shoes, we wonder how he survived, let alone thrived. How did he ultimately reach a point where he had no hatred in his heart toward his brothers, or even toward Potiphar, as evidenced by his willingness to marry his daughter? While we cannot fathom such greatness, we can be sure that Yosef paved the road for each of us to weather life's ups and downs and live with an elevated perspective during difficult times. This is what infuses us with the capacity to bounce back and thrive after setbacks. Yosef provided us with the antidote to the very worst of the Satan's poisons: *yei'ush* — despair, loss of hope.

When we defined success in an earlier chapter, we pointed out that Yosef HaTzaddik has the distinction of being the only person in the Torah to bear the title of *Ish Matzliach*, successful man. As we contemplate what he endured and how he excelled throughout his travails, we can begin to understand why he earned this coveted title. Yosef displayed remarkable resiliency and a positive attitude, traits that help to pave the road to success. Without resiliency, life wears you down and your motivation and zest for living dries up. Think of resiliency as the durability of your energy tank, and motivation as the fuel inside. If the tank cracks, all of the fuel leaks out.

☙ Attitude

Yosef's resiliency was ironclad because he applied a positive interpretation to the events that transpired in his life — not only in retrospect, but as they were happening. When we experience life's inevitable losses or setbacks, our reaction, mindset, and attitude make all of the difference. Putting matters in the right perspective spares us the emotional turmoil that causes us to lose motivation and hope. It is therefore imperative that we embrace a healthy perspective on setbacks: that they are a normal part of life and actually contribute to success.

Setbacks are part of the fabric of life

The *pasuk* (*Yechezkel* 1:14) teaches, וְהַחַיּוֹת רָצוֹא וָשׁוֹב — "and the life force flows (runs) and ebbs (returns)." These words are a fundamental element of "The *Ma'aseh Merkavah*" — "Work of the Chariot" — on which much of *Kabbalah* is based, and they tell us that life is a series of ebbs and flows. The cardiograph of the heart of all human beings consists of the repetition of peaks and valleys followed by a flat line. Our heartbeat mirrors life; ups, downs, and short periods of respite. Setbacks are par for the course, and while we don't particularly enjoy them and even pray that they don't occur, Chazal teach us that they are part of life and woven into the very fabric of creation. A constant flat line means the person *R'L* has passed away.

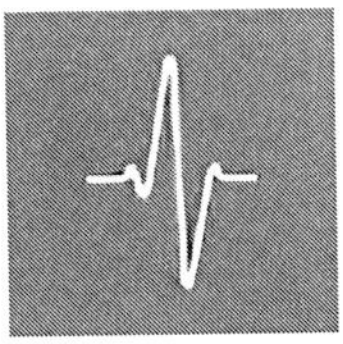

Rav Tzadok HaKohen (*Pri Tzaddik Shabbos Shuvah*) confirms the fundamental value of setbacks in his explanation of the saying, שֶׁבַע יִפּוֹל צַדִּיק וְקָם, "A righteous person falls seven times and gets up." The *tzaddik* will achieve levels of righteousness that are greater and greater with each fall and subsequent rise. This is what is meant with the words וַיֵּלֶךְ מֹשֶׁה (*Devarim* 31:1) "and Moshe went." Unlike an angel which is a static being, a human is here to move forward, and moving forward necessitates setbacks. Moshe Rabbeinu at the end of his life therefore says, לֹא אוּכַל עוֹד לָצֵאת וְלָבוֹא. Moshe Rabbeinu realized that he had reached his final destination when he was unable to "leave" his current level. He realized there was no setback forthcoming and he could no longer "arrive" at a higher level. He realized it was his time to pass from the world.

The Holy Maggid of Chernobyl, in his *sefer*, *Meor Einayim*, teaches that rising can only occur after a fall. Because our purpose is to rise, the world is created in such a way that nothing stays up forever. The fall gives birth to the even greater rise that will follow.

Rav Nachman of Breslov (*Likutei Moharan* 22:11) teaches that when a person seeks to rise from level to level, he must experience a setback, because setbacks lead to advancement. He cautions us (*Meshivas Nefesh* 5) that when we are experiencing a fall, we will firmly believe that these words were not meant for us, but only for righteous people who are on a path of constant elevation. Nevertheless, he stresses that this concept applies to every single one of us — setbacks must precede advancements.

The benefits of setbacks

Our attitude toward setbacks will improve the day we begin to view them as beneficial, as a prerequisite to success. Here are some of these benefits:

- Without challenge, life ultimately loses its luster; setbacks create challenges. Imagine a man who has a magic wand and can instantly have whatever his heart desires: a beautiful house, family, lots of money in the bank, the best foods, friends. His life is like paradise. Each day, he merely has to perform the same procedure. He waves his wand and achieves absolute perfection.

In his perfect world, there is never an argument, there's never aggravation, his stocks only go up, nothing ever breaks, his kids get straight A's. Eventually, he will feel he is dying of boredom. Life will become stale because there are no problems to solve, no challenges to overcome and no brighter future to anticipate.

The Chasam Sofer says (*Niddah* 48b), that were a person to always have whatever he desired, he would utterly despise his life. This idea in encompassed in the blessing *"Borei nefashos rabbos v'chesronan"* — which blesses Hashem, "Who created a multitude of living things and their deficiencies." Hashem created us in a way that we are always lacking something. The purpose of these deficiencies is conveyed in the subsequent words, *"L'hachayos bahem nefesh kol chai"* — "to sustain the soul of every living being." The needs and deficiencies we must face and overcome are what sustain us, by giving us motivation and excitement to live and grow.

- Great things will only come to us after we yearn and pray for them.

It is only in times of darkness that we yearn for light, because it is human nature to become accustomed to a long-term situation. Only when the situation worsens do we long for restoration of our former circumstances. That longing is the "awakening from below" which initiates an even greater light from above. Chazal tell us that the *tefillos* we undertake during periods of darkness pave the way for us to rise from the fall.

- In times of darkness we are able to activate the awesome power of hope. In the words of the Ramchal (Lecture on Hope), the hope for salvation that we muster during difficult times is what draws down blessing from above. **"Constriction was created for the sole purpose for us to be *mekaveh* — be hopeful — and in doing so, draw down the light of the Infinite, may His Name be blessed."** The word *kav*, which is the root of the word "hope," means a "line." In *Kabbalah*, the *kav* is the mechanism through which all abundance flows to us from Above.

- Times of darkness provide the setting in which the purpose of Creation can best be fulfilled. If Hashem's only intent were to create an entity into which He could shine His light, it would seem that the Heavens would have been all that was needed. However, the *Tanya* teaches (36) that the ultimate purpose of creation could not have been the existence of angels, because in their realm there is no darkness, and only in darkness can light be revealed. Darkness only exists in the realm of the human being. The *Tanya* is teaching that "*Hakadosh Baruch Hu* desired a place to live in the lower worlds," and since He is infinite light, He is revealed most intensely in times of utter darkness. The darker the situation into which we fall, the more opportunity there is to fulfill the sole purpose of all of creation — the revelation of Hashem's light.

There is a story told about the holy Rav Shlomke of Zhvill, in which he and his followers went to pray at the Kosel on a Friday night, despite the great danger in those years (1930s). After a heartfelt prayer, as the group was returning through the market, an Arab approached the Rebbe and slapped him across the face. Naturally his followers were horrorstruck, yet the Rebbe began to smile.

"Imagine a poor man that comes to ask a rich man for a donation," he explained. "If the rich man asks the poor man if he has change for 5 shekel, then the poor man knows that he isn't getting much of a donation. If the rich man asks him if he has change for 20 shekel, he knows he is getting a bit more.

"Imagine if the rich man asks him if he has change of 1,000 shekel! Sure, the poor man is going to have to hand the rich man a large sum of money, but he knows that he is getting a large donation in return. Nobody asks for that much change if they intend to give a shekel or two."

Rav Shlomke continued, "We earned something truly great through the *mesiras nefesh* that we demonstrated in coming here to *daven*. Hashem, however, wanted a bit of change back from us before He gives us our reward, and that's why I received a slap on the face. I am smiling because the greater the change, the greater the gift."

- Setbacks are often the "change" that we give back to the Ribono shel Olam, and the gift is the even greater rise that follows.
- Setbacks squeeze the greatness out of us. They teach us what we are truly capable of. They bring forth unrevealed potential that we would have never known lies dormant inside of us had we not faced adversity.
- Adversity forges us into a stronger, improved vessel that will be capable of containing the greater good that will follow. Without suffering the fall and then rising stronger, we would be too weak to contain the greater good Hashem wants to send us, and it would break us.
- Faith and trust in Hashem, and the positivity and optimism that express that exalted state, have the greatest value during periods of darkness. Although we are tested in both good and challenging times, our faith is tested most during periods of difficulty.

In the words of the Chazon Ish (*Emunah U'Vitachon*):

> *It is easy to speak of trust at times when the need to trust does not play an important role in one's life; but it is much more difficult to have trust at times when it is indeed called for… The real test that can determine whether a person really believes in what he is saying — whether he really does place his trust in Hashem or he has merely trained himself to chirp "bitachon, bitachon" without having it penetrate his heart — is when he encounters a situation that demands that he indeed place his trust in Hashem. At such times the role of trust is to guide his actions, heal, and soothe him.*

When we internalize each of these bullet points, we can ultimately come to see life's struggles and setbacks as labor pains that lead to birth and growth. The Baal Shem Tov tells us that the *nisayon,* challenge of difficult periods, comes from the loss of hope and the feeling of abandonment that permeates us. We misinterpret Hashem's intentions and in doing so we disconnect from our trust in Him.

Don't blame yourself

It is extremely important for a person to internalize that setbacks are a normal part of life because, while we are meant to learn something from both ups and downs, we are not meant to blame ourselves by thinking that we are being punished for something we have done wrong. In certain rare instances that may be the case, and challenging times should therefore motivate us toward introspection, but in most cases punishment has absolutely nothing to do with it. On the contrary, Hashem is placing an opportunity for growth and abundance before us. As Rav Nachman taught us, the Satan will not allow us to believe this when darkness falls; he will try to convince us that we are an exception to this rule. There are no exceptions to this rule — darkness always brings greater light.

Yosef HaTzaddik had many years to contemplate whether and how he may have contributed to his situation, but as the story unfolded it became obvious that he was being primed to ascend to kingship and to provide salvation for his family. Hashem loves each of us, infuses us every moment with the blessing of life. Whatever situation we face, it can and will lead to ultimate good.

Pray!

Rav Nachman of Breslov teaches (74):

> *There are two types of judgments; an impure one, the result of the snake's poison that was injected into Chava, and a pure one, as the pasuk teaches, "The one that Hashem loves He rebukes" (Mishlei 3:12)... An indication that a person is experiencing a pure setback is that he doesn't lose his motivation to pray for salvation (Talmud Berachos 5a).*

Besides the fact that prayer brings salvation, our continued connection to prayer also demonstrates that we have not lost hope or our faith in the love Hakadosh Baruch Hu has for us.

But I am so exhausted from the constant ups and downs!

Sometimes we grow so tired; matters seem so hopeless and pointless. We win a battle only to face another even bigger one; we rise only to fall even harder soon after. Why must life be this way? What is the meaning of all this? The following Torah, when I first learned it, changed my perspective on this subject.

The *Tanya* relates in Chapter 27 "***This is the task of the beinonim*** (the segment of the population that lives with the ongoing internal battle between right and wrong) ***to subdue the evil impulse and the thoughts that arise within them and to completely avert their mind from them. With every repulsion of thought, the Sitra Achra, Satan, is suppressed here below. Each arousal from below*** (our initiative to battle the Satan) ***produces a corresponding arousal above...***

Therefore, one should not ever feel depressed or troubled in his heart (i.e.: what is the point of this battle if I never experience ultimate victory) ***even if he is engaged in this battle all of the days of his life. For perhaps this is precisely why he was created, and this is the service that is demanded of him — to subdue the Sitra Achra constantly.*** (Sometimes life feels like one long game of whack a mole; we hit him over here and he pops up somewhere else.)

There are two kinds of Divine pleasure, one from the complete annihilation of the Sitra Achra **and the conversion from bitter to sweet, from darkness to light, which is accomplished by *tzaddikim*. The second is when the *Sitra Achra* is subdued while he is still in his strongest and most powerful form, soaring like an eagle, and from this height Hashem topples him in response to our human initiative. This is accomplished by the *beinonim*.**

The strength that these holy words provide is immeasurable. There are two kinds of Divine pleasures: ours and that of the *gedolim* of each generation. Hashem derives *nachas* from both and treasures both equally. Battling each day and never coming home with a trophy takes overwhelming will and perseverance. Climbing and knowing that we may never arrive at the top takes a deeper understanding of life and its true purpose. It requires a negation of the ego and thoughts of "I want to feel good about myself. I want to stand at the top and be able to say, 'I did it! I won!'

Fighting the same battles throughout our lives requires us to negate what "we" want and focus on the underlying purpose of life — to battle and overcome, and do so over and over and over, not so that we can feel victorious, but so that we can carry out the Will of Hashem. While we may not see it, the hair's breadth progress that we are making on this world is moving upper worlds in infinite ways and giving Hakadosh Baruch Hu outstanding pleasure.

There is nothing wrong with us. Battling our way out of darkness is our purpose in life. We should therefore expect this to be the case for our entire lives and even learn to look forward to it being this way.

32

Conclusion

It is difficult to say goodbye to the writing of this book. There is so much more to say and many more Torah gems to share. We have barely scratched the surface; we've delivered but a small glass of water from the Pacific Ocean. Before we end there is one last idea that I am compelled to share and that is the powerful idea of sharing. The topic is a book unto itself but a brief discussion in the context of self-actualization is a befitting way to conclude.

☙ In the Image of Hashem

Rav Dessler writes in his *Kuntress HaChesed* (Ch. 1) that when Hashem created man, He created him to be both a giver and a receiver. This ability to give is a distinctly Divine quality and serves as a profound expression of emulation of our Creator, Who gives without receiving anything in return. Furthermore, Hashem created the entire universe for the sole purpose of having to whom to give — us — and in the same manner He created us in His image. We each spend a lifetime creating a world around us through marriage, family, friends, possessions, skills, and occupations. Acting in the image of Hashem means seeing that world as a means to an end; a vehicle for giving and sharing.

☙ The Greatest Segulah There Is

I was once speaking to a crowd who came to learn ways to improve their financial situation and better their lives in general. During the Q&A, a man asked "Naftali, what is the one thing that I can do to jump-start my life?" I answered, "Start helping the people around you jump-start their lives. Act as Hashem does and blessing will follow" He retorted, "But I have nothing to share."

So many people erroneously believe that a high level of achievement is a pre-requisite for giving to and helping others. Nothing can be further from the truth. Everyone, without exception, has something that someone else needs. This axiom is woven into the fabric of the universe. *Olam chesed yibaneh* (*Tehillim* 89:3) – the world is founded on *chesed* and each of us plays his part in that perfectly designed system. For some it is a given talent or skill; creativity, humor, organizational skills, time-management... For others it is the wisdom garnered from having lived through an experience. We can each find valuable gems within ourselves and seek out those that would benefit from them. When we do so, we experience a deep sense of fulfillment unlike any pleasure that this material world has to offer. We experience the revelation of the G-dliness within us.

☙ Finding Meaning in Pain

I have seen many people pull themselves out of depression and despair through the realization that their life has great purpose and meaning; that they have what to offer the world around them. That even painful and tragic experiences such as unemployment, anorexia, loss of a loved one, childlessness, illness, and divorce can be turned into a vehicle for extraordinary good when the experience is utilized to help others. We need only look around us to see the wonderful organizations and *chesed* projects that were launched by those who experienced a setback or tragedy and then said, "I want to help those who are living through the same thing." As we learned from Yosef HaTzaddik, the ultimate definition of positive and negative in any situation is defined by our free-choice; what we make of the experience. Both great abundance and lack can serve as either transformative or destructive forces, depending on how the person leverages them.

When we make an earnest attempt to step into the role of "giver" we become a conduit for the abundance and goodness that Hakadosh Baruch Hu wants to bring into the world. We empower ourselves with the כֹּחַ הַמְשַׁלֵּחַ, the infinite strength of the Sender; Hakadosh Baruch Hu.

❧ Learning to Receive

The words of Rav Dessler also teach that receiving is a form of giving because it allows the other to emulate Hashem by acting as the giver. To those who are in need this could help to alleviate the idea that receiving and shame go hand in hand. The fact is, we are all receivers. In the words of the great Rav Shalom Schwadron *z"l*, "we are all *schnorrers*. We *schnorrer luft* (air) from Hakadosh Baruch Hu every moment. Is there a greater *schnorrer* than that?" There is no person that lives independent of those around them. We needed someone to give birth to us and nurture us for many years. We needed teachers, Rebbeim, coaches, doctors… We still do. We all need companionship, love, advice, and a simple helping hand that only another can provide. Above all else we need Hakadosh Baruch Hu, the Father we all share.

For some receiving is unnatural and pride will sometimes get in the way of reaching out or admitting that we can't go it alone. In a society that worships independence and strength, showing vulnerability can sometimes prove challenging and degrading. As Torah Jews we can strengthen ourselves with the thought that receiving and giving go hand in hand and one is not possible without the other. We are all in this together because we share a common Source in the lofty soul that we carry.

❧ My *Tefillah*

I ask Hakadosh Baruch Hu that this book achieve its intended goal and find favor in your mind and heart — that you learn to embrace the treasure trove that is our *mesorah* and go on to make more of yourself than you ever imagined.

This book was written for YOU no matter who you think you are or aren't. I have yet to meet anyone who doesn't possess the power to conquer and change his inner and outer world. May Hakadosh Baruch Hu bless YOU with the vision to see yourself for who YOU truly are and to achieve your life's mission.

Appendix 1

More on the Power of Mindful Breathing

Here are additional methods of being mindful of breathing:

1. According to the Baal Shem Tov, the *pasuk* (*Yechezkel* 1:14) — *V'hachayus ratzo v'shav* — "and the life force flows (runs) and ebbs (returns)" — relates to the inhaling and exhaling of breath. When we inhale *neshamah* we are drawing renewal into ourselves. As we exhale, we can allow that renewal to help us expel the impurity or darkness that is inside of us. We can ask Hakadosh Baruch Hu to take the impurity from us, as the *pasuk* says (*Tehillim* 55:23), הַשְׁלֵךְ עַל הַשֵּׁם יְהָבְךָ — "Throw your burdens onto Hashem."

2. Rav Levi Yitzchok of Berditchev (*Drushim L'Yom Kippur*) writes that a person should contemplate and then thank Hakadosh Baruch Hu with every breath. The reason is that each time we exhale, our *neshamah* seeks to exit our bodies for good, and return to its Source. Hakadosh Baruch Hu, in His infinite mercy, doesn't allow this to happen.

3. The Maggid of Mezeritch writes that when we exhale, the *neshamah* returns to its Source and when we inhale, Hashem returns it to us. In essence, we are reborn with each breath, which should infuse us with a sense of renewal and fervor. These are points we can contemplate when we breathe.

4. If you have ever visited the holy city of Tzefas you are able to close your eyes and see "Tzefas blue" in your mind's eye. The reason that so much of the city is painted that color is that this heavenly shade of blue — *techeiles* — is identified as the color of *kedushah*, holiness. As the Gemara says:

תַּנְיָא, הָיָה ר׳ מֵאִיר אוֹמֵר: מַה נִּשְׁתַּנָּה תְּכֵלֶת מִכָּל מִינֵי צְבָעוֹנִין? מִפְּנֵי שֶׁהַתְּכֵלֶת דּוֹמָה לַיָּם וְיָם דּוֹמֶה לְרָקִיעַ וְרָקִיעַ לְכִסֵּא הַכָּבוֹד

It is taught: R' Meir would say: Why is the color of techeiles different than other colors? Because techeiles is like the sea, the sea is like the sky, and the sky is like the heavenly throne (*Chullin* 89a).

Imagining this color can aid in contemplation: Let your mind's eye tint the air that you are inhaling with this shade of light blue, and see yourself slowly filling up with the color. You can also envision yourself exhaling the color brown, muddy from anxiety, anger, stress, fear…

Each time you "breathe in" the holiness, you will have performed a positive commandment according to the *Sefer Chareidim* (Ch.2), which was written by Rav Elazar Ezkari, a great *mekubal* who lived in Tzefas at the time of the Arizal. I will share his words; while they are extremely deep, the overall message is clear.

> *The combination of the nine sefiros are called white light, and Malchus, which is blue light, is a throne for the white light, and together they serve as a throne for the emanation of Hakadosh Baruch Hu… The nation that He has chosen, He instructed to cleave with their thoughts to this blue light because they are like a wick that is connected to blue light on which there is white light… and this is what the pasuk means, "And you who cleave to Hashem your G-d."*

There are several sources that describe the *sefirah* of *Malchus* as the color of *techeiles*. It is mentioned in the *Zohar*, as well as the *Pardes Rimonim* from the Ramak, Rav Moshe Cordovero. According to the *Sefer Chareidim*, we perform the positive commandment of *dveikus* by connecting our thoughts to the blue light, the *sefirah* of *Malchus*, which connects us directly to Hakodesh Baruch Hu. Connecting to our Creator will serve to erase all of the negativity which is occupying our minds.

Appendix 2
The Power of Positive Thinking

☙ Impact of thought

In western society, there is a saying: "Think what you like." Conversely, the Gemara (*Yoma* 29a) states, הִרְהוּרֵי עֲבֵירָה קָשִׁים מֵעֲבֵירָה — "thoughts of sin are worse than sin." To the world at large, thought is ephemeral and intangible. If it doesn't lead to action, it is believed to evaporate. The Torah teaches us, however, that in many ways thought has a greater impact than action. The Rambam explains why "Thoughts of sin are worse than sin."

> *I can offer a wonderful explanation: If a person sins, it is generally due to circumstances that result from his being a physical creature; that is, a person will sin due to his animal side. But thoughts are the treasure of a person that follow his "form" (his image of Hashem) and if a person sins with his thoughts, then he has sinned with his greatest asset ... [because] the purpose of the mind is to cling to G-d, not to slip below [to the animal level] (Moreh Nevuchim 3:8).*

The Rambam is explaining that when a person sins with his body, it is understandable because the body is physical, and therefore has all sorts of physical urges and instincts. The mind, on the other hand, is the manifestation of the image of G-d. To sin with one's mind is therefore a greater desecration than sinning with one's body.

The *Nefesh HaChaim* (Gate 1:14) teaches that a human being possesses three primary faculties. In descending order of loftiness they are thought, speech, and action, which correspond to the three levels of soul — *neshamah, ruach,* and *nefesh*. Just as *neshamah* is loftier and can effectuate a greater supernal change than *nefesh,* likewise thought carries far more potent powers than action.

Let us explore a few examples that illustrate the power of thought.

☙ Thinking Optimistically

In his commentary on *Parashas Noach,* the Apter Rav, the Oheiv Yisrael, teaches that Noach entered the ark "as a result of the flood waters." Rashi says that Noach was among the "small believers. He believed and he didn't believe and he therefore only entered the ark when the flood waters forced him to." Rashi seems to be criticizing Noach for his lack of *emunah,* which doesn't seem plausible given that the Torah bestows on him the title of "complete *tzaddik.*"

The Apter Rav explains that the word *emunah* has two meanings. Faith is the common meaning, but we find in *Megillas Esther* that the word אוֹמֵן means "nurture," when it is used to tell us that Mordechai nurtured Esther like his own child. The reason that faith and nurture go hand in hand is that with thoughts of faith, a person possesses the power to bring about good, to draw it down from above.

The Apter Rav says that Noach understood this power well. He therefore tried to hold back thoughts of faith before the coming of the flood, because he didn't want to cause it. He tried to minimize his faith, knowing its inherent power, and this is what Rashi meant by "small believer"; he consciously made his belief small. The lesson is that how we think affects what flows to us from above. We must not follow the philosophy of "think what you want," because what we think creates reality. **Positive thinking leads to positive outcomes**. *"Tracht gut vett zein gut"* as the Yiddish saying goes. And yes, the opposite is true as well.

◆§ Thinking Positively About Others

The Torah tells us that Yosef recognized his brothers when they came to Egypt, but they didn't recognize him (*Bereishis* 42:8). The Ohr HaChaim HaKadosh explains that "even though it is the nature of people that when recognition is revealed in the heart of one person the second person's heart will also become aware of this, **since hearts reveal secrets one to another**, the *pasuk* says that they did not recognize him. This was because upon seeing Yosef in an exalted state, they pushed the thought that this was him out of their minds."

The *Ohr HaChaim* further cites this same phenomenon to explain the *pasuk* in *Vayigash*, "Then Yehudah approached him (Yosef) and said...". He explains Yehudah's "approaching" Yosef as an illustration of the *pasuk* (*Mishlei* 27:19) which says, "As water mirrors the face to the face, so does the heart of man to man." Knowing that hearts communicate in this fashion, Yehudah brought to mind his feelings of friendship and closeness toward Yosef, which would in turn cause Yosef's heart to reciprocate. He drew Yosef closer using the power of thought. The lesson is that we cannot think as we wish about others because **people will know what we think of them**. Trying to hide the truth from them is an exercise in futility.

We learn from all of the above that thoughts are not "mere" thoughts; their impact on reality is greater even than that of action, because they affect higher places. If we walk around with negative thoughts in our heads, then more than likely, negativity will be the outcome. If the first thing we notice about others when we meet them are their shortcomings, then we will have few friends. If we allow nonsense to swim inside our heads, we will have wasted one of our most potent tools for life, and in doing so, many precious years of our lives. On the other hand, thoughts of optimism, faith, growth, compassion, and gratitude bring about outstanding success and salvation.

Mesorah Publications, ltd
313 Regina Avenue
Rahway, New Jersey 07065
(718) 921-9000
www.artscroll.com